OBJECT-ORIENTED PROGRAMMING AND JAVA

Springer

Singapore
Berlin
Heidelberg
New York
Barcelona
Budapest
Hong Kong
London
Milan
Paris
Santa Clara
Tokyo

OBJECT-ORIENTED PROGRAMMING AND JAVA

Danny C.C. Poo
National University of Singapore

Derek B.K. Kiong
National University of Singapore

Guest Contributor:
Dennis Lee
Lotus Consulting (Asia Pacific), IBM

Drs. Danny C.C. Poo and Derek B.K. Kiong
Department of Information Systems
  and Computer Science
National University of Singapore
Lower Kent Ridge Road
Singapore 119260

Library of Congress Cataloging-in-Publication Data

Poo, Danny C.C., 1959–
    Object-oriented programming and Java / Danny C.C. Poo, Derek B.K. Kiong
      p.   cm.
    Includes bibliographical references and index.
    ISBN 9813083964
1. Object-oriented programming (Computer science) 2. Java (Computer program
language)   I. Kiong, Derek Beng Kee, 1959–   . II. Title
QA76.64.P65   1998
005.13'3—dc21   98-18558
                                                                  CIP

ISBN 981-3083-96-4

Java®, JavaSoft® and JDBC Compliant® are registered trademarks of Sun Microsystems,
  Inc. in the United States of America and other countries.
Netscape Navigator® is a registered trademark of Netscape Communications Corporation.

© Springer-Verlag Singapore Pte. Ltd. 1998
1st reprint 1999

The publisher makes no representation, express or implied, with regard to the accuracy of
the information contained in this book and cannot accept any legal responsibility or
liability for any errors or omissions that may be made.

Typesetting: Camera-ready by the authors
Printed in Singapore
SPIN 10676829   5 4 3 2 1

To my children, Rachel and Nigel

   whose smiles always make the difference.

                    – Danny

To my wife, Susan

   who makes all instances brighter.

                    – Derek

Preface

Control abstraction was the message of the first programming revolution seen in high-level programming languages such as Algol and Pascal. The focus of the next revolution was data abstraction, which proposed languages such as Modula and Ada.

The object-oriented revolution began slowly in the 1960s with the programming language Simula, but moved onto more languages such as Smalltalk, Objective-C and C++. Java is almost a hybrid between Smalltalk and C++, and has gained widespread acceptance due to its association with the Internet, its availability to a large user base and reusable libraries for programming in a graphical environment.

Our programming lineage have passed through Pascal, C and C++. As with many other programmers, good run-time checks with automatic memory management and a reusable API made Java a very attractive option. After a half-day on the original Java Whitepaper and the early Java online tutorial, we were sold on the Java bandwagon and already writing code. In another two days' time, we were using the Abstract Windowing Toolkit (AWT) package for graphical applications. In situations where there is no large investment into older languages, we are quite happy to abandon them completely.

Effective programming in Java comes from understanding three key areas – object-oriented concepts, the syntax and semantics of the Java programming language and the Java Application Programming Interface (API). This is our emphasis when we conduct professional courses, and in this book as well.

Much of the material in this book is based on previous courses which we have conducted over the past two years to the industry and the National University of

Singapore (NUS). Courses conducted for the industry last about 5 to 7 days, depending on the amount of coaching that participants require. In the Department of Information Systems and Computer Science at NUS, a course on "Object-Oriented Methods" runs over 13 weeks.

As you might have noticed, we have taken to Java as ducks to water. Java has allowed us to think about and specify object behavior. This results in executable code which is merely secondary. What is important is the clean specification of object behavior. Similarly, in getting accustomed to working with objects, we believe that you will enjoy it too.

Overview

Chapter 1 presents an introduction to the object-oriented world consisting of objects and object communication via the exchange of messages. Object-oriented concepts and terminology used in object-oriented methodology are discussed in chapter 2. Chapter 3 shows how these concepts materialize in the form of Java code and representations. It discusses the basic features and syntax of Java and builds upon the concepts using an incremental Counter example.

Following on from language syntax, chapter 4 demonstrates the standard programming environment using the Java Development Kit (JDK), and how a class definition may be compiled and executed, integrated and reused within other code fragments. The chapter also delves into using the Java Application Programming Interface (API) to demonstrate the ease and productivity gains of code libraries.

Chapter 5 returns to the discussion of objects, in particular, the organization of objects into manageable classes. The concept of class enables a developer to organize a complex problem domain into more manageable components. Grouping objects into classes is an act known as *classification* in object-oriented modeling. When classes are formed, they can be further distinguished into *superclasses* or *subclasses,* according to their similarities or differences in properties. Class hierarchies can then be formed. The creation of superclasses and subclasses is achieved through abstraction mechanisms known as *generalization* and *specialization* respectively. Classification, generalization and specialization are thus important abstraction mechanisms for organizing objects and managing complexities.

Inheritance is discussed in chapter 6. Common properties of classes can be shared with other classes of objects via the inheritance mechanism. It is through inheritance that software component reuse is possible in object-oriented programming. Software reusability is important because code need not be produced from scratch, thereby increasing the productivity of developers.

Another topic close to the heart of object-oriented programming is *polymorphism*. This topic is concerned with object messaging and how objects of different classes respond to the same message. With polymorphism, objects of different class definition can respond to the same message with the appropriate method. In this way, generic software code can be produced, thus enhancing the maintainability of software systems. Polymorphism is supported by dynamic binding and operation overloading, topics that are central to the discussion in chapter 7.

Enhancing software maintainability is a significant software development objective. A programming technique known as Structured Programming was introduced in the 1980s, promoting modularity as a Software Engineering principle for achieving maintainable software. Modularity is emphasized in object-oriented programming in the form of method, object, and class definition. *Encapsulation* is the manifestation of modularity in object-oriented programming to the fullest. As will be made clear in chapter 8, encapsulation brings together related properties into class definitions with the structural definition of classes hidden from their users. The purpose of this approach is to hide the implementation detail of objects so that when changes in implementation of objects are called for, users of the objects will not be adversely affected.

Exception Handling is considered in chapter 9. This is especially important in object-oriented programming, as the mechanism for the glue and safety net in code integration and reuse.

The Java API is introduced in chapter 10 and continues with the core classes for input/output, networking, graphical components and applets within Web browsers. Input and output rely on InputStream and OutputStream classes, as well as Reader and Writer classes in JDK 1.1.

Chapter 11 introduces network connections via TCP/IP using the Socket class, similar to those for input and output in chapter 10, as they share behavior from InputStream and OutputStream. As multi-processing is typically used with client/server applications, we have also included the multi-threading API in this chapter, together with a skeleton Web server as the working example.

The AWT model is elaborated with descriptions of its constituents and example usage in chapter 12. There are sufficient code examples to build interfaces for most simple applications.

Applet development relate to graphical interfaces and the issue of dynamic loading of compiled Java bytecodes. This is discussed in chapter 13. Situations where applet behavior differs from Java applications, security measures and implementing a loader over the network are also considered.

Chapter 14 examines Java Object Serialization and Remote Method Invocation. The former may be viewed as a continuation of input and output facilities discussed in chapter 10, but with the focus to implement object persistence. Object Serialization is also used to move objects over a network and forms a key role in implementing Remote Method Invocation (RMI) for distributed applications. A representative client/server application framework using RMI is provided.

Chapter 15 provides an overview of Java Database Connectivity. This topic warrants a whole book, but we limit our discussion to the rationale, perspective and architecture of JDBC together with a small code example.

To encourage readers to read, modify and test out their code, the code fragments used throughout the book are available for downloading from the URL http://dkiong.comp.nus.edu.sg/oojava/.

Acknowledgement

We thank Dennis Lee, from Lotus Consulting (Asia Pacific), IBM, for contributing chapters 14 and 15, which has made this book more useful and relevant. His recent involvement in the Nagano Winter Olympic Project in which he wrote the Java Email component using IBM and Lotus Domino technology had received glowing reports from the media and even a congratulatory note from Lou Gerstner, CEO, IBM. This project is the largest deployment of Java on the Net for a major sporting event and it performed brilliantly over 16 intense days. It is testimony that Java is not just hot air.

Dennis came to know about this book project via the Web, and agreed to contribute content after several exchanges of Email, even before we met in person. For this, we thank my colleagues at the Centre for Internet Research (CIR), National University of Singapore, who work to use the Internet productively.

The lineage of CIR may be traced back to the Internet Research and Development Unit (IRDU) and even further back to Technet Unit, Computer Centre, National University of Singapore which was first to provide and promote Internet services in Singapore. In addition, Dr Thio Hoe Tong, Director of the Computer Centre, and Dr Tan Tin Wee, Head of IRDU, have supported the Java team even in the early days when we played with the Alpha release of Java. We thank Aaron Aw and Leong Kok Yong for sharing their Java insights.

Poo & Kiong
National University of Singapore
May 1998

Contents

1 Introduction

Object-oriented programming has been in practice for many years now. While the fundamental object-oriented concepts were first introduced via the `class` construct in the Simula programming language in the 1960s, the programming technique only became prominent with the advent of Smalltalk-80 more than a decade later.

More and more programs are now designed and developed using the object-oriented programming technique. What is object-oriented programming? What makes it so attractive as an alternative programming approach? How does it differ from the traditional procedural programming approach? These questions will be discussed in this chapter.

1.1 Object-Oriented Programming

In the past, programming a computer system was approached in a procedural manner. Here, code is modularized based on a system's processes. For instance, a library application system would have processes involving the checking in and out of books, reservations, cataloging of books, etc. Problem solving would involve the analysis of these processes in terms of the procedural tasks carried out and the production of a system whose representation is based on the procedural flow of the processes.

Object-oriented programming, on the other hand, models objects and their interactions in the problem space and the production of a system based on these objects and their interactions. Since the real-world problem domain is characterized by objects and their interactions, the object-oriented programming approach would result in the production of a computer system that has a closer representation of the real-world problem domain than would be the case if the procedural programming approach is used.

To illustrate, let us consider a real-world situation as outlined in the next section.

1.2 Objects and Their Interactions in the Real World

There are two persons, Benjamin and his wife, Bambie. They are customers of HomeCare, a company dealing in luxurious furniture.

HomeCare sells a variety of sofa set which are displayed in the showroom for customers. Each sofa set is labeled with an identification number and a price tag. After viewing the sofa sets for an hour, Benjamin and Bambie decided to purchase a green, cow leather, 5-seater set. They approached Sean, a salesperson at HomeCare, to make their order.

In making his request known to Sean, Benjamin sends a *message* to Sean, "I would like to purchase this green, cow leather, 5-seater set. Can you please have it sent to me by next Wednesday?".

The message that Benjamin sent to Sean is a `takeOrder` message. It contains information such as the type of sofa set (a `green`, `cow leather`, `5-seater set`) and the date of delivery (`next Wednesday`). These information are known as the *parameters* of the `takeOrder` message. In response to Benjamin's message, Sean replied with the result of Benjamin's request. We can represent the interaction between Benjamin and Sean graphically as in Figure 1-1.

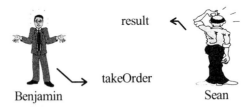

result

takeOrder

Benjamin   Sean

Figure 1-1: Interaction Between Benjamin and Sean

Sean was able to respond to Benjamin's `takeOrder` message because he understood it and has the means of handling Benjamin's request. Although Sean knew how to satisfy Benjamin's request in the message, Benjamin did not. In fact, most of the time, customers do not know how a salesperson went about satisfying their orders. All they get from salespersons are replies such as "I am sorry sir/madam, we are unable to satisfy your request because the sofa that you wanted has been sold out" or

"Sir/madam, your request has been satisfied, we will deliver the goods on Wednesday between 10 to 11am to the address indicated. Thank you for your order."

Sean, as a salesperson at HomeCare, has a responsibility towards Benjamin. He maintains his responsibility by applying a set of operations:

1. He has to determine if there is sufficient stock to satisfy Benjamin's request.

2. He has to determine if the requested date for delivery is a suitable date.

3. He has to instruct the warehouse staff to deliver the goods to Benjamin's address on the requested date, if the above conditions are satisfied.

4. Finally, he has to inform Benjamin the result of his request.

1.3 Objects and Their Interactions in Programming

The interactions between Benjamin and Sean in the above real-world situation can similarly be represented in object-oriented programming terms. For instance, Benjamin and Sean are *objects* that interact by sending *messages*. Benjamin is thus a message-sending object while Sean is a message-receiving object i.e. Benjamin is a sender and Sean is a receiver.

The `takeOrder` request from Benjamin to Sean is an example of a message. It may have additional, accompanying information known as *parameters* (or *arguments*) of the message. The fact that Sean responded to Benjamin's message indicates that the message is a valid message. Each valid message corresponds to a *method* which Sean uses to fulfill his responsibility to Benjamin.

An invalid message, on the other hand, is one which the receiver does not have the capability to respond to, i.e. the receiver does not have a corresponding method to match to the message. For example, if Benjamin had requested for a discount on the price, his request would be rejected as Sean being a salesperson does not have the capability (or a corresponding method) to respond to such a message.

A method contains a number of operations detailing how Sean is to satisfy the demand Benjamin put on him through the request. Figure 1-2 summarizes the relationships among these terms.

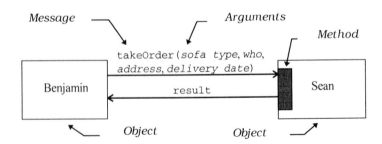

Figure 1-2: Object Interactions in Object-Oriented Programming Terms

While Benjamin may know *what* Sean can do through his methods, he may not know *how* Sean does them. This is an important principle of object-oriented programming known as *information hiding* – the sender of a message does not know *how* a receiver is going to satisfy the request in the message.

1.4 Simulation

Based on the above example, it is clear that concepts in object-oriented programming such as object, message and method, do provide a close representation of real-world objects and their interactions. These concepts are thus suitable for simulating actual object interactions in real-world situations.

It is this ability for modeling real-world problems that object-oriented programming has been deemed most suitable for simulation. The Simula programming language was designed to provide simulation facilities in the early 1970s using object-oriented concepts.

1.5 Java

Java was first introduced in 1995 as a simple and secure object-oriented programming language. It is unique in that being a new language, it has received so much interest from the computing community. Within two years, there is an estimate of 400,000 Java programmers and over 100 books on Java programming.

There are a few possible reasons for the phenomenal interest in Java. 1995 was the year of maturing WEB technologies and Java's multi-platform capability which enables a Java program to execute on any computer, was exceedingly attractive, especially on an opened network like the Internet. Java is implemented via part compilation and subsequent execution on an interpreter implemented in software.

Java applications are therefore object code portable as long as a Java virtual machine is implemented for the target machine.

The popularity of Java is also ironically due to its similarity with its close rival C++. While C++ has been the de-facto object-oriented programming language since it has been created in the same spirit as C, Java has taken the pain out of learning a new language by reusing much of C and C++. At the same time, safe programming practice in Java and language facilities for automatic memory management has been attractive to programmers on the verge of deserting their C/C++ camps.

Thus, while Java works well on the Internet, easily supporting applet execution embedded in WEB pages, it is also sufficiently attractive to use it independent of the Internet. Here, users are happy with a familiar C++-like syntax, but without the pitfalls attributed to C++ features.

In relation to the Internet, Java applets have given rise to a new generation of distributed applications with low software distribution and maintenance costs. As applets are embedded in an HTML document via <APPLET> tags, its transmission to the client machine for execution is implicitly handled by the underlying network protocols and thus makes the typical channels of distribution and installation obsolete.

While the object-oriented programming framework promotes reusability of software and code, this very practice has been demonstrated in the rich set of class libraries as seen in languages like Smalltalk-80 and Java. Java foundation class libraries provide for windowing and graphical user-interface programming, network communications, multimedia facilities demonstrate the practical and joyful productive work done in Java.

1.6 Summary

The following points were discussed in this chapter:

- An overview of object-oriented programming concepts and their applicability for modeling and representing real-world entities and their interactions in the problem solving process.

- Object-oriented concepts of object, message, and method.

- An overview of the Java programming language and the potential of productive software development.

1.7 Exercises

1. Distinguish the programming approach used in procedural programming and object-oriented programming.

2. "Object-oriented programming approach is ideal for simulating real-world problems." Discuss the validity of this statement.

3. Consider the following scenarios and outline the objects and their interactions, in terms of messages and arguments, among themselves in the scenarios:

   (a) a driver driving a car

   (b) a customer making a cash withdrawal from an Automated Teller Machine (ATM)

   (c) a customer buying a compact disk player from a vendor

   (d) a traffic policeman directing traffic at a junction

   (e) a lecturer delivering his/her lecture to a class of students

   (f) a tutorial discussion between an instructor and students.

2 Object, Class, Message and Method

We had our first introduction to objects, message and method in Chapter 1. Another concept closely associated with the concept of objects is *class*. In object-oriented programming, a class is a definition template for structuring and creating objects.

How the concept of object, message, method and class is used in a computer model is discussed in this chapter.

2.1 Objects and Class

In Chapter 1, we introduced a customer Benjamin. Now, meet Bernie, another customer at HomeCare. As customers of a furniture shop, Benjamin and Bernie share some similar information. Each has a name, an address and a budget – information that are relevant in describing customers. These information are known as object *attributes*.

An attribute definition allows for objects to have independent *attribute values*. For example, Benjamin may have a larger budget and thus a larger budget value (say, $2000) than Bernie whose budget may be $1000. Collectively, the values of an object's attributes represent the *state* of the object.

Besides attributes, Benjamin and Bernie also exhibit some behavior typical of a customer. For instance, Benjamin and Bernie would execute a *method* when making a purchase. Let us call this method purchase(). The method purchase() is made up of a set of operations which Benjamin and Bernie would use to send a purchase request to a salesperson.

Structurally, Benjamin and Bernie can be represented as follows:

```
Benjamin as an Object
  Attributes:
    name = "Benjamin"
    address = "1, Robinson Road"
    budget = "2000"
  Methods:
    purchase()    {send a purchase request to a salesperson}
    getBudget()   {return budget}


Bernie as an Object
  Attributes:
    name = "Bernie"
    address = "18, Sophia Road"
    budget = "1000"
  Methods:
    purchase()    {send a purchase request to a salesperson}
    getBudget()   {return budget}
```

name, address and budget are attributes while purchase() and getBudget() are methods of the objects. Note that both objects share a common definition of attributes and methods. In fact, all customers of HomeCare share the same set of information. They all have attributes name, address and budget, and methods purchase() and getBudget(). In defining these objects, a common definition known as *class* in object-oriented terms is used. A class is a definition template for structuring and creating objects with the same attributes and methods. Benjamin and Bernie, being customers of HomeCare, can therefore be defined by a class called Customer as follows:

```
Class Customer
  Attributes:
    name
    address
    budget
  Methods:
    purchase()    {send a purchase request to a salesperson}
    getBudget()   {return budget}
```

One major difference between objects and class is in the way attributes and methods are treated in objects and class. A class is a definition about objects; the attributes and methods in a class are thus declarations that do not contain values. However, objects are created instances from a class. Each has its own values of attributes and methods. The values of the set of attributes describe the state of the objects.

Let us now examine the salespersons. Salespersons also have attributes and methods. Sean and Sara are two salespersons at HomeCare. They are thus capable of a behavior typical of a salesperson e.g. taking orders from customers. To fulfill their role as salespersons in a purchase transaction, Sean and Sara perform a method. We shall call this method, `takeOrder()` and represent Sean and Sara as follows:

```
Sean as an Object
  Attributes:
    name = "Sean"
  Methods:
    takeOrder()        {
      check with warehouse on stock availability
      check with warehouse on delivery schedule
      if ok
      then {instruct warehouse to deliver stock(address, date)
            return ok}
      else return not ok
    }

Sara as an Object
  Attributes:
    name = "Sara"
  Methods:
    takeOrder()        {
      check with warehouse on stock availability
      check with warehouse on delivery schedule
      if ok
      then {instruct warehouse to deliver stock(address, date)
            return ok}
      else return not ok
    }
```

Being salespersons, Sean and Sara share similar information of attributes and methods as expected. Like the customers, their definition can be described by a class called SalesPerson with the following representation:

```
Class SalesPerson
  Attributes:
    name
  Methods:
    takeOrder()        {
      check with warehouse on stock availability
      check with warehouse on delivery schedule
      if ok
      then {instruct warehouse to deliver stock(address, date)
            return ok}
      else return not ok
    }
```

Note that the definition of the SalesPerson class is different from the Customer class since customers and salespersons behave differently — customers make orders and salespersons take orders.

2.2 Message and Method

Objects communicate with one another by sending *messages*. A message is a *method call* from a message-sending object to a message-receiving object. A message-sending object is a *sender* while a message-receiving object is a *receiver*.

An object responds to a message by executing one of its methods. Additional information, known as *arguments*, may accompany a method call. Such parameterization allows for added flexibility in message passing. The set of methods collectively defines the dynamic behavior of an object. An object may have as many methods as are required.

2.2.1 Message Components

A message is composed of three components:

- an object identifier which indicates the message receiver,

- a method name (corresponding to a method of the receiver), and

- arguments (additional information required for the execution of the method).

Earlier we saw that Benjamin sent a message to Sean when Benjamin wanted to buy a sofa set. The reasonable location for Benjamin to send the message to Sean is in Benjamin's purchase() method as shown below (indicated in bold):

```
Benjamin as an Object
  Attributes:
    name = "Benjamin"
    address = "1, Robinson Road"
    budget = "2000"
  Methods:
    purchase() {
      Sean.takeOrder("Benjamin", "sofa", "1, Robinson Road",
               "12 November")
    }
    getBudget()        {return budget}
```

The message Sean.takeOrder(who, stock, address, date) is interpreted as follows:

- Sean is the receiver of the message,

- takeOrder is a method call on Sean,

- "Benjamin", "stock", "address", "date" are arguments of the message.

2.2.2 Methods

A message is valid if the receiver has a method that corresponds to the method named in the message and the appropriate arguments, if any, are supplied with the message. Only valid messages are executed by the receiver. The takeOrder() message is valid because Sean has a corresponding method and the required arguments (who, stock, address, date) are supplied with the message.

Sean's takeOrder() method is made up of a set of operations (indicated in bold below) as follows:

```
Sean as an Object
  Attributes:
   name = "Sean"
  Methods:
    takeOrder(who, stock, address, date)    {
      check with warehouse on stock availability
      check with warehouse on delivery schedule
      if ok then {
        instruct warehouse to deliver stock to address on date
        return ok
      } else return not ok
    }
```

In the above description, a message is sent from Sean to a Warehouse object to inquire on the order and delivery schedule in Sean's takeOrder() method. If both conditions are satisfied, Sean would instruct the Warehouse object to arrange for delivery.

How Sean carries out the method is known only to Sean. Neither Benjamin nor the other customers know how Sean does it. For example, to check on the stock and delivery schedule with the warehouse, Sean might have called the warehouse over the phone or he might have checked them against a list he had gotten from the warehouse. What Benjamin knows of Sean is that Sean is capable of responding to his request since his message to Sean is acceptable by Sean.

In object-oriented programming, Benjamin and Sean are said to have followed the principle of *information hiding – How* Sean is going to satisfy Benjamin's request is hidden from Benjamin. In this way, Sean is free to select whatever way he chooses to satisfy Benjamin's request – he may phone the warehouse or look up the pre-prepared list and vice versa.

2.2.3   Client and Server

By executing a method, a message-receiving object (such as Sean) is said to serve the message-sending object (such as Benjamin). A message-receiving object is thus a *server* to a message-sending object and the message-sending object is thus a *client* of the server.

Figure 2-1: Object Communication Process

In any object communication, there is at least a client and a server. The client sends a message to request a server to perform a task. The task is fulfilled by a message-corresponding method of the server. In sending a message to the warehouse, Sean is said to be the client and the warehouse, the server.

Benjamin, Sean and the warehouse are three objects involved in a communication process. Benjamin is the initiator with Sean and the warehouse as partners in the communication process. Figure 2-1 depicts a typical communication process amongst objects.

2.3 Creating Objects

In object-oriented programming, objects are created from classes. Instances of Customer objects are created from a Customer class and SalesPerson objects from a SalesPerson class.

Created object instances are individuals with their own state. To illustrate, let us consider the example of counters. A counter is a device that keeps account of the number of times an event has occurred. It has two buttons: an `initialize` button that resets the counter to 0, and an add button that adds 1 to its present number. Figure 2-2 shows a counter with a number 10.

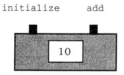

Figure 2-2: A Counter

Structurally, the first counter object can be represented as follows:

```
First Counter Object
  Attributes:
    number = 10
  Methods:
    add()              {number = number + 1}
    initialize()       {number = 0}
    getNumber()        {return number}
```

Figure 2-3 shows two more counters.

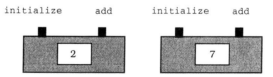

Figure 2-3: Two Additional Counters

Like the first counter, these two counters may be reset to zero and incremented through the initialize and add buttons respectively, and represented as follows:

```
Second Counter Object
  Attributes:
    number = 2
  Methods:
    add()              {number = number + 1}
    initialize()       {number = 0}
    getNumber()        {return number}
```

```
Third Counter Object
  Attributes:
    number = 7
  Methods:
    add()              {number = number + 1}
    initialize()       {number = 0}
    getNumber()        {return number}
```

All the three counters share the same definition of attributes and methods, and like in the previous examples, can be defined by a class as follows:

```
Class Counter
  Attributes:
    number
  Methods:
    add()          {number = number + 1}
    initialize()   {number = 0}
    getNumber()    {return number}
```

The Counter class has:

- an attribute, number;

- an initialize() method that causes a counter to reset its number to 0.

- an add() method that causes a counter to add 1 to its number; and

- a getNumber() method that returns the current value of the attribute number.

Suppose a new object is created from the Counter class. Although the new Counter object would have the same definition of attributes and methods as the previous three counters, its attribute value may not be the same as those other counters. This suggests that the state of the counters may be different from one another.

For the newly created fourth Counter object, it has a state represented by the attribute number with a value of 0, the value at initialization:

```
Fourth Counter Object
  Attributes:
    number = 0
  Methods:
    add()          {number = number + 1}
    initialize()   {number = 0}
    getNumber()    {return number}
```

Note that the attribute value of the fourth Counter object is different from the other three counters.

2.4 Summary

The following points were discussed in this chapter:

- Objects are defined by classes.

- Objects from the same class share the same definition of attributes and methods.

- Objects from the same class may not have the same attribute values.

- Objects from different classes do not share the same definition of attributes or methods.

- Objects created from the same class share the same definition of attributes and methods but their state may differ.

- A method is a set of operations executed by an object upon the receipt of a message.

- A message has three components: an object identifier, a method name and arguments.

- A message-receiving object is a *server* to a message-sending object known as a *client*.

2.5 Exercises

1. Distinguish the terms "Object" and "Class" .

2. Consider the scenario of buying flowers from a florist. Outline the objects in such a transaction together with the messages exchanged.

3. Given a class definition Rectangle below, describe the structure of any 3 instances of Rectangle.

```
class Rectangle {
Attributes:
  length
  width
Methods:
  getLength()  { return length }
  getWidth()   { return width }
  draw()       { ... }
```

4. How would you implement the concept of class and method in a non-object-oriented programming language such as COBOL, Pascal or C?

5. Define using the following structure a class definition for cars. A car generally has abilities to start, move forward, move backward, stop and off. A car can also return to its relative location. The starting location is a value 0.

```
class Car {
Attributes:
  ...
Methods:
  ...
}
```

6. Distinguish between a client and a server.

7. A client communicates with a server by sending a _____ to the server. The _____ is a call on a _____ of the server.

3 A Quick Tour of Java

Earlier, we introduced key object-oriented concepts such as objects, methods and classes and how these may be ultimately used in a computer model. In this chapter, we see how the Java programming language is used to construct our object model of the problem domain. This approach is advantageous in that it allows our model to operate or "come alive" under computer control.

3.1 Primitive Types

The Java programming language allows for the creation of objects which will ultimately participate in message communication. We have seen that objects may have diverse behavior and that it is more convenient to specify objects via classification, i.e. class constructs.

Before examining class definitions for user-specified objects, we should be mindful that Java also provides primitive values from which other (bigger) objects may be described in terms of and constructed from. For example, a complex number may be seen as comprising of two numbers representing the real and imaginary parts.

The primitive types `byte`, `short`, `int` and `long` defined in the Java language allow for the representation of discrete integer values of widths 8, 16, 32, and 64 bits respectively. These in turn correspond to the representation of numeric ranges -128 to 127, -32768 to 32767, -2147483648 to 2147483647, and -9223372036854775808 to 9223372036854775807 respectively.

The primitive types `float` and `double` allow for the representation of single and double precision floating-point real values with representational widths of 32 and 64 bits respectively. The adopted IEEE 754 standard includes both positive and negative sign-magnitude numbers, both positive and negative zeros and infinities and unique Not-a-Number representations.

Values of type `float` are of the form $s \cdot m \cdot 2^e$, where s is either +1 or -1, m is a positive integer less than 2^{24}, and e is an integer between -149 and 104. Similarly, values of type `double` have the similar form $s \cdot m \cdot 2^e$, but m is a positive integer less than 2^{53}, and e is an integer between -1075 and 970.

Finally, the primitive types `char` and `boolean` allow for 16-bit multi-byte characters and `false`/`true` boolean values respectively.

3.2 Object Definition

Building upon the primitive values supported by the language proper, other entities to be manipulated are user-designed objects which are defined via class constructs. A class construct in Java consists of the `class` keyword followed by the class name and braces { } which delimit the declaration of attributes and methods for its instances. The Counter class introduced in Chapter 2 would have the following form in Java:

```
class Counter {
    attribute and method declarations
}
```

Object attributes are, in turn, either nested component objects or primitive types used to represent the object. An *instance method* manipulates the object by altering its attribute values. The `number` attribute and `add()` method in the Counter class below are representative of an object's *state* and *operation* respectively:

```
class Counter {
    int number;
    void add() {
        number = number +1;
    }
}
```

The `number` attribute is also known as an *instance variable* because it occurs in every object or instance of the Counter class. This further implies that an attribute in one instance is independent from that in another instance. In the same vein, a method manipulates object attributes in the same instance. This occurs when a method is invoked and the corresponding code in its body is executed. In our recent example, invoking the add() method of an object will increment the corresponding number attribute.

3.2.1 Variable Definitions

Variable definitions in Java take the form below, where the type name T precedes the variable name v:

```
T v;
```

Typing in a programming language allows the values for a variable to be anticipated. As such, appropriate storage may be set aside for these values.

There is another subtle advantage of typing in programming languages – the values associated with the variable also imply what operations are valid and applicable. For example, multiplication and division applies to numeric values but not character values. Thus, the language compiler may flag multiplication and division of character values as erroneous.

All variables in Java are typed allowing the compiler to verify during compilation, that operations on the object associated with the variable are legitimate.

3.2.2 Methods

A method definition which occur in a class construct is made up of two distinct portions: the method signature header and its implementation code body surrounded by the braces { ... }.

The method signature portion, such as void add() in the Counter example, has the generic form below, where m is the method name, T its return type, with Rn and pn being parameter types and names respectively (n being the number of parameters):

```
T m(R1 p1, R2 p2, ... Rn pn)
```

We have seen that a method named m() is invoked to correspond to a message *m* sent to the object. Consequently, the object may return a result to the message sender. The type of this value is denoted by T. If no result needs be returned, the keyword void is used instead.

The formal parameters p1, p2...pn contain the additional values sent together with the message. They have corresponding types R1, R2...Rn, and is used by the compiler to verify that the correct parameters are supplied for each method invocation. Any number of formal parameters may be specified, but the number of actual parameters in a message must match those originally specified in the method signature.

The implementation of a method consists of a block of statements surrounded by { }. Often, such methods would modify the object's attributes. In the case of the add() method of our Counter example, it increments the variable number. A block consists of declarations of any local variable, expressions and control-flow constructs. These would be discussed in detail in following sections.

In the slightly expanded version of the Counter class below, an extra initialize() method has been added to re-initialize the Counter value so that counting can be easily restarted. This allows instances to respond to the additional *initialize* message.

```
class Counter {
  int number;
  void add() {
    number = number+1;
  }
  void initialize() {
    number = 0;
  }
}
```

If the number of times a counter is restarted is significant, we might introduce another attribute reused to maintain this information. Correspondingly, this attribute is incremented in the block of the initialize() method:

```
class Counter {
  int number = 0;
  int reused = 0;
  void add() {
    number = number+1;
  }
  void initialize() {
    number = 0;
    reused = reused+1;
  }
}
```

The previous example on the class Counter definition shows that an object may have as many attributes and methods as required to effectively model the object. In the most recent definition, objects of the class Counter have 2 attributes (number and reused, both with an initial value of 0 when created) and 2 methods (`add()` and `initialize()`).

3.3 Object Instantiation

A class construct provides a description for objects of that class, and serves as a template for objects to be created. However, no instances of the class is created, except by calling the object allocator function `new()`. The expression `new Counter()` returns a newly-created instance of the Counter class. However, in order that this new object may be referred to, it is assigned to an appropriate variable. Assuming the variable `carpark` in the fragment below, a new Counter object may be created via `new Counter()`, and then assigned to the former:

```
Counter carpark;
...
carpark = new Counter();
```

Henceforth, the newly-created object may be referred to via the variable `carpark`. Where more Counter objects are needed, the object allocator function `new()` may be repeatedly invoked, and the resultant objects assigned to other variables such as `entrance` and `exitDoor`:

```
Counter entrance, exitDoor;
...
entrance = new Counter();
exitDoor = new Counter();
```

3.4 Object Access and Message Passing

Since the attributes and methods of an object are considered its characteristics, these are accessed via the qualification operator "`.`" with respect to an object proper. Thus, the counts of the various Counters `carpark`, `entrance` and `exitDoor` are `carpark.number`, `entrance.number` and `exitDoor.number` respectively. The total numbers from these counters is:

```
carpark.number + entrance.number + exitDoor.number
```

Similarly, the `initialize()` method of Counters `carpark`, `entrance` and `exitDoor` may be invoked via:

```
carpark.initialize();
entrance.initialize();
exitDoor.initialize();
```

3.5 Representational Independence

While accessing object attributes directly is permissible, it is not ideal as it couples implementation code to the current object representation. As such, any changes in object representation propagates to dependent code, resulting in high software maintenance cost.

A common object-oriented programming practice is information hiding – to make object representations inaccessible to clients so that modifications in (server) object representations do not propagate excessively. This decoupling of dependencies reduces software maintenance cost.

Limiting access to object representations in Java is mainly achieved by the two main constraint specifiers `private` and `public`. The former limits access of the following entity to within the class construct, while the latter makes it accessible to any client code.

```
class Counter {
  private int number = 0;
  private int reused = 0;
  public void add() {
    number = number+1;
  }
  public void initialize() {
    number = 0;
    reused = reused+1;
  }
}
```

Since constraint specifiers in the above class definition hides the internal representation of Counter objects, the resultant attributes are no longer accessible, and useless for interrogation. In this case, accessor methods `getNumber()` and `getReused()` are required, as outlined in the following code fragment. They provide access to internal details, but without dependency overheads. Representation independence is maintained by confining access to private attributes to within the class construct. This topic is further discussed in Chapter 8.

```
class Counter {
  private int number = 0;
  private int reused = 0;
  public void add() {
    number = number+1;
  }
  public void initialize() {
    number = 0;
    reused = reused+1;
  }
  public int getNumber() { return number; }
  public int getReused() { return reused; }
}
```

3.6 Overloading

Attribute names of a class may be the same as those in another class since they are accessed independently. An attribute *x* in a class does not necessarily have any semantic bearing with another as they have different scopes, and does not preclude using the same attribute there.

Within a Java class construct, methods may share the same name as long as they may be distinguished either by:

- the number of parameters, or

- different parameter types.

This criterion requires a message with associated parameters to be uniquely matched with the intended method definition.

If we had wanted a Counter to be incremented other than by 1, we could define another add() method which takes an integer parameter instead.

```
class Counter {
  private int number = 0;
  private int reused = 0;
  public void add() {
    number = number+1;
  }
  public void add(int x) {
    number = number+x;
  }
  public void initialize() {
    number = 0;
    reused = reused+1;
  }
```

```
    public int getNumber() { return number; }
    public int getReused() { return reused; }
}
```

If `carpark` had been assigned an instance of Counter, `carpark.add()` would invoke the first method to increment by 1, while `carpark.add(2)` would invoke the new one just defined.

3.7 Initialization and Constructors

Currently, object creation and initialization are seen as distinct operations. The abstraction in object-oriented programming languages often allow these two operations to be implicitly combined. As such, constructors may be seen as unique methods invoked implicitly when an object instance is created. Implicit initialization relieves the programmer from performing this important function, but more importantly, prevents uninitialized objects as a result of absent-minded programmers. Carefully designed constructors allow for object invariants to be maintained regardless of how they were created.

Apart from having the same name as the class, and not having a return result type, a constructor is not different from a method. It has similar syntax for its parameters and implementation body.

In place of attribute initialization, our next Counter example uses a constructor method. This offers additional functionality compared with the former approach.

```
class Counter {
    private int number, reused;
    public void add() {
        number = number+1;
    }
    public void initialize() {
        number = 0;
        reused = reused+1;
    }
    public int getNumber() { return number; }
    public int getReused() { return reused; }
    Counter() { number = 0; reused = 0; }
}
```

While this change is not significant in our trivial example, constructors allow more flexibility such as the execution of arbitrary expressions and statements when compared with static attribute initializers. As with methods, constructors may also be overloaded. This provides for varied ways for objects to be created and initialized.

The additional new overloaded constructors in the new class definition below allows for various initial values for number and reused other than just 0.

```
class Counter {
  private int number, reused;
  public void add() {
    number = number+1;
  }
  public void initialize() {
    number = 0;
    reused = reused+1;
  }
  public int getNumber() { return number; }
  public int getReused() { return reused; }
  Counter() { number = 0; reused = 0; }
  Counter(int x) { number = x; reused = 0; }
  Counter(int x, int y) { number = x; reused = y; }
  Counter(float z) { number = (int) z; reused = 0; }
}
```

3.8 Expressions, Statements and Control-flow Mechanisms

We saw earlier that a method definition consists of the method signature and its implementation body. As an object responds to messages by executing code in the method body to affect changes in its state, assignment is a very common operation.

v = E;

Assignment consists of a left-hand variable which will contain or "hold" the value specified via the right-hand expression. It may be a literal value such as 3, a variable which holds the intended value like number, or an operator with appropriate operands, such as x+4, or even r.f or y*p(5). In the same way that + is an operator, . and () are also operators. The last expression involves nested expressions: the result of p(5) is used in multiplication.

3.8.1 Operators

We first examine the operators in Java.

(a) Arithmetic Operators

The arithmetic operators in Java include the common addition "+", subtraction "-", multiplication "*" and division "/" operations.

```
int a = 13;
int v = 7;

a+v // returns result 20
a-v // returns result 6
a*v // returns result 91
a/v // returns result 1
```

These operators apply to numeric operands, and return the type of its operands. When operands are mixed, the widest is used to prevent unexpected truncation.

```
float b = 13;
int w = 7;

b+w // returns result 20.0
b-w // returns result 6.0
b*w // returns result 91.0
b/w // returns result 1.8571428
```

The "%" operator returns the remainder of integer division.

```
int a = 13;
int v = 3;

a/v // returns result 4
a%v // returns result 1
```

When used as a unary operator, "-" negates the numeric operand.

```
int a = 13;

-a // returns result -13
```

(b) Logical Operators

The logical operators in Java include the standard *and* "&&", *or* "||" and *not* "!". Each operator returns a boolean result:

&& returns true if both operands are true.

x	y	x && y
false	false	false
false	true	false
true	false	false
true	true	true

|| returns true if at least one operand is true.

x	y	x || y
false	false	false
false	true	true
true	false	true
true	true	true

! returns true if the single operand is false.

x	! x
false	true
true	false

(c) Relational Operators

The *equality* "==" and *inequality* "!=" operators in Java operate on all values and objects to return a boolean result.

```
int h = 4;
int j = 4;
int k = 6;
Counter m = new Counter();
Counter n = new Counter();


h == j // returns true, h and j have the same value
h == k // returns false
k == k // returns true


m == n // false, m and n are different objects even if they have the
       //   same constituents
n == n // true
```

The following relational operators in Java operate on numeric values.

<	less than
>	greater than
<=	less than or equal
>=	greater than or equal

```
int h = 4;
int j = 4;
int k = 6;
```

```
h < k  // returns true
h < j  // returns false
h <= j // returns true
```

(d) Bitwise Operators

The following bitwise operators in Java operate on corresponding bits of `byte`, `short`, `int` and `long` values.

&	bitwise "and"
^	bitwise exclusive "or"
|	bitwise inclusive "or"
~	bitwise one's complement

>> <<	right and left bitwise shift
>>>	right bitwise unsigned shift

```
int a = 15; //   binary     000001111
int v = 34; //   binary     000100010

a & v       // returns result 2     000000010
a ^ v       // returns result 45    000101101
a | v       // returns result 47    000101111
~a          // returns result -16
            //    11111111111111111111111111110000

v >> 3      // returns result 4     000000100
v << 3      // returns result 272   100010000

~a >> 3     // returns -2
            //    11111111111111111111111111111110
~a >>> 3    // returns 536870910
            //    01111111111111111111111111111110
```

(e) Assignment

Having seen the basic means of providing new values to variables, assignment "=" is more correctly viewed as an *operator* rather than a statement. In addition to assigning the right-side value to the left-side variable, it also returns the value assigned. As such, the assignment expression may appear in the context of an enclosing expression. (In the example below, the result of the assignment operator to variable a is not used.)

```
int a, b;                                  int a, b;
                      implies
a = b = 2;                                 a = (b = 2);
```

The code fragments above assign 2 to b and the result of 2 is assigned to a. This is because unlike the common arithmetic operators which associate from left-to-right, the assignment operator associates from right-to-left. This is highlighted in the next section on operator precedence.

In general, an assignment operator results in a side-effect since it changes the value of the variable being assigned. Other related assignment operators have the special form "*op=*", where *op* is a typical operator.

```
x op= f;      has the same meaning as      x = x op f;
```

In the above equivalent form, *op* may be operators such as +, -, *, /, %, >>, <<, &, ^ or |. Thus +=, -=, *=, /=, %=, >>=, <<=, &=, ^=, and |= are also valid assignment operators.[1]

The other two operators related to assignment are auto-increment "++" and auto-decrement "--". Since they are used in either postfix and prefix forms, four scenarios are as illustrated in the code fragments below.

The postfix form (such as f++) returns the result before the increment/decrement operation, whereas the prefix form (such as ++f) returns the results after the increment/decrement operation. In the code fragments below, f is either incremented or decremented. However, g is either assigned a "pre"- or a "post"-value depending on whether the postfix or prefix forms are used.

```
int f, g;                                  int f, g;

f = 6;                                     f = 6;
g = f++;                                   g = ++f;
// g has 6                                 // g has 7
// f has 7                                 // f has 7

int f, g;                                  int f, g;

f = 6;                                     f = 6;
g = f--;                                   g = --f;
// g has 6                                 // g has 5
// f has 5                                 // f has 5
```

---

[1] There is a subtle difference between x[i++] += 4 and x[i++] = x[i++] + 4, in that i++ is evaluated once in the former but twice in the latter.

(f) Conditional Expression

The conditional expression operator ? : returns one of two values depending on the boolean condition. For example, the expression *A?B:C* returns the value of *B* if *A* is true, else the value of *C* is returned.

(g) Typecast

The typecast operator *(type)E* performs 2 basic functions at run-time depending on the source expression *E*. For a numeric type (such as int, float, or double), it converts the value to another of the specified type.

```
int k = 5;
double d = 4.16;

k = (int) d*k;
```

The resultant expression of d*k is double value, and the typecast operation converts it to an integer. For variable, the operator confirms that the object referenced is compatible with the specified class.

```
Object x = new Counter();
Counter c;

c = x;              // illegal since not all Objects are Counters
c = (Counter) x;    // legitimate because x is at run-time
                    //    verified to reference a Counter
```

(h) Precedence and Associativity

Since most operators have operands which could be (nested) expressions, *operator precedence* and *associativity rules* are necessary to define the evaluation order. For example in evaluating "a+b*c", "b*c" is evaluated before its result is added to a because multiplication "*" has higher precedence than addition "+". Table 3-1 summarizes the operators discussed so far.

The operators at the top of the table have higher precedence than those at the bottom. It is as though precedence pulls operands, so that operators with a higher precedence are evaluated before those with lower precedence. All binary operations are left-associative, except assignment operators which associate right-to-left.

Operator
[] . *(params)* E++ E--
unary operators: -E !E ~E ++E --E
new *(type)* E
* / %
+ -
>> << >>>
< > <= >=
== !=
&
^
|
&&
||
? :
= += -= *= /= %= >>= <<= &= ^= |=

Table 3-1: Operator Precedence

Precedence allows the expression "a>>b+c" to be unambiguously interpreted as "a>>(b+c)", and not "(a>>b)+c". Similarly, "!m&&n" is interpreted as "(!m)&&n" and not "!(m&&n)".

Associativity rules come into effect when equal precedence levels do not help in resolving evaluation order. Due to associativity rules (which is left-to-right for "/" and "*", i.e. evaluating the left operator and then right), "a/b*c" is interpreted as "(a/b)*c" and not "a/(b*c)".

Similarly, due to right-to-left associativity, "~y++" is interpreted as "~(y++)" instead of "(~y)++".

3.8.2 Expression Statements

The simplest and most common statements in Java are expression statements, which consist of an assignment expression, method invocation or instance creation followed by a semicolon. The following are expression statements:

```
int a, b;
T c;

a = 1;          // assignment expressions
a++;
c = new T();

new T();        // instance creation

c.m();          // method invocation
```

3.8.3 Control-flow Statements

Apart from the simple statements, there are control-flow statements which affect the execution order of statements. These statements are commonly grouped under conditional and iterative statements.

(a) Conditional Statements

Conditional statements allow for conditions to be attached to a statement as to whether it would be executed. The most basic form is the if statement. In the code fragment below, the statement S is executed only if the boolean condition E evaluates to true:

```
if (E)
    S;
```

A slight variation is the if-else statement which allows for an *either-or* choice. If the boolean condition E evaluates to is true and S is executed, then R would not. If S is not executed, then R would be:

```
if (E)
    S;
else
    R;
```

Apart from 1-way and 2-way branches in flow-control, the switch statement allows for multi-way selection:

```
switch (E) {
  c1: S1;
      break;
  c2: S2;
      break;
  c3: S3;
  c4: S4;
      break;
  default: Sd;
}
```

Generally, the `switch` statement allows for the execution of a choice of statements depending on the expression *E*: *S1* when *E* evaluates to the constant *c1*, *S2* when *c2*, ...etc., the mappings given by each switch limb. The `break` statement causes flow-control to leave the switch statement immediately.

In the case of the execution of statement *S3* when *E* evaluates to *c3*, the absence of a `break` statement causes execution to continue to *S4* instead. The `default` limb is used when the evaluated value of *E* does not match any constant values in the limbs.

(b)   Iterative Statements

Iterative statements allow for constituent statements to be executed repeatedly. In the most basic way, the body of the `while`-statement below is repeatedly executed when the boolean condition *E* is true. The loop terminates when *E* is `false`, after which execution proceeds to the next statement:

```
while (E)
    S;
```

The `while`-statement is known as a *pre-test* loop since the constituent *S* is only executed if the condition *E* evaluates to is `true`. Thus, if *E* was false in the first instance, the statement *S* is never executed.

On the other hand, the `do-while` statement is a *post-test* loop. *R* is first executed and subsequently while the boolean expression *F* evaluates to `true`, *R* is executed again. Again, the loop terminates when *F* evaluates to `false`. Thus, this control flow construct will execute *R* at least once.

```
do {
    R;
} while (F);
```

3.9 Blocks

A block, indicated by { }, may occur at any location where a statement is valid. It is considered the sequential construct as the group of statements it surrounds is treated as a single statement or processing unit.

Thus, while the various control-flow constructs merely show a single statement as the constituent body, a block may be used where such constructs should contain more than one statement. For example, *factorial* may be computed by the following while-statement:

```
f = 1;
while (k > 1) {
   f = f*k;
   k--;
}
```

Blocks allow for control-flow constructs to be nested within bigger constructs. In the code fragment below, the nested if-else statement allows for the number of even numbers and sum of odd numbers in the range to be computed.

```
even = 0; sumOfOdd = 0;
f = 1;
while (k > 1) {
   f = f*k;
   if (k % 2 == 0)
     even++;
   else
     sumOfOdd = sumOfOdd + k;
   k--;
}
```

3.9.1 Local Declarations

In treating a statement sequence as a single statement, a block may also be thought of as a sub-machine which fulfills a specific task. As such, the scope of local variable declarations is the rest of the block in which the declaration occurs. This allows declarations and associated references to be localized, thereby aiding maintainability.

```
while (k > 1) {
  f = f*k;
  if (k % 2 == 0) {
    double d = 4.5;
    ....
    even++;
  } else {
    long d = 23546;
    ...
    sumOfOdd = sumOfOdd + k;
  }
  k--;
}
```

The code fragment above is legitimate because both local declarations of d have been confined to their respective nested blocks – d is a double in the first block, while d is a long in the second.

With instance variables, a local declaration has the same form below, where T is the declared type of variable v.

```
T v;
```

For notational convenience, declarations may have two variations:

- a list of variables with the same type separated by commas, and;

- an initial value may be provided via an expression following an assignment operator.

```
T v, w = n(), z;
```

3.10 More Control-flow Statements

Three other control-flow statements are commonly used: for-statement, break and continue. The for-statement is often used as a counter-controlled loop to iterate through a loop a fixed number of times, even though it does not have explicit mechanisms for counter control.

For example, the earlier *factorial* example could be re-coded as follows:

```
for (f = 1; k > 1; k--)
  f = f*k;
```

The generic form of the for-statement

```
for (Q; R; S)
    T;
```

is often easier thought of as a transformed while-statement, where Q, T, and S are the initializer, conditional and re-initializer expressions:

```
Q;
while (R) {
    T;
    S;
}
```

The break-statement was encountered when the switch-statement was discussed. Its more generic function is to transfer control out of the innermost switch, while, do or for-statement. This is why using the break-statement ensures that only the statements associated with the case-limb are executed.

For the situation with the while, do or for-statements, the break-statement allows for a quick exit from the iteration. In many situations, its use can result in a simpler program structure. For example, the following two code fragments have similar effects.

```
finished = false;              while (E) {
while (E && !finished) {          S;
    S;                            if (F) {
    if (F) {                          U;
        U;                            break;
        finished = true;          }
    }                             T;
    if (!finished)            }
        T;
}
```

Finally, the continue-statement transfers control to the beginning of the innermost iterative loop so as to reevaluate the boolean condition for the next iteration. Unlike, the break-statement, control-flow does not exit from the loop. As such, the following two code fragments have similar effects.

```
while (E) {                              skip = false;
  S;                                     while (E) {
  if (F) {                                 S;
    U;                                     if (F) {
    continue;                                U;
  }                                          skip = true;
  T;                                       }
}                                          if (!skip)
                                             T;
                                           else
                                             skip = false;
                                         }
```

While the differences between program structures in the above examples might seem mild for the `break` and `continue`-statements to be useful, it is more pronounced for program structures which are deeply nested.

3.11 Arrays

Just as objects are created dynamically (i.e. it happens at run-time during program execution), arrays in Java are similarly created. The size of an array need not be specified or computed during compilation.

An array is thus declared using the subscript operator, but without indication of the upper bound:

```
Counter gates[];
```

An array is created via the `new` operator, but with the array size within square brackets:

```
gates = new Counter[8];
```

The array size associated with `gates` is 8, but this does not imply 8 Counter objects. Instead, it is important to understand a Counter array as being similar with multiple variables, i.e. it is an object which does not further contain Counter objects but merely referencing eight potential Counter objects.

Thus, individual array elements must be created explicitly:

```
Counter gates[];
gates = new Counter[8];
for (int i=0; i<8; i++);
  gates[i] = new Counter();
```

3.12 Result Returned by Method

Now that we have examined the statement constructs in Java, we return to see how a method may return a result to its sender. A method in a class definition has the following general form, with the return-statement returning control-flow back to the message sender:

```
T foo(gT g, hT h ...)
{
    // local definitions

    // statements

    return v;
}
```

The value returned v, must be of the type T as indicated in the method signature. If the sender does not require any results, the keyword void should be used as the return type. In this case, the returning expression v would be omitted in the return statement.

The return-statement need not be the last statement in the block as implied in the previous example. In a non-trivial structure, multiple return-statements might be used as in the next example, but the programmer must evaluate if the situation improves program structure and readability.

```
T foo(gT g, hT h ...)
{
  for (E; F; G)
    if (H)
      return v;
    else if (J) {
      b;
      return w;
    }
  return x;
}
```

3.13 Summary

The following topics were discussed in this chapter:

- primitive types in Java

- `class` constructs

- definition of instance variables and methods

- object instantiation

- message passing and expressions

- statements and control-flow mechanisms

Generally, these constructs are representative of what Java offers. The `class` construct is key in Java because it allows for objects to be defined to model the problem domain. Below that, variables and methods are defined, which correspond to data and code. Code abstraction result in hierarchical statement blocks (with optional local variables) and control flow mechanisms. Figure 3-1 illustrates this hierarchy.

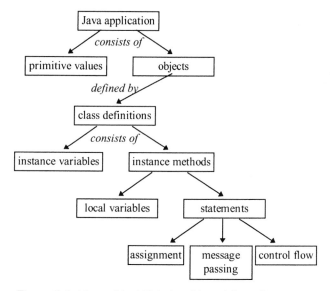

Figure 3-1: Hierarchical Relationships of Java Constructs

3.14 Exercises

1. Which of the following are valid variable names in Java?

   _object
   object–oriented
   object_oriented
   Object.oriented
   $java
   java
   Integer
   String
   Int
   933
   fm90.5
   1fm

2. Define a Square class with the length of its side as an instance variable. Include an appropriate constructor method and methods to enlarge an instance as well as compute its area.

3. Using the Square class in Question 2, create 10 randomly sized squares, and find the sum of their areas.

   (The method `Math.random()` returns a random number between 0.0 and 1.0 each time it is invoked.)

4. Add the functionality for a Square object to draw itself via ASCII characters. For example, a Square of length 4 could be drawn as:

   ```
   ****
   *  *
   *  *
   ****
   ```

   or:

   ```
   XXXX
   X++X
   X++X
   XXXX
   ```

The `System.out.print()` and `System.out.println()` methods would be useful.

5. Find a number with 9 digits $d_1d_2d_3...d_9$ such that the sub-string number $d_1...d_n$ is divisible by n, $1<=n<=9$. Note that each of the digits may be used once.

4 Implementation in Java

In Chapter 3, we demonstrated how object-oriented concepts may be implemented via notations in the Java programming language. For validation purposes, it allows for objects in our system to be operational. We now proceed to see how it may be practically applied to example problems as typical programs.

4.1 Calculator

We first consider how a simple calculator with the basic 4 arithmetic functions, as illustrated in Figure 4-1, might be implemented. Most generic machines allow adding *11* to *13* to be accomplished via the buttons [1][3][+][1][1][=].

For a simple implementation, we will initially not concern ourselves with the non-essentials of external looks (e.g. keypad layout or casing specifics as in real calculators), but instead concentrate on the core calculating engine. Enhancements involving mechanisms for user-interface may be subsequently considered. This is consistent with the software engineering principle of *abstraction*.

Conceptually, the core calculator engine may be viewed as comprising of registers to hold values, together with built-in operators such as addition and subtraction to manipulate such values. Having operations involving two operands, the calculator needs at least two registers.

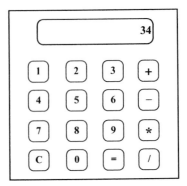

Figure 4-1: Four-function Calculator

Four arithmetic operations imply at least four operators. A *compute* operator is required to get its execution started, together with a *clear* operator to prepare the registers for new computations. These correspond to the equal and clear keys on a calculator. Lastly, the digits form the basic input mechanism for numeric operands. We would assume that the *display* operator will retrieve a value for display on the calculator panel.

Object initialization may be easily accomplished via constructor methods. In this case, a CalculatorEngine object is initialized via invoking the *clear* operator. The resultant Java code skeleton for CalculatorEngine objects with this basic representation is shown in Listing 4-1. Note that all operators easily correspond to instance methods, as well as to buttons on the face on a conventional calculator. Code represented by ellipses will be elaborated in due course.

```
class CalculatorEngine {
   int value;
   int keep;        // two calculator registers
   void add()           { ... }
   void subtract()      { ... }
   void multiply()      { ... }
   void divide()        { ... }
   void compute()       { ... }
   void clear()         { ... }
   void digit(int x)    { ... }
   int display()        { ... }
   CalculatorEngine()   { clear(); }
}
```

Listing 4-1: CalculatorEngine skeleton

4.1.1 The `clear()` method

The `clear()` method initializes the CalculatorEngine object to the state for a calculator to begin the key sequence for next calculation. It is thus intuitive to set the variables `value` and `keep` to 0.

```
void clear() {
  value = 0;
  keep = 0;
}
```

4.1.2 The `display()` method

To implement the `display()` method to provide computation results, we must first clarify the purposes of the instance variables `value` and `keep`. The former is updated as a result of new inputs from numeric keys or the result of an operator, and thus is used to update the display area.

As expressions are keyed in using an infix notation (e.g., $\boxed{1}\boxed{3}\boxed{+}\boxed{1}\boxed{1}\boxed{=}$), the first operand must be stashed away before it is overwritten by the entry of the second operand. The `keep` instance variable serves this purpose.

```
int display() {
  return(value);
}
```

4.1.3 The `digit()` method

The `digit()` method accumulates digits keyed in via the numeric keypad. A new digit shifts existing digits in the `value` instance variable one place to the left. This manipulation is accomplished by multiplication by 10 and followed by addition of the last digit.

```
void digit(int x) {
  value = value*10 + x;
}
```

While this method stands out amongst the other methods as it expects an integer parameter to indicate which numeric key was pushed, it can be circumvented by using wrapper methods such as `zero()`, `one()`, `two()`, `three()`, ...`nine()`.

```
void one() {
  digit(1);
}


void two() {
  digit(2);
}

...
```

4.1.4 Operator Methods

The infix mode of the *add*, *subtract*, *multiply* and *divide* operators require that the specified operation be stashed away to be applied **after** input of the second operand. For this purpose, we define another instance variable `toDo` which records the action to be associated with the next compute operation.

```
char toDo;

void add() {
  keep = value;    // keep first operand
  value = 0;       // initialise and get ready for second operand
  toDo = '+';      // this is what we should do later
}

void subtract() {
  keep = value;    // keep first operand
  value = 0;       // initialise and get ready for second operand
  toDo = '-';      // this is what we should do later
}
```

Since all the binary operations have the same form, it is again natural to adopt abstraction techniques to relocate common code in a `binaryOperation()` method:

```
void binaryOperation(char op) {
  keep = value;    // keep first operand
  value = 0;       // initialize and get ready for second operand
  toDo = op;
}

void add()      { binaryOperation('+');  }
void subtract() { binaryOperation('-');  }
void multiply() { binaryOperation('*');  }
void divide()   { binaryOperation('/');  }
```

Lastly, we conclude with the compute operation which provides the answer to applying the operator in `toDo` on the operands `value` and `keep`.

```java
void compute() {
  if (toDo == '+')
    value = keep + value;
  else if (toDo == '-')
    value = keep - value;
  else if (toDo == '*')
    value = keep * value;
  else if (toDo == '/')
    value = keep / value;
  keep = 0;
}
```

4.2 Code Execution

In the previous chapter, the `new` operator creates an object instance of the class that it is applied to. Thus,

```java
CalculatorEngine c = new CalculatorEngine();
```

creates an instance and associates it with the variable `c`. Subsequently, the code sequence

```java
c.digit(1);
c.digit(3);
c.add();
c.digit(1);
c.digit(1);
c.compute();
```

computes the value of the expression *13+11*. For verification purposes, the Java API (Application Program Interface) method `System.out.println()` may be used to produce output on the screen:

```java
System.out.println(c.display());
```

There is however a slight snag: the CalculatorEngine object instance is the only object in existence, yet which object would send it messages to compute expressions? Or even more fundamental, at the very commencement of program execution when no objects existed, how was the first object created?

Java solves this issue through the introduction of *class methods* which are invoked with respect to the class it is associated with rather than object instances. More specifically, the body of the static method named `main()` is the first code sequence to be executed. As such, the previous code sequence must be brought into `main()` and rearranged as follows:

```
public static void main(String arg[]) {
  CalculatorEngine c = new CalculatorEngine();
  c.digit(1);
  c.digit(3);
  c.add();
  c.digit(1);
  c.digit(1);
  c.compute();
  System.out.println(c.display());
}
```

The various code fragments may be brought together within a class construct in the file `CalculatorEngine.java` as shown in Listing 4-2.

```
class CalculatorEngine {
  int value;
  int keep;        // two calculator registers
  char toDo;

  void binaryOperation(char op)  {
    keep = value;    // keep first operand
    value = 0;        // initialize and get ready for second operand
    toDo = op;
  }

  void add()       { binaryOperation('+'); }
  void subtract()  { binaryOperation('-'); }
  void multiply()  { binaryOperation('*'); }
  void divide()    { binaryOperation('/'); }

  void compute() {
    if (toDo == '+')
      value = keep + value;
    else if (toDo == '-')
      value = keep - value;
    else if (toDo == '*')
      value = keep * value;
    else if (toDo == '/')
      value = keep / value;
    keep = 0;
  }

  void clear() {
    value = 0;
    keep = 0;
```

```
        }

        void digit(int x)   {
          value = value*10 + x;
        }

        int display() {
          return(value);
        }

        CalculatorEngine() { clear(); }

        public static void main(String arg[]) {
          CalculatorEngine c = new CalculatorEngine();
          c.digit(1);
          c.digit(3);
          c.add();
          c.digit(1);
          c.digit(1);
          c.compute();
          System.out.println(c.display());
        }
    }
```

Listing 4-2: CalculatorEngine class

With the Java Development Kit (JDK) version 1.1.x appropriately installed, it may
be compiled via:

```
$ javac CalculatorEngine.java
```

where `CalculatorEngine.java` is the name of the file containing Java source and `$`
is the system's command line prompt. Similarly, execution of the resultant Java
bytecode may proceed via:

```
$ java CalculatorEngine
```

4.3 Simple User Interface

While the code in `static void main()` does execute to show the behavior of a
CalculatorEngine object instance, it is an absolutely clumsy situation. Each
evaluation of a new arithmetic expression requires editing code and recompilation.
Ideally, we should be compiling the source once, but inputting different expressions
for evaluation.

It is common to have an user-interface object to work cooperatively with the CalculatorEngine. This separation of concerns allow for the CalculatorEngine to be independent of interface issues. We will initially consider a line-mode user interface and subsequently enhance it for a windowing environment.

To this end, a CalculatorInterface object fulfills this role. It has the role of a middleman which does not work too much, but instead accepts input and passes it onto the CalculatorEngine. Similarly, feedback from the CalculatorEngine is collected and becomes output for the CalculatorInterface object.

The implementation of CalculatorInterface consists of an initializing phase where a CalculatorEngine object is bound to an CalculatorInterface object, and an execution phase which performs the necessary dispatching. These are implemented by the constructor and `run()` methods of CalculatorInterface respectively, as illustrated in Listing 4-3.

```
import java.io.*;

class CalculatorInput {

  BufferedReader stream;
  CalculatorEngine engine;

  CalculatorInput(CalculatorEngine e) {
    InputStreamReader input = new InputStreamReader(System.in);
    stream = new BufferedReader(input) ;
    engine = e;
  }

  void run() throws Exception {
    for (;;) {
      System.out.print("[" + engine.display() + "]");
      String m = stream.readLine();
      if (m == null) break;
      if (m.length() > 0) {
        char c = m.charAt(0);
        if (c == '+') engine.add();
        else if (c == '-') engine.subtract();
        else if (c == '*') engine.multiply();
        else if (c == '/') engine.divide();
        else if (c >= '0' && c <= '9') engine.digit(c - '0');
        else if (c == '=') engine.compute();
        else if (c == 'c' || c == 'C') engine.clear();
      }
    }
  }
}
```

```
public static void main(String arg[]) throws Exception {
  CalculatorEngine e = new CalculatorEngine();
  CalculatorInput x = new CalculatorInput(e) ;
  x.run();
}
}
```

Listing 4-3: CalculatorInput class

While the code for CalculatorInterface relies on facilities for exception and input/output handling which have not been described, these may initially be ignored. Nevertheless, the code serves two immediate purposes here:

- It demonstrates the context of a *test harness* and how it is easily constructed to aid incremental development.

- It shows the synergistic cooperation of two objects with distinct concerns in an object-oriented design environment.

Until these topics are discussed in Chapters 9 and 10, it is not harmful that at present, they be taken by faith. The "throws Exception" signature suffix allows for Java exceptions to be for the moment ignored. It is useful for modular and secure programming methodology. It also suffices that the BufferedReader class facilitates input, and that the readLine() method allows an input line to be read.

The new user-interface class may be compiled via

```
$ javac CalculatorInput.java
```

It provides the added flexibility of arbitrary computations via keyboard input sequences. The calculator display is indicated within square brackets "[ ]":

```
$ java CalculatorInput
[0] 1
[1] 3
[13] +
[0] 1
[1] 1
[11] =
[24]
```

4.4   Another Interface for CalculatorEngine

The separation of concerns between CalculatorEngine and CalculatorInterface allows for the former to be reused in different environments. To show the ease of code reusability when a neat modular structure is adopted, another user-interface framework to work with CalculatorEngine is introduced in this section.

Similar to CalculatorInput, CalculatorFrame provides an environment for a CalculatorEngine object to execute. The major difference is that CalculatorFrame caters for a windowing environment, and gives the illusion that the calculator "hides" behind the frame.

Windowing facilities in Java will be discussed in Chapter 12. However, this graphical calculator example is still appropriate since its objective is to show the benefits of modular code and reusable API libraries in Java. Code in the constructor method sets up a calculator frame with buttons and a display at appropriate locations. Using a graphical user interface in this instance is fairly straight-forward since mouse clicks on calculator buttons are mapped to actionPerformed() method. As such, code which performs the necessary dispatching to CalculatorEngine shown in Listing 4-4 is similar to that in the run() method in CalculatorInput.

```java
import java.awt.*;
import java.awt.event.*;

class CalculatorFrame extends Frame implements ActionListener {

    CalculatorEngine engine;
    TextField display;

    WindowListener listener = new WindowAdapter() {
        public void windowClosing(WindowEvent e)   { System.exit(0); }
    };
```

```
    CalculatorFrame(CalculatorEngine e) {
      super("Calculator");
      Panel top, bottom; Button b;

      engine = e;
      top = new Panel();
      top.add(display = new TextField(20));
      bottom = new Panel();
      bottom.setLayout(new GridLayout(4,4));
      bottom.add(b = new Button("1")); b.addActionListener(this);
      bottom.add(b = new Button("2")); b.addActionListener(this);
      bottom.add(b = new Button("3")); b.addActionListener(this);
      bottom.add(b = new Button("+")); b.addActionListener(this);
      bottom.add(b = new Button("4")); b.addActionListener(this);
      bottom.add(b = new Button("5")); b.addActionListener(this);
      bottom.add(b = new Button("6")); b.addActionListener(this);
      bottom.add(b = new Button("-")); b.addActionListener(this);
      bottom.add(b = new Button("7")); b.addActionListener(this);
      bottom.add(b = new Button("8")); b.addActionListener(this);
      bottom.add(b = new Button("9")); b.addActionListener(this);
      bottom.add(b = new Button("*")); b.addActionListener(this);
      bottom.add(b = new Button("C")); b.addActionListener(this);
      bottom.add(b = new Button("0")); b.addActionListener(this);
      bottom.add(b = new Button("=")); b.addActionListener(this);
      bottom.add(b = new Button("/")); b.addActionListener(this);
      setLayout(new BorderLayout());
      add("North", top);
      add("South", bottom) ;
      addWindowListener(listener) ;
      setSize(180, 160) ;
      show();
    }

    public void actionPerformed(ActionEvent e) {
      char c = e.getActionCommand().charAt(0);
      if (c == '+') engine.add();
      else if (c == '-') engine.subtract();
      else if (c == '*') engine.multiply();
      else if (c == '/') engine.divide();
      else if (c >= '0' && c <= '9') engine.digit(c - '0');
      else if (c == '=') engine.compute();
      else if (c == 'C') engine.clear();
      display.setText(new Integer(engine.display()).toString());
    }

    public static void main(String arg[]) {
      new CalculatorFrame(new CalculatorEngine());
    }
}
```

Listing 4-4: CalculatorFrame class

4.4.1 Event-driven Programming

While much code may be presently skipped, it is of great encouragement to readers that the API libraries allow for windowing applications to be developed with minimal user-code. Much code occur in the constructor and `actionPerformed()` methods, which sets up the calculator buttons and respond to mouse clicks.

The code in the CalculatorFrame class looks somewhat strange because it is not completely procedural in its specification. In particular, while the body of the `actionPerformed()` method resembles that in `run()` in CalculatorInput, the former is not explicitly invoked from within the class, such as from `static void main()` (as was the case for CalculatorInput) .

Procedural programming is the paradigm where actions are specified in a step-by-step sequence like a baking recipe. Within each Java method, code is specified procedurally and execution order may be easily determined.

In event-driven programming, code fragments are instead associated with events and invoked when these events occur. In a typical graphical environment with windowing facilities, events correspond to mouse movements, mouse clicks and keystrokes from the keyboard. It is impossible to determine or plan in advance what course of actions users might take to accomplish a certain task. Instead, we associate code fragments with significant events so that their side-effects would be appropriate response to such external events.

In an object-oriented system, methods are convenient units of code, and are used to receive stimuli from external devices. In Java, an ActionListener keeps a lookout for events involving mouse clicks. This is relevant to our CalculatorFrame, and we in turn implement the `actionPerformed()` method as a trigger point for mouse clicks on calculator buttons.

Thus, for each push as a calculator button, `actionPerformed()` is invoked, and it uses the `getActionCommand()` to identify which button. The framework for windowing using the AWT API will be further elaborated in Chapter 12.

Similarly, WindowAdaptor is used to monitor events involving windows, and `windowClosing()` is the corresponding method which is invoked when the user clicks to close the calculator window. Execution is terminated via `System.exit(0)` .

4.5 Summary

This chapter demonstrates Java syntax and semantic covered earlier in Chapter 3. The calculator case study example shows how:

- a class construct might be developed and compiled for execution by the virtual machine

- execution commences with the `static void main()` method

- objects are instantiated and appropriately coordinated for cooperative message passing to model

- the BufferedReader class is used for input

- the AWT package is used for GUI programming using frames and involving event-handling.

4.6 Exercises

1. The operators for CalculatorEngine are binary and require two operands. How would unary operators which require one operand be incorporated?

   Modify the CalculatorEngine class to add the following capabilities.

   - squareOf

   - factorial

2. Choose two interface characters most apt for squareOf and factorial and incorporate the additional capability into the CalculatorInput class.

3. Rearrange the layout of the calculator panel in the CalculatorFrame class to accommodate the new capabilities, and modify the appropriate event-handlers to take advantage of these functions.

4. The CalculatorFrame class produces the result of 247 corresponding to the key input sequence 1 3 + 1 1 = 7 . Explain the reason for this observation, and suggest how it may be corrected.

5 Classification, Generalization and Specialization

Objects of similar definition have been grouped and defined into classes. The act of identifying and categorizing similar objects into classes is known as *classification* in object-oriented modeling. In this chapter, we shall examine how objects are grouped into classes and how the relationships of classes can be organized into a class hierarchy using abstraction mechanisms *generalization* and *specialization*. In addition, we shall discuss the concept of *superclass* and *subclass* as a prelude to discussing generalization and specialization.

5.1 Classification

In Table 5-1, there are 18 instances of animal. Each entry has a name and a short description. Some of the animals share common information among themselves. We shall group the animals based on their commonality with each other.

We shall begin with Mighty, Flipper, Willy, Janet, Jeremy, Bunny, and Smudge. These objects are grouped together into the Mammal category since they share some common information typical of a mammal:

- their youngs are born alive;

- they are warm-blooded;

- they breathe through their lungs; and

- their body is covered with hair.

Object	What is it?	Object	What is it?
Angel	a fish	Mighty	an elephant
Bunny	a rabbit	Smudge	a cat
Janet	a female person	Jaws	a shark
Jeremy	a male person	Swift	an eagle
Flipper	a dolphin	Willy	a whale
Heather	a hen	Parry	a parrot
Wise	an owl	Sally	a snake
Kermit	a frog	Lily	a lizard
Beatle	a bug	Ben	a bee

Table 5-1 : A List of Objects

Similarly, Parry, Heather, Wise and Swift are grouped into a Bird category as they share common information typical of a bird:

- they have a beak;

- they have two legs;

- they have two wings;

- their wings and body are covered with feathers;

- they can fly;

- they lay eggs; and

- they are warm-blooded.

In like manner, we group:

- Angel and Jaws into a Fish category;

- Sally and Lily into a Reptile category;

- Beatle and Ben into an Insect category; and

- Kermit into an Amphibian category.

Six categories were eventually produced as shown in Figure 5-1. In object-oriented modeling, the act of categorizing objects is known as *classification*. The categories formed are known as classes. From a modeling perspective, classes form meaningful abstractions for organizing information – any reference to the classes would indirectly refer to the objects in the class.

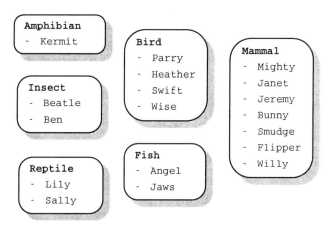

Figure 5-1: Categories of Animal

5.2 Hierarchical Relationship of Classes

Classes formed can be organized in a hierarchical manner. Depending on the position of a class in the hierarchy, it may be known as a superclass or a subclass of a class. We shall now examine the notion of superclass and subclass here.

5.2.1 Superclass and Subclass

In Chapter 2, we introduced Sean and Sara as salespersons of HomeCare. We also mentioned that Sean and Sara are objects of the SalesPerson class. We shall now introduce two more employees – Simon and Sandy. Specifically, Simon and Sandy are managers with properties that are slightly different from Sean and Sara. We shall classify Simon and Sandy as objects of a different class: Manager. Nevertheless, all four persons are, employees of HomeCare and objects of another class: Employee. The relationships of these classes and objects are illustrated in Figure 5-2.

Note that Sean and Sara are shown as instances of the SalesPerson class while Simon and Sandy are instances of the Manager class. The enclosing boundary of the Employee class over these objects indicates that the objects are also instances of the Employee class.

Sean and Sara therefore belong to two classes: the Employee class and SalesPerson class. Likewise, Simon and Sandy belong to the Employee and Manager class. This implies that the information about Sean and Sara as employees is also true of them as salespersons. We can thus refer to Sean as an employee or a salesperson.

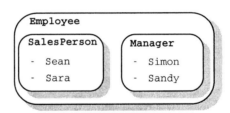

Figure 5-2: Employee, SalesPerson and Manager Class

Which class Sean is referred to is a matter of generality. When Sean is referred to as an employee, we are being general about who he is but when he is referred to as a salesperson, specific information about his role and employment is specified. For example, Sean takes orders and earns a commission for each sale since he is a salesperson but this does not apply to Sandy who is a manager, despite both of them being employees of HomeCare. Similarly, when we speak of an object as an employee, we are being general and its differences with objects of other classes are ignored.

The Employee class is said to be a *generalized* class of SalesPerson and Manager. Conversely, SalesPerson and Manager are said to be *specialized* classes of the Employee class. Generalized and specialized classes can be organized into a class hierarchy with the generalized classes placed toward the top of the hierarchy and the specialized classes toward the bottom of the hierarchy.

A specialized class is known as a *subclass* of a class while the generalized class is known as a *superclass* of a subclass in object-oriented terms. For example, SalesPerson is a subclass of the Employee class which is also the superclass of SalesPerson.

5.2.2 A Class Hierarchy Diagram

The hierarchical relationships among classes can be seen in a class hierarchy diagram in Figure 5-3. A box in the diagram represents a class while a triangle denotes the hierarchical relationship between classes with a superclass positioned at the top. Subclasses are placed toward the bottom of a class hierarchy diagram.

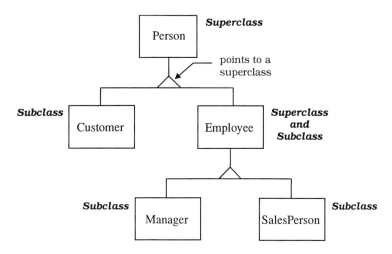

Figure 5-3: A Class Hierarchy Diagram

A class can be a superclass to a class or a subclass of another class or both depending on its position in the hierarchy. For example in Figure 5-3:

- Manager and SalesPerson are subclasses of the Employee class.

- Employee is a subclass of the Person class.

- Person is a superclass of Customer and Employee class.

- Employee is thus a superclass (to Manager and SalesPerson) and a subclass (of Person) in the hierarchy.

5.3 Generalization

Generalization is the act of capturing similarities between classes and defining the similarities in a new generalized class; the classes then become subclasses of the generalized class. For example, the Mammal, Fish, Bird, Reptile, and Amphibian classes introduced earlier, are similar in that all objects from these classes have a backbone. Based on this similarity, we can refer to them via a new superclass, say Animal-with-Backbone. Hence, we can refer to Kermit (an object of the Amphibian class) as an object of the Animal-with-Backbone class too. Similarly, the Insect class can be generalized into an Animal-without-Backbone class since objects from the Insert class are without a backbone. Figure 5-4 summarizes the relationships of these classes.

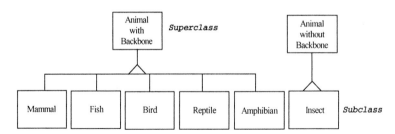

Figure 5-4: Generalizing Classes

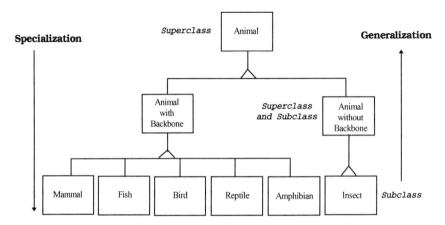

Figure 5-5: A Class Hierarchy for Animals

Animal-with-Backbone class and Animal-without-Backbone class can be further generalized by considering the similarities of objects from these two classes. Let us call the generalized class, Animal. The generalization of properties of Animal-with-Backbone class and Animal-without-Backbone class into the Animal class is shown in Figure 5-5.

The Animal class, being the topmost class in the class hierarchy, is thus the most general class of the entire Animal class hierarchy. This means that Swift, which is an object of the Bird class, is also an object of the Animal-with-Backbone class and Animal class, for example. When we refer to Swift as an object of the Animal class, we are being general about it and we would be ignoring specific information about Swift as a bird in this reference.

5.4 Specialization

In contrast, *specialization* is the act of capturing differences among objects in a class and creating new distinct subclasses with the differences. In this way, we are specializing information about objects of the superclass into subclasses. For example, in creating Animal-with-Backbone class and Animal-without-Backbone class from the Animal class, we are distinguishing information about objects with a backbone from others without a backbone into Animal-with-Backbone and Animal-without-Backbone classes. Eventually, only objects with a backbone would be classified into the Animal-with-Backbone class and the others into the Animal-without-Backbone class.

Similarly, objects from the Animal-with-Backbone class can be further classified into the Mammal, Fish, Bird, Reptile, or Amphibian classes depending on their definition of properties.

5.5 Organization of Class Hierarchy

Classes in a class hierarchy diagram are organized in such a way that generalized classes are placed toward the top of the hierarchy.

As we traverse higher into a class hierarchy, the classes become more general in definition and more objects can be classified into them. As we traverse lower into the class hierarchy, the subclasses become more specialized in definition and fewer objects can be classified into them.

5.6 Abstract and Concrete Classes

There are classes in a class hierarchy that are so general that there is really no intention to create objects from them. Such classes are meant to contain common attributes or methods of subclasses for reuse purpose. These classes are known as *abstract classes* in object-oriented modeling. For example, the Animal-with-Backbone class has been included into the class hierarchy to contain properties similar to objects in classes Mammal, Fish, Bird, Reptile, and Amphibian. Similarly, the Animal-without-Backbone class abstract general information about insects and finally, the Animal class generalizes all common properties of classes in its definition.

While classes Animal, Animal-with-Backbone and Animal-without-Backbone abstract the common properties of objects, object instances are actually created from the lowest level subclasses. Such classes from which objects are instantiated are known as *concrete classes*. Thus, Mammal, Fish, Bird, Reptile, Amphibian and Insect are concrete classes for the above class hierarchy on animals.

Abstract classes are implemented in Java using the `abstract` keyword as follows:

```
abstract class Animal {
...
}

abstract class Animal-with-Backbone extends Animal {
...
}

abstract class Animal-without-Backbone extends Animal {
...
}
```

and concrete classes are defined in the usual way:

```
class Mammal extends Animal-with-Backbone {
  Mammal(String name) {}
  ...
}

class Fish extends Animal-with-Backbone {
 Fish() {}
  ...
}

class Bird extends Animal-with-Backbone {
  Bird() {}
  ...
}

class Reptile extends Animal-with-Backbone {
 Reptile() {}
  ...
}

class Amphibian extends Animal-with-Backbone {
 Amphibian() {}
  ...
}

class Insect extends Animal-without-Backbone {
  Insect() {}
  ...
}
```

Intuitively,

```
Animal a = new Animal();
```

is not valid while

```
Mammal j = new Mammal("John");
```

is valid.

5.7 Summary

The following concepts were discussed in this chapter:

- *Classification* – categorizing of objects into a class.

- A *subclass* is a specialized class of a superclass and a *superclass* is a generalized class of a subclass.

- *Generalization* – the act of capturing similarities between classes and defining the similarities in a new generalized class; the classes then become subclasses of the generalized class.

- *Specialization* – the act of capturing differences among objects in a class and creating new distinct subclasses with the differences.

- *Abstract class* – a class from which no object instances will be created.

- *Concrete class* – a class from which object instances will be created.

5.8 Exercises

1. In your own words, describe generalization and specialization.

2.   Information about some objects is given below. Classify the objects into these classes: Bird, Insect, Fish, and Four-Legged Animal.

Object	What is it?	Data	Methods
Aaron	an Ant	a, b, d, f	X(),Z()
Beatle	a Bug	a, b, d, f	X(),Z()
Smudge	a Dog	a, b, d, l	X(),Z()
Swift	an Eagle	a, b, c, e	X(),Y()
Herman	a Hawk	a, b, c, e	X(),Y()
Oscar	an Orange	u	N()
Rosie	a Rose	v	O()
Tora	a Tiger	a, b, d, l	X(),Z()
Goldie	a Goldfish	a, b, d, g	X(),Z()
John	a Male-Person	a, b, d, h, i	X(),Z()
Jack	a Jaguar	a, b, d, l	X(),Z()
Angel	a Goldfish	a, b, d, g	X(),Z()

3.   Create generalized classes for the classes in Question 2 and produce a class hierarchy.

4.   Indicate in your class hierarchy for Question 3 abstract classes and concrete classes.

6 Inheritance

In Chapter 5, we discussed generalization/specialization as an abstraction mechanism for modeling classes and their hierarchical relationships with one another. We also introduced superclasses as generalized classes of subclasses.

In this chapter, we shall discuss *inheritance* as a mechanism for enabling properties (attributes and methods) of superclasses to be propagated downward to their respective subclasses and made them available as part of the subclasses' definition. From an implementation standpoint, inheritance encourages software reuse. The impact of inheritance on software development will also be discussed.

6.1 Common Properties

A class hierarchy on persons and employees was earlier introduced in Chapter 5. This hierarchy is reproduced but with attribute and method definitions added onto it as illustrated in Figure 6-1.

We can make the following observations about the class diagram:

- attribute `name` and method `getName()` are common in all three classes,

- attribute `employee number` and method `getEmployeeNumber()` are common in Employee and SalesPerson class.

- attribute `commission` is specific to SalesPerson class and does not appear in other classes.

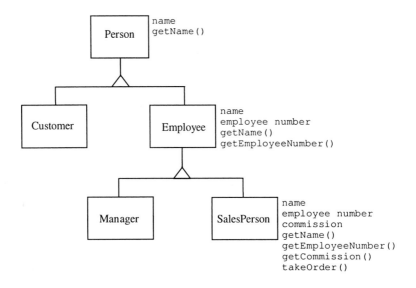

Figure 6-1: Common Properties in Classes

6.2 Inheritance

From a software reuse standpoint, generalized properties defined in superclasses should be made available to subclasses without having to declare them explicitly in the subclasses. In object-oriented programming, such reuse is possible via inheritance.

Inheritance is the ability of a subclass to take on the general properties of superclasses in the inheritance chain as part of the subclass' definition. Inheritance enables superclasses' properties to be propagated downward to the subclasses in a class hierarchy, and makes the properties available as part of the subclasses' definition. These properties are said to be *inherited* (or taken on) by the subclasses.

Using inheritance, the SalesPerson class of Figure 6-1 can now be defined by a combination of properties from:

- the Employee class,

- the Person class, and

- its own specific attribute and method definition.

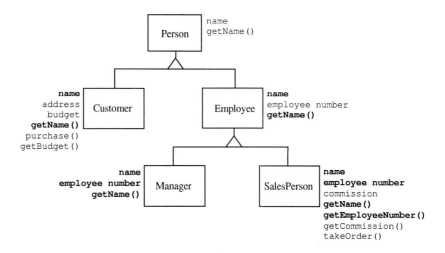

Figure 6-2: Classes with Inherited Properties

Figure 6-2 shows the modified class hierarchy for persons (with inherited properties highlighted in bold). The Person class has the following definition:

```
Class Person {
  Attributes :
    name
  Methods :
    getName()      {return name}
}
```

The Employee class is reduced to (with inherited properties highlighted in bold):

```
Class Employee {
  Attributes :
    name                          (inherited from Person class)
    employee number
  Methods :
    getName()      {return name} (inherited from Person class)
    getEmployeeNumber(){return employee number}
}
```

The SalesPerson class is simplified into (with inherited properties highlighted in bold):

```
Class SalesPerson {
  Attributes :
    name                          (inherited from Person Class)
    employee number               (inherited from Employee class)
    commission
  Methods :
    takeOrder(who, stock, address, date)    {
      check with warehouse on stock availability
      check with warehouse on delivery schedule
      if ok
      then {instruct warehouse to deliver stock
            to address on date
          return ok}
      else return not ok
    }
    getName()     {return name} (inherited from Person class)
    getEmployeeNumber(){return employee number}
                                (inherited from Employee class)
    getCommission() {return commission}
}
```

Note that attributes `name` and `employee name`, and methods `getName()` and `getEmployeeNumber()` of the SalesPerson class are not explicitly defined in the SalesPerson class but propagated downward from the superclasses through inheritance.

Only downward propagation of properties from superclasses to subclasses are permissible. There is no upward propagation of properties in object-oriented programming. Therefore, information specific to subclasses are unique to subclasses and are not propagated to superclasses. For this reason, attribute `commission` and method `getCommission()` of the SalesPerson class do not form part of the Employee class definition.

6.3 Implementing Inheritance

We shall now extend the Person class hierarchy to include a new class, Secretary. Figure 6-3 shows the modified class hierarchy with inherited properties highlighted in bold. The information in the extended hierarchy suggests that all employees have a basic salary except managers and salespersons who are paid an allowance and commission respectively.

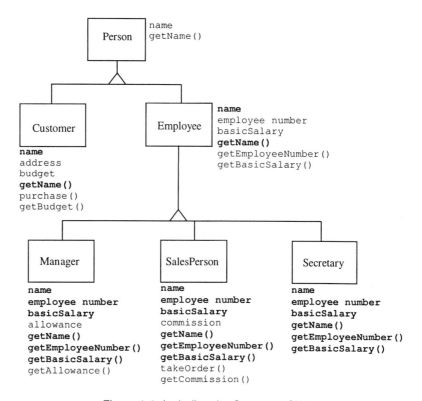

Figure 6-3: Including the Secretary Class

Superclass-Subclass relationship in a class hierarchy is denoted in the code by the keyword extends. This suggests that a subclass is an extension of a superclass. For example, the following code fragment suggests that Employee is an extension of the Person class; Manager, SalesPerson and Secretary, being subclasses, are extensions of the Employee class:

```
class Employee extends Person {
    ...
}
class Manager extends Employee {
    ...
}
class SalesPerson extends Employee {
    ...
}
class Secretary extends Employee {
    ...
}
```

Listing 6-1 is the code implementing the Person hierarchy. Code execution begins with the Employee class since it is the only class that contains `static void main()`. To execute `main()`, type the following at the command prompt line:

```
$ java Employee
```

Executing the code produces the following output:

```
The Manager Simon (employee number 01234M) has a salary of 9000
The Secretary Selene (employee number 98765S) has a salary of 2500
The Manager Simon also has an allowance of 2000
```

The output suggests that some information was made available from the superclasses in deriving the manager's and secretary's salary. Objects instantiated from the Manager or Secretary class were able to respond to requests for their `basicSalary` having inherited from the Employee class the attribute `basicSalary` and method `getBasicSalary()`.

Let us closely examine `main()`. The code begins with the instantiation of two objects, a manager and a secretary. The manager object is referenced by variable `m` while the secretary object is referenced by variable `s`:

```
Manager m = new Manager("Simon", "01234M", 9000.0f, 2000.0f);
Secretary s = new Secretary("Selene", "98765S", 2500.0f);
```

The state of the two objects is depicted in Figure 6-4.

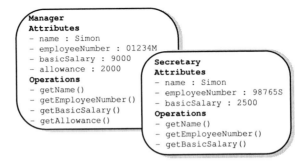

Figure 6-4: State of Manager and Secretary Object

```
class Person {
  private String name;
  Person(String aName) {name=aName;}
  public String getName() { return name; }
}

class Employee extends Person {
  private float basicSalary;
  private String employeeNumber;

  Employee(String aName, String aEmployeeNumber,
           float aBasicSalary) {
    super(aName);
    employeeNumber = aEmployeeNumber;
    basicSalary = aBasicSalary;
  }
  public String getEmployeeNumber() { return employeeNumber; }
  public float getBasicSalary() { return basicSalary; }

  public static void main(String argv[]) {
    Manager m = new Manager("Simon", "01234M", 9000.0f,2000.0f);
    Secretary s = new Secretary("Selene", "98765S", 2500.0f);
    System.out.print("The Manager "+m.getName()+
                     " (employee number "+m.getEmployeeNumber()+")");
    System.out.println(" has a salary of "+m.getBasicSalary());
    System.out.print("The Secretary "+s.getName()+
                     " (employee number "+s.getEmployeeNumber()+")");
    System.out.print("The Manager "+m.getName());
    System.out.println(" also has an allowance of " +m.getAllowance());
  }
}

class Manager extends Employee {
  private float allowance;

  Manager(String aName, String aEmployeeNumber,
          float aBasicSalary, float aAllowanceAmt) {
    super(aName, aEmployeeNumber, aBasicSalary);
    allowance = aAllowanceAmt;
  }
  public float getAllowance() {
    return allowance;
  }
}

class Secretary extends Employee {
  Secretary (String aName, String aEmployeeNumber,
             float aBasicSalary) {
    super(aName, aEmployeeNumber, aBasicSalary);
  }
}
```

Listing 6-1: Inheritance in the Extended Person Hierarchy

The remainder of `main()` are output statements. Some methods from various classes, invoked in producing the outputs, e.g. `getName()` from the Person class, and `getEmployeeNumber()` and `getBasicSalary()` from the Employee class, are propagated through the inheritance mechanism to the subclasses, Manager and Secretary.

6.4 Code Reuse

By allowing information of a superclass to be taken on by subclasses, the information is said to be reused at the subclass level. All newly created instances of the subclasses would have as part of their definition the inherited information. For example, `employee number`, `basic salary`, and `getEmployeeNumber()` of the Employee class and `name` and `getName()` of the Person class are said to be *reused* by the Manager and Secretary class.

6.5 Making Changes in Class Hierarchy

Changes to software specification are inevitable. We shall now consider how changes in a class hierarchy impact software maintenance as a whole. The following situations will be discussed:

- Change in property definition for *all* subclasses.

- Change in property definition for *some* subclasses.

- Adding/deleting a class.

6.5.1 Change in Property Definition for All Subclasses

Suppose a change in representational scheme of the `employee number` in Figure 6-3 is required. This change will affect not only the attribute `employee number` but also the method `getEmployeeNumber()` and possibly other classes that inherit `employee number`. We shall examine this change in two possibilities:

a. inheritance is not available

b. inheritance is available.

a) Inheritance Not Available

In the case where inheritance is not available, the attribute `employee number` and method `getEmployeeNumber()` would have to be defined in all the relevant classes e.g. Employee, Manager, SalesPerson and Secretary. The change in representational scheme of `employee number` would thus have to be effected individually on these classes. The redundancy arising from the multiple definition of `employee number` and `getEmployeeNumber()` may lead to inconsistency in definition if the change is not carried out properly.

b) Inheritance Available

With inheritance, the situation is different. We would first define attribute `employee number` and method `getEmployeeNumber()` in Employee class and let subclasses Manager, SalesPerson and Secretary inherit these definitions from Employee class. The required change in representational scheme for attribute `employee number` would be limited to the Employee class. The change would be propagated to the subclasses via inheritance. In this way, the change is thus limited to the superclass, enabling a uniform and consistent property definition for all subclasses. In addition, redundancy in property definition at the subclass level can be minimized and software maintenance enhanced.

6.5.2 Change in Property Definition for Some Subclasses

In some situations, a change in property definition at the superclass level may not necessarily apply to all subclasses. The above solution would therefore not apply in these situations. To illustrate, let us extend the Person class hierarchy further to include two more employee classes: Technician and Clerk.

Let us assume the following for a HomeCare employee:

- a manager   – basic salary plus allowance

- a salesperson – basic salary plus commission

- a secretary   – basic salary

- a technician – basic salary

- a clerk   – basic salary

At the Employee class, a `getPay()` method is defined to return the monthly pay of an employee since the method applies to all classes of employee. The definition of the Person class remains the same as before:

```
class Person {
  private String name;
  Person(String aName) {name=aName;}
  public String getName() { return name; }
}
```

Employee extends Person as follows:

```
class Employee extends Person {
  private float basicSalary;
  private String employeeNumber;

  Employee(String aName, String aEmployeeNumber,
           float aBasicSalary) {
    super(aName);
    employeeNumber = aEmployeeNumber;
    basicSalary = aBasicSalary;
  }
  public String getEmployeeNumber() { return employeeNumber; }
  public float getBasicSalary() { return basicSalary; }
  public float getPay() { return basicSalary; }

  public static void main(String argv[]) {
    Manager m = new Manager("Simon", "01234M", 9000.0f, 2000.0f);
    Secretary s = new Secretary("Selene", "98765S", 2500.0f);
    Technician t = new Technician("Terrence", "42356T", 2000.0f);
    Clerk c = new Clerk("Charmaine", "68329C", 1200.0f);
    System.out.print("The Manager "+m.getName()+
                     " (employee number "+m.getEmployeeNumber()+")");
    System.out.println(" has a pay of "+m.getPay());
    System.out.print("The Secretary "+s.getName()+
                     " (employee number "+s.getEmployeeNumber()+")");
    System.out.println(" has a pay of "+s.getPay());
    System.out.print("The Technician "+t.getName()+
                     " (employee number "+t.getEmployeeNumber()+")");
    System.out.println(" has a pay of "+t.getPay());
    System.out.print("The Clerk "+c.getName()+
                     " (employee number "+c.getEmployeeNumber()+")");
    System.out.println(" has a pay of "+c.getPay());
  }
}
```

As before, `main()` is defined in the Employee class with additional code for Technician and Clerk class highlighted in bold.

There is no change in class definition for Manager and Secretary. Technician and Clerk extend Employee, since they are subclasses of Employee:

```
class Technician extends Employee {
  Technician (String aName, String aEmployeeNumber,
             float aBasicSalary) {
    super(aName, aEmployeeNumber, aBasicSalary);
  }
}
class Clerk extends Employee {
  Clerk (String aName, String aEmployeeNumber,
        float aBasicSalary) {
    super(aName, aEmployeeNumber, aBasicSalary);
  }
}
```

Executing `main()` produces the following output:

```
The Manager Simon (employee number 01234M) has a pay of 9000
The Secretary Selene (employee number 98765S) has a pay of 2500
The Technician Terrence (employee number 42356T) has a pay of 2000
The Clerk Charmaine (employee number 68329C) has a pay of 1200
```

A cursory examination of the output reveals an inaccuracy in manager's pay: an omission of allowance amount of $2000. What had gone wrong?

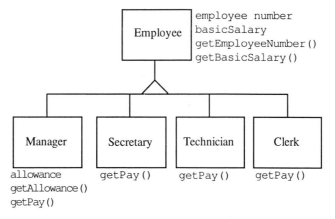

Figure 6-5: Extended Employee Class Hierarchy

The above problem can be approached in two ways:

- Remove the getPay() method from the Employee class and define it individually in the subclasses (Secretary, Technician, Clerk, and Manager).

- Maintain the definition of getPay() method in Employee class and *redefine* it in the Manager class.

Figure 6-5 illustrates a class diagram for the first approach. Each of the subclasses has its own implementation of the getPay() method. One disadvantage of this approach is that the definition of the getPay() method has to be repeated in all the subclasses. This is highly inefficient and can be difficult to maintain especially in situations where the number of subclasses is large.

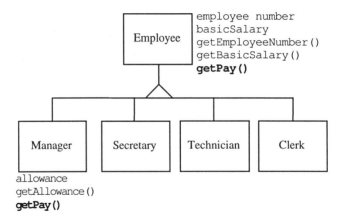

Figure 6-6: Redefining getPay() method of Manager

In the second approach, the definition of the getPay() method is maintained at the Employee class but redefined in the Manager class. This ensures that the getPay() method is inherited by all subclasses of Employee, including the Manager class.

Since a similar getPay() method is defined in Manager, the getPay() method of the Manager class would be used in the resolution of method call by the object-oriented system instead. This is depicted in Figure 6-6 and Listing 6-2.

The getPay() method of Manager class is said to redefine the getPay() method of Employee class. Note that a redefined method has the same method name and parameter definition of a redefining method. While a redefining method has the same method signature with the redefined method, the implementation of the methods may differ. In this case, the getPay() method of Manager class includes an additional computation of the allowance component.

```
class Person {
  ...
}
class Employee extends Person {
  ...
  public float getPay() { return basicSalary; }
  public static void main(String argv[]) {
  ...
  }
}
class Manager extends Employee {
  private float allowance;

  Manager(String aName, String aEmployeeNumber,
          float aBasicSalary, float aAllowanceAmt) {
    super(aName, aEmployeeNumber, aBasicSalary);
    allowance = aAllowanceAmt;
  }

  public float getAllowance() {
    return allowance;
  }

  public float getPay() {
    return (basicSalary + allowance);
  }
}
class Secretary extends Employee {
  ...
}
class Technician extends Employee {
  ...
}
class Clerk extends Employee {
  ...
}
```

Listing 6-2: Redefining getPay() Method

Judging from the output of the two solutions, both approaches are correct:

```
The Manager Simon (employee number 01234M) has a pay of 11000
The Secretary Selene (employee number 98765S) has a pay of 2500
The Technician Terrence (employee number 42356T) has a pay of 2000
The Clerk Charmaine (employee number 68329C) has a pay of 1200
```

However, the second approach is better than the first approach as it enhances software reuse and minimizes the effect of change on other classes. Redefinition of methods is supported in object-oriented programming and closely connected with operation overloading. We shall further discuss *operation overloading* in the next chapter.

6.5.3 Adding/Deleting a Class

Adding a class into an existing class hierarchy can be detrimental to the stability of the hierarchy. It is always recommended that the addition of a new class be created as a subclass in the class hierarchy. The definition of existing classes will not be adversely affected by this approach. To illustrate, let us consider an example of geometrical shapes.

Figure 6-7 is a class hierarchy of shapes. Shape is a generalized class of Circle and Square. All shapes have a name and a measurement by which the area of the shape is calculated.

The attribute `name` and method `getName()` are defined as properties of Shape. Circle and Square, being subclasses of Shape, inherit these properties (highlighted in bold in Figure 6-7).

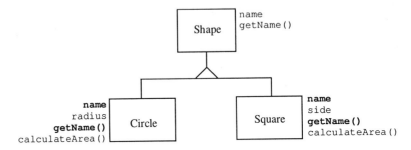

Figure 6-7: Class Hierarchy Diagram of Shape, Circle and Square

The Shape class has the following definition:

```
class Shape {
  private String name;
  Shape(String aName) {name=aName;}
  public String getName() {return name;}
  public float calculateArea() {return 0.0f;}

  public static void main(String argv[]) {
    Circle c = new Circle("Circle C");
    Square s = new Square("Square S");
    Shape shapeArray[] = {c, s};
    for (int i=0; i<shapeArray.length; i++) {
      System.out.println("The area of " + shapeArray[i].getName()
              + " is " + shapeArray[i].calculateArea()+" sq. cm.\n");
    }
  }
}
```

Note that the attribute name is declared as private in the Shape class. To make it known to other objects, a getName() method is defined in the Shape class to return the value of attribute name. The keyword private is an access control specifier which was first introduced in Chapter 3 and discussed in Chapter 8.

Circle and Square extend Shape and have the following definition:

```
class Circle extends Shape {
  private int radius;
  Circle(String aName) {
    super(aName);
    radius = 3;
  }

  public float calculateArea() {
    float area;
    area = (float) (3.14 * radius * radius);
    return area;
  }
}

class Square extends Shape {
  private int side;
  Square(String aName) {
    super(aName);
    side = 3;
  }

  public float calculateArea() {
    int area;
    area = side * side;
    return area;
  }
}
```

As usual, program execution begins with `main()` and the following output is produced when `main()` is executed:

```
The area of Circle C is 28.26 sq. cm.
The area of Square S is 9 sq. cm.
```

Two objects are created in main() – a Circle object referenced by the variable c and a Square object referenced by the variable s. The creation of a Circle object involves a call to the Circle class constructor method via the `new` keyword. A `name` parameter is required to activate the Circle constructor method. For Circle, the `name` parameter is the string `"Circle C"`.

A call is made to the Circle's superclass' constructor method via the statement

```
super(aName);
```

The call assigns the value of the parameter (`"Circle C"`) to the Circle object's attribute `name`. When the assignment is done, control returns to the Circle class' constructor method. Subsequently, the `radius` attribute of the Circle object is assigned the value 3 via the statement:

```
radius = 3;
```

Likewise, the Square object is created and its attributes updated in the execution. By now, the Circle and Square objects have a state as illustrated in Figure 6-8.

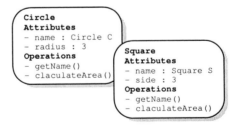

Figure 6-8: State of Circle and Square Object

An array `shapeArray` is declared in the next statement. The reference variables c and s are assigned into the array elements. Iterating through the array (via the `for`-loop), the area of the respective shape is produced by the statement

```
System.out.println("The area of " + shapeArray[i].getName()
           + " is " + shapeArray[i].calculateArea()+" sq. cm.\n");
```

We shall explain the implications of `shapeArray` and `calculateArea()` in the next chapter when the topic of *Polymorphism* is discussed. For now, we shall focus on the impact arising from the addition of classes to an existing class hierarchy.

Supposing we want to add to the Shape class hierarchy, a new class called Triangle. Listing 6-3 shows the modified code with new additions highlighted in bold.

```
class Shape {
  ...

  public static void main(String argv[]) {
    Circle c = new Circle("Circle C");
    Square s = new Square("Square S");
    Triangle t = new Triangle("Triangle T");
    Shape shapeArray[] = {c, s, t};
    for (int i=0; i<shapeArray.length; i++) {
      System.out.println("The area of " + shapeArray[i].getName()
                + " is " + shapeArray[i].calculateArea()+" sq. cm.\n");
    }
  }
}

class Circle extends Shape {
...
}

class Square extends Shape {
  ...
}

class Triangle extends Shape {
  private int base, height;

  Triangle(String aName) {
    super(aName);
    base   = 4;  height = 5;
  }

  public float calculateArea() {
    float area = 0.5f * base * height;
    return area;
  }
}
```

Listing 6-3: Adding a Triangle

To add the new Triangle class, the following is involved:

1. Add a statement to create a Triangle object in `main()`.

2. Add a statement to include the newly created triangle into `shapeArray` in `main()`.

3. Create a new Triangle class as a subclass of Shape.

It is clear that subclassing the new Triangle class into the class hierarchy does not affect the definition of the other three classes. Subclassing is specialization and is thus a desired design practice in Object-Oriented Software Engineering as it has minimal impact on software maintenance.

Thus the deletion of subclasses that are not superclasses to other classes has minimal impact on software maintenance.

6.6 Accessing Inherited Properties

Inherited properties form part of the definition of subclasses but they may not necessarily be accessible by other classes. Accessibility of inherited properties can be controlled using access control specifiers which will be discussed in Chapter 8.

6.7 Inheritance Chain

We have so far discussed class hierarchies whose classes have only one parent or superclass. Such hierarchies are said to exhibit *single inheritance*. The path of inheritance over the classes is known as the inheritance chain.

A single inheritance chain can be *single* or *multi-level*. In a single-level single inheritance chain, there is only one level of superclass a subclass can inherit properties from. In contrast, in a multi-level single inheritance chain, a subclass can inherit from more than one level of superclasses. The difference is illustrated in Figure 6-9.

Besides single inheritance, there is also multiple inheritance. A class hierarchy is said to exhibit *multiple inheritance* if a subclass in the hierarchy inherits properties from two or more superclasses in more than one inheritance path.

http:// java.sun.com/docs/books/ tutorial/index.html

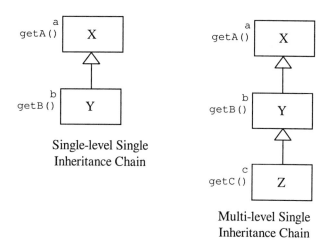

Figure 6-9: Single and Multi-Level Single Inheritance Chain

6.7.1 Multiple Inheritance

To appreciate the concept of multiple inheritance, let us consider the example of frogs. A frog is an amphibian that takes on characteristics typical of a land animal and a water animal. A frog can live both on land and in water. We can thus represent frogs as instances of a Frog class and specialize it as a subclass of Land-Animal class and Water-Animal class. The Frog class will inherit from the Land-Animal class — the ability to live on land and from the Water-Animal class — the ability to survive in water. Figure 6-10 shows the position of the Frog class in relation to its superclasses in a class hierarchy.

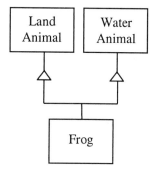

Figure 6-10: Multiple Inheritance

By inheriting properties from more than one superclass, the Frog class is said to exhibit multiple inheritance. All properties of the Land-Animal and Water-Animal classes are now part of the definition of the Frog class.

6.7.2 Problems Associated with Multiple Inheritance

Consider the example of a sales manager. A sales manager can take orders from a customer (as a salesperson would) and authorize orders (as a manager would). Thus, a SalesManager class is a subclass of two superclasses namely, the Manager class and the SalesPerson class, as shown in Figure 6-11. The class diagram can be read as "a sales manager is both a salesperson and a manager". The SalesManager class would inherit from the Manager class the method `authorize()` and from SalesPerson class the method `takeOrder()`.

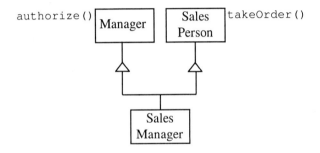

Figure 6-11: Class Hierarchy for SalesManager

Assuming that the concept of multiple inheritance is not available. We would have to represent SalesManager as a subclass in a single inheritance chain as shown in Figure 6-12.

Although the properties inherited in this hierarchy is the same as that of Figure 6-11, the class hierarchy of Figure 6-12 is semantically incorrect – a sales person is not a manager.

While it is clear from the above example that multiple inheritance is useful for a more natural approach to modeling information about the real world, it has its problems, particularly in situations where the same attributes or methods are redefined in the multiple inheritance paths. To illustrate, let us consider the class hierarchy of Figure 6-13.

The attribute `a` and method `getA()` have been redefined in class X and Y. Which copy of `a` should a Z object inherit from? Or, which `getA()` method should a Z object use? Here, the Z object can be an X object or a Y object at some point in time.

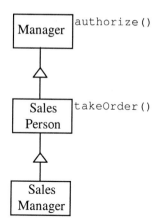

Figure 6-12: A SalesManager Class Hierarchy Using Single Inheritance

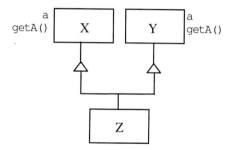

Figure 6-13: Redefined Attribute and Method in Multiple Inheritance Paths

In like manner, we can extend the class hierarchy for sales managers to that shown in Figure 6-14. We say that a sales manager is a manager and a salesperson. A manager and a salesperson in turn are employees in general.

By means of inheritance, the definition of a SalesManager object would include:

- attribute `name`; and

- inherited methods `getName()`, `authorize()`, `takeOrder()` and `collectPayment()`.

Since the method `collectPayment()` occurs in two superclasses – Manager and SalesPerson – it would be difficult from a language implementation point of view to determine which of the `collectPayment()` method a SalesManager object should inherit.

There are thus ambiguities in language implementation when multiple inheritance paths redefine the same attributes or methods in multiple inheritance.

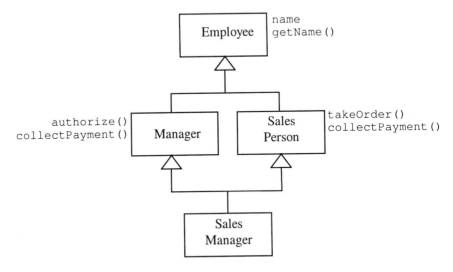

Figure 6-14: Extended Class Hierarchy for SalesManager

6.7.3 Contract and Implementation Parts

Basically, a method has two parts – *contract* and *implementation*.

The contract part is also known as the method signature and specifies the name of the method, its return type and formal parameters (if any).

The implementation part contains statements that are executed when a method is called. It is through the implementation of the method that the state of an object is changed or accessed. By changing the implementation of a method, the behavior of an object is altered, even though the contract part remains unchanged. In Listing 6-4,

```
public int getA()
```

is the contract part, while the two statements:

```
a = a+1;
return a;
```

enclosed within the block form the implementation part of the getA() method.

```
class X {
  int a;
  public int getA() {
    a = a+1;
    return a;
  }
}
```

Listing 6-4: Class X and Method getA()

Similarly, an attribute has a definition and an implementation: the name of an attribute defines the attribute while its structure specifies the implementation of the attribute.

6.7.4 Contract and Implementation Inheritance

A class inherits property definitions and the way the properties are implemented from its superclasses in a single inheritance chain. In other words, a class in a single inheritance chain inherits both the contract and implementation parts of the superclasses' properties.

The inheritance of implementation causes the ambiguities in multiple inheritance. When the same attributes or methods are redefined in the multiple inheritance paths, there is a need to determine which implementation of the redefined properties should be used.

To avoid the problems of multiple inheritance, Java does not support it *explicitly*. Instead Java supports single inheritance and provides a means by which the effects of multiple inheritance can be realized. This contingency is exercised when single inheritance alone may not be sufficient for representing real-world situations.

The approach in Java allows subclasses to inherit contracts but not the corresponding implementation. Subclasses must provide the implementation part of methods. Multiple inheritance is thus indirectly supported in Java with subclasses self-implementing the appropriate behavior. The implementation to be inherited is therefore resolved at the subclass level.

For redefined attributes in multiple inheritance paths, only constant values are allowed in Java. By definition, constants are not modifiable.

6.8 Interface

Contract inheritance is supported in Java via the interface construct. An interface definition is similar to a class definition except that it uses the `interface` keyword:

```
interface I {
  void j();
  int k();
}
```

All methods in an interface are *abstract methods*, i.e. they are declared without the implementation part since they are to be implemented in the subclasses that use them.

6.8.1 Multiple Inheritance Using Interface

The interface construct in Java is used with single inheritance to provide some form of multiple inheritance. To illustrate, we shall refer to the example on sales managers introduced earlier and examine how we can resolve the problems encountered in the single-inheritance solution.

The SalesManager class is first defined as a subclass of SalesPerson in a single inheritance chain. SalesPerson is in turn declared as a subclass of Employee. Given this inheritance hierarchy, a sales manager is a salesperson who in turn is an employee in general.

In order that a sales manager has the ability to manage, we add to the SalesManager class, appropriate behavior in an interface which is then inherited by the SalesManager class. We shall call that interface `Manage` as follows :

```
interface Manage {
  boolean authorize();
}
```

Figure 6-15 shows the class hierarchy for SalesManager which is described as a salesperson with *additional* ability to authorize orders.

In using the `Manage` interface, the subclass SalesManager must implement the abstract methods of the interface. This is reflected in the class declaration of Sales Manager:

```
class SalesManager extends SalesPerson implements Manage {
  ...
}
```

This indicates that a class, SalesManager, derived from the SalesPerson class implements the `Manage` interface.

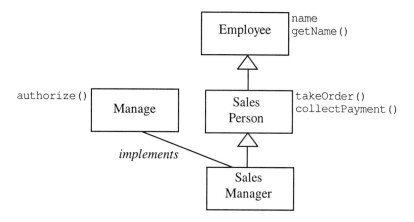

Figure 6-15: Single Inheritance with Interface

The code for the classes in Figure 6-15 is illustrated in Listing 6-5. For illustration purposes, the code for `takeOrder()` and `collectPayment()` methods has been simplified to produce output to indicate their execution. The abstract method `authorize()` of the `Manage` interface has been implemented in the SalesManager class has been embolden.

As expected, the following output was produced:

```
Order taken
Order authorized
Payment collected
SalesManager Sara took order, authorized it and collected payment.
```

The `collectPayment()` method of the SalesPerson class has been pre-determined and used in the above solution. A sales manager is basically a salesperson with an additional behavior to authorize payments (via the `authorize()` method).

```
interface Manage {
  boolean authorize();
}

class Employee {
  String name;
  Employee() {}
  String getName() {return name;}
}

class SalesPerson extends Employee {
  boolean takeOrder() {
    System.out.println("Order taken");
    return true;
  }
  void collectPayment() {
    System.out.println("Payment collected");
  }
}

class SalesManager extends SalesPerson implements Manage {
  SalesManager(String n) {name = n;}
  public boolean authorize() {
    // authorisation by a sales manager
    System.out.println("Order authorized");
    return true;
  }

  public static void main(String args[]) {
    SalesManager sm = new SalesManager("Sara");
    if (sm.takeOrder())
      if (sm.authorize()) {
        sm.collectPayment();
        System.out.println("SalesManager "+sm.getName()+
          " took order, authorized it and collected payment. ");
      }
      else System.out.println("SalesManager "+sm.getName()+
          " did not authorize order. No payment collected. ");
  }
}
```

Listing 6-5: SalesManager Class and Manageable Interface

An alternative implementation would be to consider SalesManager as a subclass of Manager taking on methods `authorize()` and `collectPayment()`, as shown in Figure 6-16. `takeOrder()` is derived from implementing the `CanTakeOrder` interface instead. Note that the implementation of `collectPayment()` method in this case is different from the implementation of `collectPayment()` method in Figure 6-15.

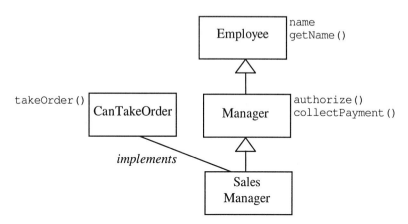

Figure 6-16: Inheriting from Manager Class

Which of these two solutions is preferred is a modeling problem and can be resolved if more information on the problem domain and requirements is provided.

6.8.2 Attributes in an Interface

Data attributes declared in an interface construct are always `static` and `final`. They are `static` as there can only be one copy of the data available and `final` since they are not modifiable. By declaring data attributes in an interface, constant declarations for use in methods is possible. Constants are names for values with a specific meaning.

As all data attributes are implicitly declared as `static` and `final` in an interface definition, these keywords need not precede their declaration:

```
interface Colourable {
    int RED = 1;
    int GREEN = 2;
    int BLUE = 3;

    void setColour (int c);
    int getColour();
}
```

6.8.3 Methods in an Interface

All methods in an interface are abstract methods and any class that uses the interface must provide an implementation for them. Like data attributes, an interface does not have to explicitly declare its methods abstract using the keyword `abstract`.

Similarly, interface methods are always public, and the access modifier `public` keyword is not required since it is implied in the interface declaration. However, in contrast with data attributes in an interface, methods may not be `static` since static methods, being class specific, are never abstract.

6.8.4 Abstract Class and Interface

A class implementing an interface must implement all the abstract methods declared in an interface; otherwise, the class is considered as an *abstract* class and must be declared using the `abstract` keyword as follows:

```
abstract class ColourTest implements Colourable {
  int i;
  ColourTest() {}

  public void setColour (int c) {
    i=c;
  }

  public static void main(String args[]) {
    ...
  }
}
```

The class ColourTest is declared `abstract` since the `getColour()` method of the `Colourable` interface is not implemented. Note that the `setColour()` method has to be declared `public` as it is a method of the `Colourable` interface.

There are some differences between an abstract class and an interface. These differences are summarized as follows:

Abstract Class	Interface
May have some methods declared `abstract`.	Can only have abstract methods.
May have `protected` properties and `static` methods.	Can only have `public` methods with no implementation.
May have `final` and non-final data attributes.	Limited to only constants.

An abstract class can enhance inheritance as some or all parts of the class can be implemented and inherited by subclasses. An interface, on the other hand, is generally used for achieving multiple inheritance in Java.

An abstract class cannot be used to instantiate objects since it may contain parts that are not implemented. Given a declaration of an abstract class LandVehicle below,

```
public abstract class LandVehicle {
    int doors;
    LandVehicle() { doors = 4; }
    void drive();
}
```

the following statement will be considered as invalid:

```
LandVehicle l = new LandVehicle();
```

6.8.5 Extending Interface

Does a subclass of a class that implements an interface also inherit the methods of the interface? Consider the code in Listing 6-6:

```
interface I {
    void x();
}

class A implements I {
    public void x() { System.out.println("in A.x"); }
    public void y() { System.out.println("in A.y"); }
}

class B extends A {
    void z() {
        x();
        y();
    }

    public static void main(String args[]) {
        A aa = new A();
        B bb = new B();
        bb.z();
    }
}
```

Listing 6-6: Extending Interface to Subclasses

The following output

```
in A.x
in A.y
```

proceduced suggests that the methods x() and y() of class A have been invoked. Class B, being the subclass of class A, inherited not only method y() but also method x() which is a method of the interface I.

6.8.6 Limitations of Interface for Multiple Inheritance

Although the interface feature in Java provides an alternative solution to achieving multiple inheritance in class hierarchies, it has its limitations:

a.   An interface does not provide a natural means of realizing multiple inheritance in situations where there is no inheritance conflict.

b.   While the principal reason for inheritance is code reusability, the interface facility does not encourage code reuse since duplication of code is inevitable.

a) No Inheritance Conflict

Consider the situation in Figure 6-17 where there is no inheritance conflict in attributes or methods.

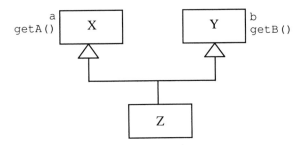

Figure 6-17: No Inheritance Conflict

A Z object has attributes a and b together with methods getA() and getB(). Without the support of multiple inheritance in Java, such class hierarchy cannot be realized.

b) No Code Reuse

Let us, as examples, consider land vehicles such as motor cars and trucks. A class hierarchy showing Motor Car and Truck as subclasses of LandVehicle is given in Figure 6-18.

Motor Car and Truck have been declared as subclasses to distinguish the different brake system used. By means of inheritance, data attributes `regnNumber` and `numberOfPassenger` of LandVehicle are inherited by Motor Car and Truck as part of their properties.

Let us extend this example in our discussion of the issue – no code reuse and further extend the class hierarchy to include information that distinguishes the drive system between the land vehicles. We shall consider three alternative representation.

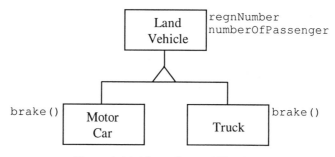

Figure 6-18: Motor Car and Truck

In the first representation, the front-drive feature of a vehicle is defined as a superclass in Figure 6-19. The implementation of `drive()` method for the vehicles is indicated by the two statements:

```
frontWheelSys.engage();
this.accelerate();
```

The Front-Wheel-Drive class is an abstract class with a `drive()` method. This suggests that all motorcars and trucks are front-wheel-drive vehicles. This is incorrect as some motorcars and trucks may be back-wheel-drive vehicles. The class hierarchy in Figure 6-19 is therefore inappropriate for representing motor cars and trucks.

In the second representation, the front-drive feature is contained within a subclass, Front-Wheel-Drive Car or Front-Wheel-Drive Truck in Figure 6-20. While this is semantically correct in satisfying the requirement, it does not take full advantage of inheritance – the `drive()` method is duplicated in Front-Wheel-Drive Car and Front-Wheel-Drive Truck class.

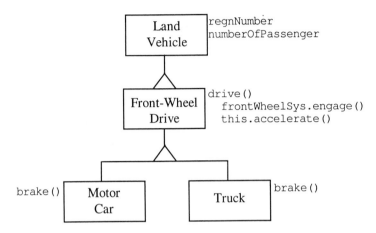

Figure 6-19: "Front-Wheel Drive Class as Superclass" Representation Scheme

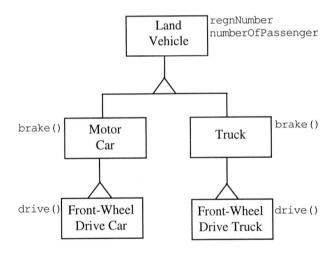

Figure 6-20: "Front-Wheel Drive as Subclasses" Representation Scheme

In the last representation, the `drive()` method is abstracted into a separate superclass and inherited by Front-Wheel-Drive Car and Front-Wheel-Drive Truck through a multiple inheritance chain in Figure 6-21.

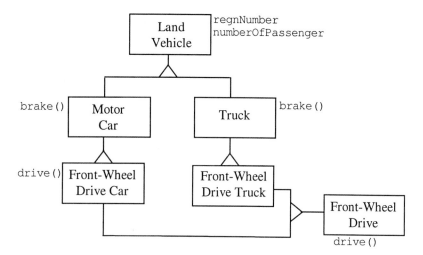

Figure 6-21: "Multiple Inheritance" Representation Scheme

This hierarchy is obviously desirable but implementing the solution with the interface construct would result in the definition of `drive()` method as an abstract method of a Front-Wheel-Drive interface and implemented in Front-Wheel-Drive Car and Front-Wheel-Drive Truck class. The effect is the same as that for "Front-Wheel Drive as Subclasses" representation scheme where the implementation of the `drive()` method is duplicated in the two subclasses.

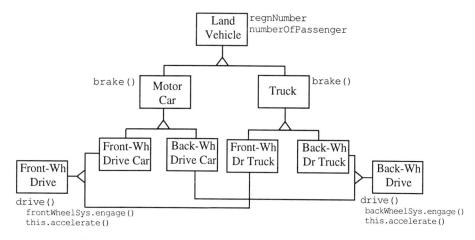

Figure 6-22: Front-Wheel and Back-Wheel Drive Vehicles

The problem with the interface solution is further amplified when we consider the need to implement the `drive()` method for Back-Wheel-Drive vehicles as well (see Figure 6-22). Using the interface solution, we need to implement the `drive()` method in Front-Wheel-Drive Car, Back-Wheel-Drive Car, Front-Wheel-Drive Truck, and Back-Wheel-Drive Truck. This approach can be error-prone.

From the above example, it is clear that the interface construct does not encourage code reuse and duplication of method implementation is inevitable. If multiple inheritance had been available in Java, implementing the `drive()` method would be easier.

6.9 Summary

The following points were discussed in this chapter:

- A class can take on the properties of a superclass via the *inheritance* mechanism.

- Inheritance is the ability of a subclass to take on the general properties of classes higher up in a class hierarchy.

- Properties can only be propagated downward from a superclass to a subclass.

- Inheritance enables code reuse.

- Inheritance enhances software maintainability.

- Inheritance enables class extension through subclassing.

- A class that takes on properties from only one superclass is said to exhibit *single inheritance*.

- A class that takes on properties from two or more superclasses is said to exhibit *multiple inheritance*.

- Multiple inheritance is not implemented in Java, hence, the interface construct implemented via the `interface` keyword is an alternative solution to achieve multiple inheritance. However, this solution has its limitations.

6.10 Exercises

1. Define and distinguish the terms "single inheritance" and "multiple inheritance".

2. Give an example of multiple inheritance in a real-life situation.

3. A and B are two classes. A inherits properties from B, so A is a _____ class of B and B is a _____ class of A.

   If A has attributes a1 and a2, methods getA1() and getA2(), and B has attributes b1 and b2, methods getB1() and getB2(), then by means of inheritance, the actual definition of A and B would be:

   ```
   class A {                          class B {
   Attributes:                        Attributes:
   _____                        _____
   _____                        _____
   _____                        _____
   _____
   Methods:                           Methods:
   _____                        _____
   _____                        _____
   _____                        _____
   _____
   ```

4. Given the following information on classes A and B, declare A and B in Java:

   - attributes a1, b1 are integers

   - attributes a2, b2 are strings

   - method getA1(), getA2(), getB1(), getB2() returns a1, a2, b1, and b2 respectively.

5. How does inheritance contribute to software reusability?

6. Given the following class hierarchy diagram,

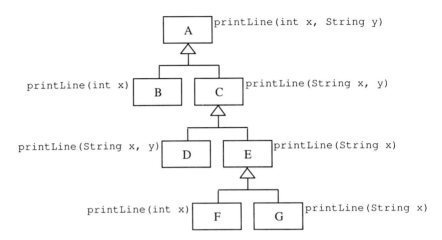

which class' `printLine()` method would be used for each of the message below
(Assuming z is an object instantiated from class F):

a) `z.printLine(1)`

b) `z.printLine(2, "Object-Oriented Programming")`

c) `z.printLine("Java")`

d) `z.printLine("Object-Oriented Programming", "Java")`

e) `z.printLine("Object-Oriented Programming", 3)`

7. What can you say about the method `printLine(String x)` of class **G** in
    Question 6?

8. Distinguish between contract inheritance and implementation inheritance.

9. Discuss the problem associated with multiple inheritance. How does Java
    overcome it and what feature is provided in Java to achieve multiple inheritance?
    Discuss the limitation of this feature.

10. An abstract class contains one or more _____ methods. Distinguish
    between an abstract class and an interface. Which is better and why?

11. What is the expected output for the code in Listing 6-7.

```
interface I {
  void x();
  void y();
}

class A implements I {
  A() {}
  public void w() {System.out.println("in A.w");}
  public void x() {System.out.println("in A.x");}
  public void y() {System.out.println("in A.y");}
}

class B extends A {
  B() {}

  public void y() {
    System.out.println("in B.y");
  }

  void z() {
    w();
    x();
  }

  static public void main(String args[]) {
    A aa = new A();
    B bb = new B();
    bb.z();
    bb.y();
  }
}
```

Listing 6-7

7 Polymorphism

Up till now we have been assuming all code are bound during compilation. Binding variables to operations at compile time is known as *static binding*. Besides static binding, there is *dynamic binding* in which binding takes place at run time.

Static binding is limited and may lead to difficulty in software maintenance. Dynamic binding, on the other hand, provides design flexibility and may enhance software maintainability.

In this chapter, we shall discuss static binding and dynamic binding. We shall also examine how dynamic binding contributes to *polymorphism* which is the ability of objects to respond to the same message with the appropriate method based on their class definition.

7.1 Static Binding

In Chapter 6, we introduced an example on shapes. Let us now examine how the conventional procedural programming approach would handle the code for the Shape example.

In Listing 7-1, we list the pseudo-code for the Shape example using procedural declaration. Two shapes, a circle and a square, in the form of a record structure have been declared in the Data Section. Each shape has a shape name. The shape name for circle c is "Circle C" and the shape name for square s is "Square S". Circle C has a variable radius while Square s has a variable side. In addition, an array, shapeArray, has been declared to contain up to 5 characters, each character to reference a shape.

```
Data Section
Type
  Circle = Record
              String name;
                int radius;
          End
  Square = Record
              String name;
                int side;
          End
Variable
  shapeArray : Array [1..5] of char;
  c : Circle;
  s : Square;


Main Code Section
  c.name  = "Circle C";
  c.radius = 2;
  s.name  = "Square S";
  s.side   = 3;
  A[1] = 'c';
  A[2] = 's';
  For int i = 1 to 2 do  {
    Switch shapeArray[i]
      'c' : calculateCircleArea();
      's' : calculateSquareArea();
      'n' : do nothing;
    End (Case)
  }

Routine Section
calculateCircleArea()   {
  float area = 3.14 * c.radius * c.radius;
  writeln ("The area of ", c.name, " is ", area, " sq. cm.");
}

calculateSquareArea()   {
  float area = s.side * s.side;
  writeln ("The area of ", s.name, " is ", area, " sq. cm.");
}
```

Listing 7-1: Procedural Declaration of Shape Example

In the Main Code Section, the circle and square have been initialized with some parameters. Iterating through the array, the area of Circle C and Square S is produced and printed.

```
Data Section
Type
   ...
   Triangle = Record
                String name;
                int base, height;
              End
Variable
   ...
   t : Triangle;

Main Code Section
   ...
   t.name   = "Trianlge T";
   t.base   = 4;  t.height = 5;
   ...
   A[3] = 't';
   For int i = 1 to 3 do   {
     Switch shapeArray[i]
        'c' : calculateCircleArea();
        's' : calculateSquareArea();
        't' : calculateTriangleArea();
        'n' : do nothing;
     End (Case)
   }

Routine Section
calculateCircleArea()   {
   ...
}

calculateSquareArea()   {
   ...
}

calculateTriangleArea()   {
   float area = 0.5f * t.base * t.height;
   writeln ("The area of ", t.name, " is ", area, " sq. cm.");
}
```

Listing 7-2: Static Binding – Adding a Triangle

Since each array element may reference a circle, a square or something else (which we do not really care), a case statement for determining which of the shape's calculate area routine to execute given a choice has to be coded in the program and bound at compile time. For example, a calculateCircleArea() routine has to be called for a circle and a `calculateSquareArea()` routine has to be called for a square, etc.

Two distinct `calculate area` routines are required because the method for calculating the area of a circle is different from that for a square. Also, most procedural programming languages do not have two routines with the same name. Different routine names therefore have to be devised.

We say that the variable `shapeArray[i]` (or the choices) is *statically bound* to the routine `calculateCircleArea()` in the case when the value of `shapeArray[i]` is 'c' and `calculateSquareArea()` when the value of `shapeArray[i]` is 's'.

With static binding, problems may arise in code maintenance. To illustrate, let us now add another shape, Triangle, to the code. Listing 7-2 shows the solution with changes highlighted in bold. Note that changes were made at the following points:

- in the Data Section where a triangle is defined;

- in the Main Code Section where the detection of a triangle and the appropriate routine call have to be included in the `switch` statement; and

- in the Routine Section where the specific routine for calculating the area of the triangle has to be included.

Multiple places are affected as a result of extending shape types. This indicates that "static binding" approach is prone to programming error in such situations.

7.2 Dynamic Binding

An alternative approach to static binding is *dynamic binding*. Here, the binding of variables to routines (or methods in object-oriented programming terms) is done at run time. In Listing 7-3, an object-oriented version of the previous Shape example is produced. The code here resembles the one used in Chapter 6.

```
class Shape {
  private String name;
  Shape(String aName) {name=aName;}
  public String getName() {return name;}
  public float calculateArea() {return 0.0f;}

  public static void main(String argv[]) {
    Circle c = new Circle("Circle C");
    Square s = new Square("Square S");
    Shape shapeArray[] = {c, s};
    for (int i=0; i<shapeArray.length; i++) {
      System.out.println("The area of " + shapeArray[i].getName()
              + " is " + shapeArray[i].calculateArea()+" sq. cm.\n");
    }
  }
}

class Circle extends Shape {
  private int radius;
  Circle(String aName) {
    super(aName);
    radius = 3;
  }

  public float calculateArea() {
    float area;
    area = (float) (3.14 * radius * radius);
    return area;
  }
}

class Square extends Shape {
  private int side;
  Square(String aName) {
    super(aName);
    side = 3;
  }

  public float calculateArea() {
    int area;
    area = side * side;
    return area;
  }
}
```

Listing 7-3: Dynamic Binding — Shape, Circle and Square Class

Two objects, a circle and a square, are created by the first two statements of main(). Object variables for the circle and square are kept in the array, shapeArray, and iterating through the array, the area of the respective object is produced and printed by the statement:

```
System.out.println("The area of " + shapeArray[i].getName()
                  + " is " + shapeArray[i].calculateArea()+" sq. cm.\n");
```

While the actual routine for the choice of shape in the array elements has to be pre-determined via a `switch` statement in static binding, it is different with dynamic binding. `switch` statement is not required in this solution.

Based on the output from the code, it is clear that the appropriate method for responding to the choice in `shapeArray` has been used:

```
The area of Circle C is 28.26 sq. cm.
The area of Square S is 9 sq. cm.
```

The method has been selected based on the class of the shape referenced in `shapeArray` at run time. This is only possible in programming languages that support dynamic binding. With dynamic binding, the variable `shapeArray[i]` is bound to an object's method only at run time when the class definition of the shape referenced is known.

7.3 Operation Overloading

Circle and Square have similar `calculateArea()` method in their class definition. Although both methods have the same method signature, they have different method implementation, since the formula for calculating area of each is not the same.

While it is impossible in conventional imperative programming languages to have two routines having the same name, it is allowed in object-oriented programming. The ability to use the same name for two or more methods in a class is known as *operation overloading* in object-oriented terms (see also Section 3.6).

7.3.1 Same Method Signature

Two methods are said to have the same method signature if :

* the name of the methods are the same; and

* the number and type of formal parameters are the same.

The `calculateArea()` method of the Shape, Circle and Square class, in Listing 7-3, is said to have the same method signature.

7.3.2 Overloading Method Names

Methods having the same method signature may pose problems in the compilation process depending on where they are used in the program. In this section, we shall consider various situations and report on the validity of overloaded method names.

In the code fragment below, method `A()` is overloaded by `A(int x)`, `A(int x, int y)`, and `A(String s)`. These four methods are distinguished in the compilation process by the number and type of parameters present in the method call.

```
class A {
  ...
  A() { ... }
  A(int x) { ... }
  A(int x, int y) { ... }
  A(String x) { ... }
  ...
}
```

Indicated below are the actual methods called given the message on the left:

`A thisA = new A();`	➜	`A()`
`A thisA = new A(3);`	➜	`A(int x)`
`A thisA = new A(4, 5);`	➜	`A(int x, int y)`
`A thisA = new A("hello");`	➜	`A(String x)`

In the code fragment below, the definition of method `a1()` is reported as a duplicate method declaration by the compiler since the two methods have been declared in the same class. It is thus considered as invalid.

```
class A {
  A() {}
  public void a1() {}
  public void a1() {}
}
```

The return type of a method does not distinguish overloaded methods from one another as the following example shows. Method `a1()` is flagged as invalid by the compiler as both of them are considered similar.

```
class A {
  A() {}
  public void a1() {}
  public int a1() {return 0;}
}
```

However, declaring methods of the same signature in different classes are considered as valid in object-oriented programming:

```
class A {
  A() {}
  public void a1() {}

  public static void main(String args[]) {
  }
}

class B {

  B() {}
  public void a1() {}
  public void b1() {}
}
```

Finally, consider the following code fragment:

```
class C {
  C() {}
  public void c1() {System.out.println("C.c1()");}
}
class D extends C {
  D() {}
  public void c1() {
    super.c1();
    System.out.println("D.c1()");
  }
  public void d1() {}

  public static void main(String args[]) {
    D thisD = new D();
    thisD.c1();
  }
}
```

Although method c1() is defined in two different classes, the situation is different from the previous case. In this case, method c1() is defined in subclass D and superclass C. The declaration of method `c1()` in this case is considered valid as in the previous case. The expected output is:

```
C.c1()
D.d1()
```

Method `c1()` in subclass D is said to *redefine* method `c1()` of superclass C. For a method to redefine a superclass' method, the method signature of the two methods must be the same; otherwise, they are considered as two different methods as shown by the output from the code below:

```
class C {
  C() {}
  public void c1() {System.out.println("C.c1()");}
}

class D extends C {
  D() {}
  public void c1(int i) {
    super.c1();
    System.out.println("D.c1()");
  }
  public void d1() {}

  public static void main(String args[]) {
    D thisD = new D();
    thisD.c1();
    thisD.c1(3);
  }
}
```

Output

```
C.c1()
C.c1()
D.d1()
```

7.4 Polymorphism

We noted earlier in Section 7.2 that code binding can be effected at run time with dynamic binding. Also, appropriate method call can be made without making any direct reference to it in the message. As is evident in the output of the code, the appropriate `calculateArea()` method for the respective object was selected.

It is apparent that the message (`calculateArea()`) from the sender (`main()`) has been interpreted appropriately by the receiver. A circle receiving the message has used its own method `calculateArea()` to calculate the area and a square receiving the same message has done the same with its own `calculateArea()` method. The ability of *different* objects to perform the appropriate method in response to the *same message* is known as *polymorphism* in object-oriented programming.

7.4.1 Selection of Method

In polymorphism, the interpretation of a message is not affected by a sender. What a sender knows is that an object can respond to a message but it does not know which class the object belongs to or *how* it will respond to the message. For example, the message `shapeArray[i].calculateArea()` of `main()` (see Listing 7-3) is sent to a Shape object (a circle or a square). The sender (`main()`) does not know which of the Shape object will respond to the message, let alone *how* it will perform the method.

The selection of the appropriate method depends on the *class* the object belongs to. For a circle object, the `calculateArea()` method of the Circle class will be called and for a square object, the `calculateArea()` method of the Square class will be called. Since the first element in `shapeArray` is a circle, the `calculateArea()` method of the Circle class is executed producing an area of 28.26 square centimeters. Similarly, the `calculateArea()` method of the Square class is performed for the second element of `shapeArray`, resulting in a value of 9 square centimeters. The `calculateArea()` method of the Circle and Square class is thus said to be *polymorphic*.

7.4.2 Incremental Development

Polymorphism is facilitated by dynamic binding and the ability to use the same name for similar methods across class definitions. It would not be possible to achieve polymorphism if a programming language does not support these facilities.

Polymorphism encourages programmers to specify *what* method should happen rather than *how* it should happen. This approach allows flexibility in code design and promotes incremental program development. To illustrate, we shall consider adding a new Triangle object type into the code of Listing 7-3. Listing 7-4 is the modified code with additional code highlighted in bold.

Note that minimal changes were made to the original code of Listing 7-3. The main changes occur in the following areas:

- A new Triangle class was added. The addition of the class does not affect the other parts of the program.

- A statement was added in `main()` to create the Triangle object.

- A statement was added in `main()` to include the newly-created triangle into the shapeArray.

No change was made in the `println` statement in `main()`. No `switch` statement is required to determine which method to use too. This example shows that adding new object type is made easy with polymorphism, and there is greater scope for incremental development.

```
class Shape {
  ...
  public static void main(String argv[]) {
    Circle c = new Circle("Circle C");
    Square s = new Square("Square S");
    Triangle t = new Triangle("Triangle T");
    Shape shapeArray[] = {c, s, t};
    for (int i=0; i<shapeArray.length; i++) {
      System.out.println("The area of " + shapeArray[i].getName()
                + " is " + shapeArray[i].calculateArea()+" sq. cm.\n");
    }
  }
}

class Circle extends Shape {
...
}

class Square extends Shape {
  ...
}

class Triangle extends Shape {
  private int base, height;

  Triangle(String aName) {
    super(aName);
    base  = 4;  height = 5;
  }

  public float calculateArea() {
    float area = 0.5f * base * height;
    return area;
  }
}
```

Listing 7-4: Dynamic Binding — Adding a Triangle

7.4.3 Increased Code Readability

Polymorphism also increases code readability since the same message is used to call different objects to perform the appropriate behavior. The code for calling methods is greatly simplified as much of the work in determining which class' method to call is now handled implicitly by the language. The simplicity of the code is evident in the `println()` statement of Listing 7-3.

7.5 Summary

In this chapter, we discussed :

- *Static binding* – the binding of variables to operations at compile time,

- *Dynamic binding* – the binding of variables to operations at run time,

- *Operation overloading* – the ability to use the same name for two or more methods in a class, and

- *Polymorphism* – the ability of *different* objects to perform the appropriate method in response to the *same message*.

7.6 Exercises

1. Discuss the two facilities required in programming languages for supporting polymorphism.

2. How does polymorphism contribute to software maintainability?

3. Contrast between "method redefinition" and "operation overloading".

8 Modularity

We have so far discussed the basic facilities of Java for creating objects through class definitions and reusing code by inheriting properties of similar but more general classes.

In this chapter, we look at the important issue of modularity and the related mechanisms available in Java. Modularity is important because it forms the basis of how programs are developed and impacts on software maintenance.

8.1 Methods and Classes as Program Units

A method comprises of statement sequences and is often viewed as the smallest program unit to be considered as a subprogram. It is self-contained and designed for a particular task which represents an object behavior.

Together with data to hold object states, a coordinated set of methods completes the specification for object behavior of that class of objects. As we have seen, these are the constituents of a class definition. Compared to a method, a class definition is the next bigger unit under design.

Properties defined in a class can be distinguished into object and class properties. Object properties are definitions that are specific to objects and apply to all objects from the same class. Class properties, on the other hand, apply only to the class even though the structure and behavior of objects of a class is defined by the class.

8.2   Object and Class Properties

In this section, we shall examine the distinction between object and class properties.

8.2.1   Counting Instances

Listing 8-1 contains the code for an example that counts the number of objects instantiated from the SalesPerson class.

```
class SalesPerson {
  String employeeId;

  SalesPerson(String aEmployeeId) {
    employeeId = aEmployeeId;
  }

 public static void main(String arg[]) {
    int count = 0;
    SalesPerson s1 = new SalesPerson("12345S");
    count = count+1;
    SalesPerson s2 = new SalesPerson("33221K");
    count = count+1;
    System.out.println(count + " salespersons have been created");
  }
}
```

Listing 8-1: Counting Instances

The code begins with the declaration of a variable count. This variable is used to continually create the number of SalesPerson objects. For each creation of a SalesPerson object, count is incremented via the statement:

```
count = count+1;
```

This statement is executed twice since two SalesPerson objects were instantiated. Finally, the code prints out the number of SalesPerson object instantiated via the statement

```
System.out.println(count + " salespersons have been created");
```

The output:

```
"2 salespersons have been created"
```

suggests that two SalesPerson objects were created and this is clearly correct.

While the solution is correct, it is cumbersome since for each new instantiation of a SalesPerson object, a fresh:

```
count = count+1;
```

statement has to be added into `main()`.

An alternate class organisation is given in Listing 8-2, where `count` is incremented within the constructor method of the SalesPerson class. This strategy supports abstraction and is advantageous because the user does not have to bother with operations on `count`.

```
class SalesPerson {
    String employeeId;
    int count = 0;

    SalesPerson(String aEmployeeId) {
        employeeId = aEmployeeId;
        count = count + 1;
    }

    int getCount() { return count; }

    public static void main(String argv[]) {
        SalesPerson s1 = new SalesPerson("12345S");
        SalesPerson s2 = new SalesPerson("33221K");
        System.out.println(s1.getCount() +
                        " salespersons have been created");
    }
}
```

Listing 8-2: Alternative Solution to Counting Instances

It is clear from the output:

```
"1 salespersons have been created"
```

that the result is incorrect[1].

---

[1] Even if `s1.getCount()` has been substituted with `s2.getCount()` in the `println()` method, the result would still be incorrect.

The variable `count` in the alternative solution is declared as an object attribute rather than a local variable of the static method `main()` as was the case for the previous solution. As an object attribute, `count` can now be incremented in the constructor method of the SalesPerson class. However, with each instantiation of a SalesPerson object, the `count` variable of each newly created object is incremented. Since two instances of SalesPerson object were created, two independent copies of `count`, each having the value 1, were present. Figure 8-1 shows the state of the two created SalesPerson objects.

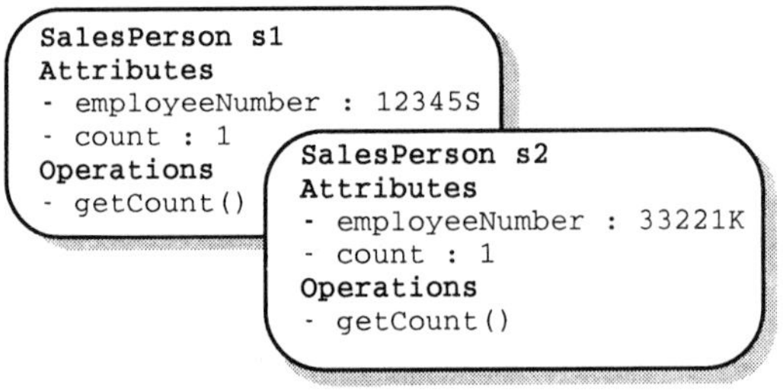

```
SalesPerson s1
Attributes
- employeeNumber : 12345S
- count : 1
Operations         SalesPerson s2
- getCount()       Attributes
                   - employeeNumber : 33221K
                   - count : 1
                   Operations
                   - getCount()
```

Figure 8-1: State of SalesPerson Objects

Although only one copy of `count` is required, it is unclear which copy of the two instances should be used.

8.2.2 Shared Attributes

Another solution can be found in Listing 8-3 whereby `count` is declared as `static`. Declaring `count` as `static` allows the variable `count` to be shared among all instances of the SalesPerson class. Thus, `s1.count` refers to the same memory location as `s2.count`. The statement:

```
count = count+1;
```

in the constructor method therefore increments the same shared copy of `count` as shown in Figure 8-2. The output from the code:

```
"2 salespersons have been created"
```

is correct.

```
class SalesPerson {
    String employeeId;
    static int count = 0;

    SalesPerson(String aEmployeeId) {
        employeeId = aEmployeeId;
        count = count + 1;
    }

    int getCount() { return count; }

    public static void main(String argv[]) {
        SalesPerson s1 = new SalesPerson("12345S");
        SalesPerson s2 = new SalesPerson("33221K");
        System.out.println(s1.getCount() +
                        " salespersons have been created");
    }
}
```

Listing 8-3: Shared Attributes

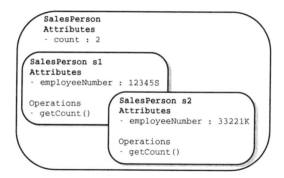

Figure 8-2: Shared Variable count

8.2.3 Class Attributes

The static variable count is also known as a class attribute. While a class definition specifies the structure and behavior of objects within, it may have its own attribute and method definitions.

An attribute definition that is preceded with the keyword static is a class attribute. While we previously viewed the static variable count as shared amongst all instances, its association with the class is consistent. As a class attribute, it is also accessible to instances of the class.

8.2.4 Class Methods

In another change in Listing 8-4, we make getCount() a class method by prefixing it with the static keyword. The results from the code is the same as that of Listing 8-3 with just static count.

```
class SalesPerson {
    String employeeId;
    static int count = 0;

    SalesPerson(String aEmployeeId) {
        employeeId = aEmployeeId;
        count = count + 1;
    }

    static int getCount() { return count; }

    public static void main(String argv[]) {
        SalesPerson s1 = new SalesPerson("12345S");
        SalesPerson s2 = new SalesPerson("33221K");
        System.out.println(s1.getCount() +
                        " salespersons have been created");
    }
}
```

Listing 8-4: Class Methods

Note the difference in representation between the getCount() method of Figure 8-3 for Listing 8-4 and Figure 8-2 for Listing 8-3. In Figure 8-3, both SalesPerson objects s1 and s2 do not own the getCount() method since the method belongs to the SalesPerson class as represented by the outermost bubble surrounding instances s1 and s2.

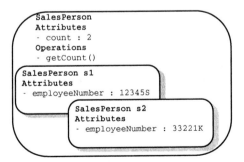

Figure 8-3: Class Method getCount()

8.2.5 Name Aliases

Within the class definition of SalesPerson in Listing 8-4, the method names `getCount()`, `s1.getCount()`, `s2.getCount()` and `SalesPerson.getCount()` are all aliases which reference the `static` method `getCount()`. `getCount()` is typically the most convenient usage within the class construct. Outside of the class definition (where there may be several `getCount()` methods in other class definitions), qualification by the class name as in `SalesPerson.getCount()` is the only way to access the method.

Thus within `static void main()`, the `println()` method could have been:

```
System.out.println(getCount() + " salespersons have been created");
```

8.3 Controlling Visibility

Except for the discussion on "Representational Independence" in Section 3.5, we have mostly ignored the issue of visibility of attributes and methods. Any discussion on modularity is not complete without discussing visibility issues.

First, while modules should be as independent as possible with minimal coupling, no module can be totally isolated from other code since it is unusual for a module to work in isolation. Thus, there must be entities on an object which is accessible externally.

On the other hand, objects should reveal as little as possible of its internal workings so that there would be minimal dependence on such details. Ideally, objects would reveal information on a need-to-know basis.

We have earlier seen the use of the visibility specifiers `private` and `public` in Section 3.5. They precede attribute and method definitions. Both access control specifiers function at the extreme ends of the visibility spectrum. The `private` specifier makes entities that follow it hidden from code fragments external to the class. The `public` specifier makes entities that follow it fully visible from all other Java code.

We modify our SalesPerson class in Listing 8-5 so that `count` has the `private` access specifier, while `employeeId` and `getCount()` are declared as `public`. This means that the variable `count` is not visible by any code outside the class definition. As such, any part of the program outside the class definition of SalesPerson cannot *directly* access the `count` variable.

```
class SalesPerson {
    public String employeeId;
    private static int count = 0;

    SalesPerson(String aEmployeeId) {
        employeeId = aEmployeeId;
        count = count + 1;
    }

    public static int getCount() { return count; }

    public static void main(String argv[]) {
        SalesPerson s1 = new SalesPerson("12345S");
        SalesPerson s2 = new SalesPerson("33221K");
        System.out.println(s1.getCount() +
                        " salespersons have been created");
    }
}
```

Listing 8-5: Restricted Access of Count

Private variables are either used within the class definition, or a `public` accessor method is implemented to provide the access required outside the class definition. We assume the latter to be the case and provided a publicly accessible `getCount()` to return the value of `count`.

Between the `public` and `private` extremes, Java also allows for two more categories: `protected` and the default visibility of "friendly".

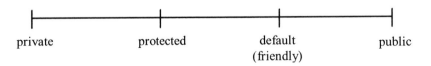

Keyword	Visibility
private	Access to a `private` variable or method is only allowed within the code fragments of a class.
protected	Access to a `protected` variable or method is only allowed within the code fragments of a class and its subclass.
(friendly)	Access to a friendly variable or method (with no access specifier) is only allowed within the code fragments of a class and any other class in the same package.
public	Access to a `public` variable or method is unrestricted. It may be accessed from the code fragments of any class.

Table 8-1: Access Specifiers

While the `public` and `private` specifiers allow for an all-or-nothing access outside of the class definition, the `protected` keyword makes entities which follow it accessible to code fragments with its immediate subclass. For entities with no access specifier, friendly access is assumed. Here, access is given to code fragments within the same package. Table 8-1 summarizes accessibility rules from most restrictive to least restrictive.

8.4 Packages

While class definitions are practical modular units, the Java programming language has another mechanism which facilitates programming teams and reusable software units. The package facility allows for appropriate classes to be grouped into packages. As with standard design rationale for objects where relevant methods are placed in the same class definition, packages in Java form the next level of software containment for classes with logically related functionality.

Packaging also partitions the name space to avoid name clashes. Computations in Java are reliant on objects, and the result of system design is a set of class definitions. Where teams of programmers work independently with the intention of the results to be subsequently integrated, there is a chance that they may choose the same name for their classes. Packaging thus allows for the names of classes to be confined to the originating package.

8.4.1 The `package` Keyword

Package hierarchy is specified via the `package` keyword preceding a class definition as shown below. Here, class XYZ belongs within package A. Its complete qualified name is thus A.XYZ.

```
package A;
class XYZ {
  int h;
  void j() { ... }
}
```

It follows that a "`package B.C`" prefix before "class RST" definition makes class RST belong to the C package which is in the B package.

```
package B.C;
class RST {
  int y;
  void z() { ... }
}
```

Thus far, we have been using class definitions but without any package prefix. Such classes belong to the top-level anonymous package.

As to locating and loading code files, the Java virtual machine maps the package hierarchy onto its directory structure. As such code for A.XYZ will be at XYZ.class in directory A, or more succinctly, the pathname A/XYZ.class. Similarly, B.C.RST will be found at B/C/RST.class.

8.4.2 *The* `import` *Keyword*

The `import` keyword provides the complement function of the package facility. While the `package` keyword places succeeding class definitions in a separate name space of the said package, the `import` keyword makes package constituents visible.

Continuing from our earlier RST example, any client code outside of package B.C must either refer to it in its qualified form:

```
class another {
    B.C.RST x = new B.C.RST();
    ...
}
```

or, import the complete name space of the B.C package

```
import B.C.*;
class another {
    RST x = new RST();
    ...
}
```

or, import just the single class

```
import B.C.RST;
class another {
    RST x = new RST();
    ...
}
```

Since the class RST is now used outside its package, RST must be a public class.

```
package B.C;
public class RST {
    int y;
    void z() { ... }
}
```

8.5 Encapsulation

Another concept in object-oriented programming closely associated with modularity is *encapsulation*. Simply, encapsulation means the bringing together of a set of attributes and methods into an object definition and hiding their implementational structure from the object's users. Therefore, how an object structure and implement its attributes and methods is not visible to other objects using it. Direct access to an object's attributes is not permitted and any changes to the object's data can only be effected indirectly via a set of publicly available methods.

Analogically speaking, encapsulation can be compared to the way an egg is formed. Within an egg is a yolk which is covered by the white. To get to the yolk, one has to traverse through the white that surrounds the yolk. Using the egg as an example, the data of an object is analogous to the yolk and the methods to the white. Data is thus protected by methods — access to the data is only permissible via the methods.

Access control specifiers introduced in Section 8.3 facilitate encapsulation by controlling the visibility of data and methods by other objects.

8.5.1 Bundling and Information Hiding

Encapsulation is supported by two subordinate concepts: *Bundling* and *Information Hiding*. Bundling is the act of associating a set of methods with a set of data as the only means of affecting the values of the data. Related data and methods are therefore brought together in bundling, thus increasing the cohesiveness of object definition.

Information hiding refers to the hiding of internal representation of data and methods from the users of these data and methods. By exercising information hiding, data access on an object is limited to a set of publicly available methods. While the client is aware of the existence of the methods, it does not know how the methods are internally structured. In this way, information hiding enables the separation of the WHAT from the HOW of object definition. WHAT specifies what behavior an object is capable of and HOW specifies how the data and methods of an object is implemented.

8.5.2 Enhanced Software Maintainability

By separating WHAT from HOW, a client's access on an object is not affected by changes in the internal implementation of the object. This would enhance software maintainability. To illustrate, let us consider an example using stack, which is a software construct with operations such as push(), pop(), empty(), full() and size(). Push() adds an item into a data structure in the stack. Pop() removes the

most recently pushed item. Empty() returns true if the stack is empty and full()
returns true if the data structure has reached its limit. Size() returns the current
number of items pushed into the stack.

```
class Stack {
  private int contents[];
  private int top, size=10;

  public int pop() {
    int x = 0;
    if (empty()) System.err.println("stack underflow");
    else x = contents[top--];
    return(x);
  }
  public void push(int x)   {
    if (full()) System.err.println("stack overflow");
    else {contents[++top] = x;
          System.out.println("Pushed "+x+" into Stack");}
  }
  public int size() { return(top+1); }
  public boolean empty() { return(size() == 0); }
  public boolean full() { return(size() == contents.length); }

  Stack() { contents = new int[size]; top = -1; }

  public static void main(String argv[]) {
    int i, numberOfItem;
    numberOfItem=Integer.parseInt(argv[0]) ;
    Stack s = new Stack();
    for (i = 0; i<numberOfItem; i++)
      s.push(i);
    System.out.println("\nDetails of Stack : ");
    for (i = numberOfItem; i>0; i--)
      System.out.println("Item popped = "+s.pop());
  }
}
```

Listing 8-6: Stack using an Array Implementation

There are two possible ways of implementing the stack – using array or linked list to
store items pushed into the stack. The array implementation is shown in Listing 8-6.
In this implementation, a number indicating the number of items for the array is
entered via the main prompt and converted into an integer via the statement:

```
numberOfItem = Integer.parseInt(argv[0]);
```

numberOfItem is later used in a for loop

```
for (i = 0; i<numberOfItem; i++) s.push(i);
```

to push integers into a stack created by the statement:

```
Stack s = new Stack();
```

The push() method first checks if the stack is already full, if not, the item pushed is inserted into the array contents. An error message indicating "stack overflow" is displayed if the stack is already full. Finally, the pushed items are popped via the for statement:

```
for (i = numberOfItem; i>0; i--)
     System.out.println("Item popped = "+s.pop());
```

To test the program, a value 5 was entered:

```
$ java Stack 5
```

The output is as follows:

```
Pushed 0 into Stack        Details of Stack :
Pushed 1 into Stack        Item popped = 4
Pushed 2 into Stack        Item popped = 3
Pushed 3 into Stack        Item popped = 2
Pushed 4 into Stack        Item popped = 1
                           Item popped = 0
```

It indicates that the implementation is correct with an input value 5. However, when an input value 12 is entered, the weakness of the array implementation is reflected in the output:

```
Pushed 0 into Stack        Details of Stack  :
Pushed 1 into Stack        Item popped = 9
Pushed 2 into Stack        Item popped = 8
Pushed 3 into Stack        Item popped = 7
Pushed 4 into Stack        Item popped = 6
Pushed 5 into Stack        Item popped = 5
Pushed 6 into Stack        Item popped = 4
Pushed 7 into Stack        Item popped = 3
Pushed 8 into Stack        Item popped = 2
Pushed 9 into Stack        Item popped = 1
stack overflow             Item popped = 0
stack overflow             stack underflow
                           Item popped = 0
                           stack underflow
                           Item popped = 0
```

The problem with the above implementation lies in the size of the declared array –
twelve items cannot be pushed into an array with a size of 10. The extra two items
resulted in "stack overflow" during the push operation and "stack underflow" during
the pop operation.

In the second implementation, the internal structure keeping the items is changed
from an array to a linked-list. Listing 8-7 is the code for the second implementation.
A separate StackItem class is needed in this solution to create space for storing
integers pushed into the stack. As before, the solution works well with an input value
5 but unlike the previous implementation, no "stack overflow" or "stack underflow"
messages were reported with an input value of 12:

```
Pushed 0 into Stack        Details of Stack  :
Pushed 1 into Stack        Item popped = 11
Pushed 2 into Stack        Item popped = 10
Pushed 3 into Stack        Item popped = 9
Pushed 4 into Stack        Item popped = 8
Pushed 5 into Stack        Item popped = 7
Pushed 6 into Stack        Item popped = 6
Pushed 7 into Stack        Item popped = 5
Pushed 8 into Stack        Item popped = 4
Pushed 9 into Stack        Item popped = 3
Pushed 10 into Stack       Item popped = 2
Pushed 11 into Stack       Item popped = 1
                           Item popped = 0
```

Note that when the internal implementation of the stack was changed from an array to
a linked-list representation, no change was required in main(), the client or user of
the stack. Any change to the stack definition had been carried out on the
implementation part, without a change to the contract part, of the stack. We say that
the design of Stack class exhibits *information hiding* by hiding the internal
representation of the stack from its client, main().

```
class Stack {
  private StackItem top, temp;
  private int size;

  public int pop() {
    int x = 0;
    if (empty()) System.err.println("stack underflow");
    else {x = top.getItem(); top=top.getPrevious();size=size-1;}
    return(x);
  }
  public void push(int x)   {
    if (full()) System.err.println("stack overflow");
    else {temp=top; top=new StackItem();
          top.setPrevious(temp); top.setItem(x);
          size=size+1;
          System.out.println("Pushed "+x+" into Stack");}
  }
  public int size() { return(size); }
  public boolean empty() { return(size() == 0); }
  public boolean full() { return(false); }

  Stack() {
    top = null;
    size = 0;
  }

  public static void main(String argv[]) {
    int i, numberOfItem;
    numberOfItem=Integer.parseInt(argv[0]) ;
    Stack s = new Stack();
    for (i = 0; i<numberOfItem; i++)
      s.push(i);
    System.out.println("\nDetails of Stack : ");
    for (i = numberOfItem; i>0; i--)
      System.out.println("Item popped = "+s.pop());
  }
}

class StackItem {
  private int item=0;
  private StackItem previous;
  public int getItem() {return item;}
  public void setItem(int x) {item=x;}
  public StackItem getPrevious() {return previous;}
  public void setPrevious(StackItem p) {previous=p;}
  StackItem() {previous=null;}
}
```

Listing 8-7: Stack using a Linked-List Implementation

8.5.3 Trade-Off

Encapsulation therefore enhances software maintainability by limiting the ripple effects, resulting from a change in object definition, from affecting other objects. This is done by:

- increasing the cohesiveness of data and methods through bundling; and

- reducing the strength of coupling between software components by hiding implementation details of objects from their users.

Enhanced software maintainability comes with a price. The trade-off to software maintainability using encapsulation is performance since access to data is carried out indirectly via the methods and their execution would involve the execution of additional statements resulting in reduced performance efficiency.

8.6 Summary

The issues of modularity were discussed in this chapter. In particular, we noted that:

- A method is the smallest program unit to be considered as a whole. A class is the next bigger unit.

- Attribute and method definitions are distinguished into object attributes and methods; and class attributes and methods.

- Class attributes and methods are denoted in Java using the `static` keyword.

- The visibility of attributes and methods to code fragments external to a class can be controlled using access control specifiers — `private`, `public`, `friendly` and `protected`.

- The `private` specifier makes entities that follow it hidden from code fragments external to the class.

- The `public` specifier makes entities that follow it visible from all other Java code.

- The `protected` specifier makes entities that follow it accessible to code fragments of its subclass.

- For entities with no access specifier, the default specifier `friendly` is assumed. The `friendly` specifier makes entities that follow it accessible to code fragments within the same package.

- Appropriate classes with logically related functionality can be grouped together using the package facility. Package hierarchy is specified via the `package` keyword preceding a class definition.

- The `import` keyword provides the complement function of the package facility. The `import` keyword makes package constituents visible in program code.

- Encapsulation is the bringing together of a set of attributes and methods into an object definition and hiding their implementational structure from the object's users.

- Encapsulation is supported by two subordinate concepts: *Bundling* and *Information hiding*. Bundling is the act of associating a set of methods with a set of data as the only means of affecting the values of the data. Information hiding refers to the hiding of internal representation of data and methods from the users of these data and methods.

- Encapsulation enhances software maintainability by limiting the ripple effects, resulting from a change in object definition, from affecting other objects.

8.7 Exercises

1. What is encapsulation? How does encapsulation contribute to software maintainability?

2. How does the code in Listing 8-8 measure up to the principle of encapsulation? Comment.

3. How would you enhance the code in Listing 8-8 to achieve the desired effect of encapsulation? What is the trade-off of your enhancement? What are its advantages?

```
class time {
  int hour;
  int minute;

  time() {};

  public static void main (String arg[]) {
    time t = new time();
    t.hour = 3;
    t.minute = 25;
    System.out.println("The time now is "+t.hour+":"+t.minute);
  }
}
```

Listing 8-8: time.java

9 Exception Handling

We have so far discussed the concept of object-oriented programming involving class definitions, object instantiation, the use of instance variables and methods, and the practice of code reusability via inheritance from superclasses.

This practice has given rise to payoffs in terms of the software engineering ideas of abstraction and modularity. The former allows a programmer to focus his thoughts on issues which are crucial and relevant, and delaying decisions on other less pressing concerns. The latter characteristic ensures a degree of decoupling amongst software components, which leads to better maintainability.

This chapter examines the exception handling mechanism in Java and is very important in supporting the object-oriented software development. The fact that software modules should be robust and working under every situation, yet flexible to work under any condition and even those not yet conceived is indeed a tall order. The exception handling mechanism is key in achieving this goal.

9.1 Using Exceptions

The ideas of modularity and packaging are seen to promote software engineering, but there is a subtle conflict of requirements. While the advantages of modularity stem from reusability of well-tested and proven code, this is only achieved if class definitions are never modified once they are committed into the code repository.

While it may be true that the bulk of code may not typically require modifications, a single (or sometimes simple) modification is all it takes to introduce unintended side-effects. Yet, code modules typically require minor modifications before they are used in a different scenario or project.

In general, generic portions of code, say searching or sorting an array, often require no modifications even across different applications. However, it is in the contingency plans, say an empty array, a missing target during searching or popping an empty stack, that requirements change and different measures are necessary.

A traditional solution to using generic status code in the face of different contingencies as in this situation relies on status codes via parameter passing. This approach is unfortunately clumsy, and in some situations require constant polling.

The exception mechanism in Java allows for contingency situations to be anticipated or identified within the class construct, but its handling of that condition is implemented elsewhere. It solves the dilemma we just discussed so that only generic code and the detection of contingencies are within the class construct, but handling of these contingencies be located at application specific modules.

Many API libraries such as input/output and networking rely on exception handling for flexible error handling. This mechanism is thus a key feature in reusable software development using Java.

9.2 Exception Terminology

Using the exception handling mechanism in Java involves:

- identifying exception *conditions* relevant to the application,

- locating exception handlers to *respond* to potential conditions, and

- monitoring when such conditions *occur*.

As with all representations in Java, exception conditions are denoted by objects. Similar with all objects, exceptions are also defined by class constructs, but inheriting attributes from the Exception superclass. While exception objects may be identified by object tags, additional attributes may be included for custom manipulation.

Exception handling is dynamically enabled for statement blocks within a `try`-block. Within it, normal facilities and rules for blocks apply but, control-flow within may be transferred to associated exception handlers. An appropriate statement block prefixed by a `catch`-clause is then executed when the associated exception condition occurs.

The occurrence of an exception condition is indicated by a `throw`-statement. It allows for an exception object to be dynamically propagated to the most recent exception handler. Flow-control does not return following a `throw`-statement. Instead, execution control proceeds at the statement following the `try`-block which handles the exception.

9.3 Constructs and Exception Semantics in Java

We now consider the language primitives for realizing the exception handling framework in Java. As seen,

- exception objects are defined via class constructs which inherit from the Exception class,

- exception handling is enabled within a `try`-block, with handlers indicated by `catch` clauses, and

- an exception condition is identified by a `throw` statement. (Some predefined exception conditions are thrown implicitly by the Java Virtual Machine.)

9.3.1 Defining Exception Objects

The smallest exception object in Java merely extends from the Exception superclass, as outlined in the class definition for TransmissionError below:

```
class TransmissionError extends Exception {
}
```

Logically, its objects have the same structure as objects of the Exception parent class which implements the basic functionality of exception objects. However, subclass objects are appropriately tagged (as part of Java semantics), so that objects may be subsequently distinguished. It is often more productive to define a richer structure so that such exception objects may be accurately identified as well as easily manipulated.

```
class TransmissionError extends Exception {
    int errorKind;
    TransmissionError() { errorKind = 0; }
    TransmissionError(int x) { errorKind = x; }
    String toString() { return("Transmission Error: " + errorKind); }
}
```

Encapsulating exception conditions in objects allow for rich representations and functionality (via instance variables and methods respectively). An appropriate design for such objects would reduce any overheads of coupling between conditions and handlers.

9.3.2 Defining Exception Handlers

Exception handlers are introduced by `catch`-clause within a `try`-block prefix, of which the following code fragment is representative.

```
class X {
  ...
  T m() {
    ...
    try {
      Y b = new Y();
      b.performOperation();
      ...
    } catch (TransmissionError t) {
      errorRecovery();
      ...
    } catch (IOException e) {
      errorReport();
      ...
    }
    n();
  }
}
```

Code within the `try`-block, as well as code dynamically invoked from there, are regions where exception handling is enabled. In the representative class definition for X above, this region includes the statements within the `try`-block and other blocks within methods invoked from there such as `performOperation()`.

Exception objects thrown from a `try`-block may be potentially caught by a `catch`-block exception handler as long as the type of the former matches that expected for the latter as indicated by its formal parameter. In our previous example, the first handler catches TransmissionError exception objects, while the second handler catches IOException exception objects. Since objects of a subclass share the characteristics and are also considered objects of the base class, the said handlers will also cater to subclasses of TransmissionError and IOException objects respectively.

The placement order of `catch`-blocks is significant. Due to the inheritance mechanism, `catch`-blocks work in a sieve-like manner and handlers for subclasses should appear before handlers for superclasses.

When exception objects are caught, control-flow is transferred to the exception handler concerned. Control-flow then resumes at the statement following the try-block – in our example, this is method n().

9.3.3 Raising Exceptions

An exception condition is ultimately represented by an exception object derived from the predefined Exception class[1]. A condition is made known by throwing an appropriate object via a throw statement, to be subsequently caught by an associated handler.

```
class Y {
  ...
  void performOperation() {
    ...
    if (F)
      throw new TransmissionError();
  }
}
```

In the event that the thrown exception object does not match what is expected by event handlers, it is further propagated to the caller of the method which contains the try-block. This caller chain (which forms a back-trace) proceeds until static void main() method is encountered. The predefined environment supplies a default exception handler which aborts program execution with a execution back-trace from the run-time stack, and an appropriate error message.

TransmissionError is the typical case of a programmer-defined exception condition. The Java API also contains various exception classes which are used within the API, e.g. MalformedURL and thrown from methods like performOperation(). These are accessible via the normal mechanisms.

There is also a unique set of exceptions which are thrown directly from the Java Virtual Machine. For example, integer division is translated into an operator for the Java Virtual Machine. Thus, if a 0 divisor is encountered in an expression, a DivideByZero exception is raised from the Java Virtual Machine without any corresponding throw-statement from the application code.

---

[1] Actually, objects that can be thrown by the throw statement must be derived from the Throwable superclass. However, in addition to the Exception class, Throwable also includes the Error class which indicates serious problems that a reasonable application should not try to catch. As such, we will continue to work from the Exception class.

9.4 A Simple Example

We will now piece together the various Java constructs described in the previous section to provide the context for their usage. As a working example, we consider a stack object which allows for items to be placed, but removed in the reverse of placement order. Like a stack of plates, it allows for pushing and popping items from the "top".

Two situations may be anticipated during stack usage: when the stack is empty and no items are available for retrieval, and when the stack is full and cannot accommodate further items. The exception mechanism is ideal in that exceptions may be raised independently of how clients using a stack object may want to respond to such contingencies. This framework physically separates server code from client code, but yet provides for conceptual association so that contingencies in the server may be easily propagated and handled by the client.

To begin, the two stack conditions may be defined as follows:

```
class EmptyStack extends Exception {
}

class FullStack extends Exception {
}
```

A stack object may be implemented using an array to hold items pushed to it. By default, stacks will hold a maximum of 10 items, unless otherwise specified via its constructor.

```
class Stack {

  int height;
  Object items[];

  void push(Object x) throws FullStack {
    if (items.length == height)
      throw new FullStack();
    items[height++] = x;
  }
  Object pop() throws EmptyStack {
    if (height == 0)
      throw new EmptyStack();
    return(items[--height]);
  }
```

```
        void init(int s) {
          height = 0;
          item = new Object[s];
        }

        Stack (int s) { init(s); }
        Stack() { init(10); }
      }
```

Note the throws suffix in the method signature forewarns callers of the possibility of an exception. Consistent with secure programming practice, Java would insist that coding within the client either sets up an appropriate exception handler, or appends the throws suffix in the caller method so that the stack exception is propagated.

The programming style in class Stack allows it to be used in varied situations without the concern for acceptable or "correct" responses to stack errors. As usage of Stack is available to various client classes, the code fragments may implement appropriate handlers for each application.

We first consider a scenario involving a parser for arithmetic expressions. A full stack arising from a deeply nested expression might cause parsing to be aborted with an appropriate message.

```
    class Parser {
      ...
      void Expression() {
        Stack s = new Stack();
        try {
          ...
          s.push(x);
          ...
        } catch (FullStack e) { // respond to full stack condition
          error("expression nesting exceeds implementation limit");
          abort();
        } catch ... // other possible exceptions
      }
      ...
    }
```

In a situation where an error might not be fatal, a value from the stack could be substituted with another by the exception handler so that processing may continue. Such recovery processing is strategically focused.

```
class Evaluator {
  Stack s = new Stack();
  ...
  void operand() {
    Integer value;
    ...
    try {
      value = (Integer) s.pop();
    } catch (EmptyStack e) { // respond to empty stack condition
      value = new Integer(0);
    }
    ...
  }
}
```

9.5 Paradigms for Exception Handling

We have seen exception handling in Java as comprising of exception definition via a class definition, exception handlers via try- and catch-blocks, and raising exception incidents by throwing appropriate objects.

A general framework for exception handling has been outlined in the previous section. Ideally, the framework should be extended to fit various scenarios, which lead us to present various usage patterns.

9.5.1 Multiple Handlers

To facilitate monitoring more than one exception condition, a try-block allows for multiple catch-clauses. Without the exception handling mechanisms of Java, error handling code would be untidy, especially so for operations where a sequence of erroneous situations can occur.

For example, when sending email to a user happy@xyz.com, an email client program must:

- initiate a socket connection to the host machine xyz.com,

- specify the recipient; and

- send the contents of the mail message.

Complications arise when xyz.com is not a valid email host, happy is not a legitimate user on the host, or premature closure of the socket connection.

```
class EMail {
  ...
  void send(String address) {
    errorCode = 0;
    makeHostConnection(emailHostOf(address));
    if (connectionError) {
      errorMessage("host does not exist");
      errorCode = 1;
    } else {
      verifyUser(emailUserof(address));
      if (noUserReply {
        errorMessage("user is not valid");
        errorCode = 2;
      } else {
        while ((!endofInputBuffer()) && errorCode != -1) {
          line = readInputBuffer();
          sendContent(line);
        }
        if (networkError) {
          errorMessage("connection error occurred");
          errorCode = 3;
        }
      }
    }
  }
  ...
}
```

The above skeletal code for email processing may be structurally improved and made more transparent by using exception handling mechanisms. It is also useful from the maintenance point of view to separate processing logic from error processing. The code fragment below which uses multiple exception handlers is tidier if the appropriate exception objects are thrown by the methods makeHostConnection(), verifyUser() and sendContent().

```
class EMail {
  ...
  void send(String address) {
    try {
      errorCode = 0;
      makeHostConnection(emailHostOf(address));
      verifyUser(emailUserof(address));
      while (!endofInputBuffer()) {
        line = readInputBuffer();
        sendContent(line);
      }
    } catch (SocketException s) {
      errorMessage("host does not exist");
      errorCode = 1;
    } catch (NoUserReply n) {
      errorMessage("user is not valid");
      errorCode = 2;
```

```
        } catch (WriteError) {
          errorMessage("connection error occurred");
          errorCode = 3;
        }
      }
      ...
    }
```

The resultant structure is clearer – normal processing logic in the try-block, and error handling in catch-clauses.

9.5.2 Regular Exception Handling

Where there are multiple code fragments with similar error handling logic, a global exception handler would again be neater.

```
class EMail {
  ...
  void makeHostConnection(String host) {
    openSocket(host);
    if (!IOerror()) {
      checkResponse();
      giveGreetings();
    }
  }
  void giveGreetings() {
    writeMessage("HELO " + hostname);
    if (IOerror())
      errorCode = 9;
    else
      checkResponse();
  }
  void verifyUser(String user) {
    writeMessage("VERIFY " + user);
    if (IOerror())
      errorCode = 9;
    else
      checkResponse();
  }
  ...
}
```

In the code above, a transaction from an email client involves writing a message to the server and then reading if it receives an appropriate response. However, each message to the server might be unsuccessful due to a network error such as the termination of the connection.

With the exception handling mechanism in Java, generic errors may be handled by a common network error handler, e.g. an IOException exception handler, so that such errors need not be constantly monitored.

```
class EMail {
   ...
   void send(String address) {
      try {
         errorCode = 0;
         makeHostConnection(emailHostOf(address));
         verifyUser(emailUserof(address));
         ...
      } catch (IOException x) {
         // network error detected
      }
   }

   void makeHostConnection(String host) {
      openSocket(host);
      checkResponse();
      giveGreetings();
   }

   void giveGreetings() {
      writeMessage("HELO " + hostname);
      checkResponse();
   }

   void verifyUser(String user) {
      writeMessage("VERIFY " + user);
      checkResponse();
   }
}
```

9.5.3 Accessing Exception Objects

So far, we have discussed how a catch-block responds to exceptions specified in its parameter type T, but without reference to the parameter name e.

```
try {
   ...
      throw new X();
} catch (X e) {
   ... // e refers to exception object thrown earlier
}
```

The fact that the parameter name of a catch-block is bound to the current exception object thrown allows for the means of transferring information to the exception handler.

9.5.4 Subconditions

We have seen that exception conditions are represented by objects which are described via class constructs. Since objects are dynamically distinguished from one another by their built-in class tags, this is a viable and productive method for representing different conditions.

As with other classes, a new exception condition may also be subclassed from an existing class to indicate a more specific condition. Incorporating the inheritance mechanism to exception handling allows for logical classification and code reusability in both condition detection and handler implementation. CommError and ProtocolError in the skeletal fragment below are typical examples of rich representations using inheritance.

```
class CommError extends Exception {
    int errorKind;
    Date when;
    CommError(int a) ...
}
class ProtocolError extends CommError {
    int errorSource;
    ProtocolError(int a, int b) ...
}
```

The language mechanism which allows exception conditions and subsequently flow of control to propagate to an appropriate handler provides for powerful and flexible processing.

```
try {
    ...
        throw new CommError(errorCode);
    ...
        throw new ProtocolError(errorCode, extraInformation);
    ...
} catch (ProtocolError e) {
    ... // handle ProtocolError by inspecting e appropriately
} catch (CommError f) {
    ... // handle CommError by inspecting f appropriately
}
```

Due to inheritance rules, the exception handlers of the above try-block are ordered so that specific (subclass) exceptions are caught first. If generic (superclass) exceptions were caught first, the handler for the specific exceptions would never be used.

Note that while the exception object thrown is caught within the same `try`-block in the above, in practice, a `throw`-statement may also be deeply nested within methods invoked from the `try`-block.

9.5.5 Nested Exception Handlers

Since an exception handler comprises mainly of a statement block, the sequence of statements within it may also contain other `try`-blocks with associated nested `catch`-blocks.

```
try {
   ...
     throw new X(errorCode);
   ...
} catch (X f) {
   ...
   try {
      ...
        throw new Y(errorCode, m);
      ...
   } catch (Y e) {
      ...
   }
}
```

As illustrated above, the scenario occurs when exceptions are anticipated within exception handlers.

9.5.6 Layered Condition Handling

Just as `catch`-blocks may be nested, we consider a related situation where a more specific exception handling is required. This can occur when the current handlers are not sufficient, and the new `try`-block is nested within another to override it.

```
try {
   ...
     throw new X(errorCode);
     try {
        ...
        throw new X(errorCode);
        ...
     } catch (X e) {
        ...
     }
} catch (X f) {
   ...
}
```

There are two applicable exception handling paradigms here:

- the nested handler may perform all necessary processing so that the enclosing handler does not realize that an exception has occurred; or

- the nested handler may perform processing relevant to its conceptual level and leave the remaining processing to the outer handler.

The former has been illustrated in the previous fragment, while the latter has been outlined in the framework below, where the nested handler throws the same exception after sufficient local processing.

```
try {
  ...
  try {
    ...
      throw new X(errorCode);
    ...
  } catch (X e) {
    ...
    throw e;
  }
  ...
} catch (X f) {
  ...
}
```

9.6 Code Finalization and Cleaning Up

The model for control-flow mechanisms involving statement sequences, conditional branching and iteration are unchanged for the Java programming language. The exception handling facilities in Java may be considered an advanced control-flow facility which allows control to be dynamically transferred out of well tested code modules. We continue to examine two more features relating to control-flow.

9.6.1 Object Finalization

The role of constructor methods was discussed in Chapter 3 in providing the necessary initialization for all newly created objects. This language feature imposes an invariant for all objects of the class. The default constructor with no parameters is the simplest and typically provides baseline initialization. Other constructors provide the means of initialization by various input parameters.

The complement of the constructor mechanism is a destructor facility. Its main purpose is to undo at the onset of object disposal, what was performed during initialization. If storage had been allocated during object initialization, the appropriate destructor behavior should dispose of such storage for subsequent use.

Such language mechanisms are typically in place for modular languages, and more so, object-oriented languages. However, destructor methods in Java are less necessary due to the automatic garbage collection scheme at run-time. Any storage areas which might have been allocated but are non-accessible, are reclaimed for subsequent reuse.

This technique is indeed useful when storage recycling is not always clear to the programmer, but instead, is assured that unusable memory fragments will be ultimately recovered by the language run-time system. Thus, the Java programmer may allocate storage at will, and is not obliged to keep track of usage, nor required to de-allocate them.

De-allocating memory (which is no longer needed) is only one aspect of housekeeping for objects. Managing memory and variables happens to be an issue which is internal to a program, but can be handled automatically by the Java Virtual Machine.

There are other aspects of housekeeping which are external to a program, e.g. releasing unused file descriptors or relinquishing a network socket connection. As such resources are also external to the Java Virtual Machine, automatic de-allocation is not practical.

In place of destructor methods, Java allows for finalization methods. Each class definition may include a parameterless method called `finalize()`. The run-time system ensures that this method will be invoked before the object is reclaimed by the garbage collector.

```
class Email {
   Email() {
      // open network connection
   }
   ... other methods
   void finalize() {
      // close network connection
   }
}
```

9.6.2 Block Finalization

As described in the previous section, a `finalize()` method performs the last wishes for data before it is destroyed. Java also provides a similar mechanism for code blocks. A `finally` clause may optionally follow a `try` block. It guarantees that its code would be executed regardless of whether an exception was thrown in the `try` block, and if thrown, whether it was caught by an associated handler.

```
try {
  // processing
} catch (TransmissionError t) {
  // handle TransmissionError exception
} finally {
  // perform clean up before leaving this block
}
```

This mechanism allows for a neat program structure, e.g. when there are mandatory code fragments in both normal processing and exception handling. In elaborating our transmission example below, normal processing might involve opening transmission channel, performing all the required transmission and then terminating transmission by closing the channel. In the unfortunate event of a transmission error, we initiate contingency processing before closing the transmission channel. Maintenance is error prone due to the repetition of `channel.close()` in both `try`- and `catch`-blocks.

```
try {
  channel = openTransmissionChannel();
  channel.transmit();
  channel.close();
} catch (TransmissionError t) {
  hasError = true;
  channel.close();
} catch (NoReplyError x) {
  toRepeat = true;
  channel.close();
}
```

The improved style using a `finally`-block avoids repetition of `channel.close()`.

```
try {
  channel = openTransmissionChannel();
  channel.transmit();
} catch (TransmissionError x) {
  hasError = true;
} catch (NoReplyError x) {
  toRepeat = true;
} finally {
  channel.close();
}
```

9.7 Summary

In this chapter, we discussed advanced control-flow facilities. The most significant of these is exception handling since it allows for flexible integration of modular code. The language primitives allow for:

- the definition of exception conditions,

- raising of exceptions within the virtual machine, as well as via the throw statement, and

- catching of exception objects via try- and catch-blocks.

Other control-flow facilities for neater program structures include finalization for objects and code blocks.

- A finalize() method is invoked before an object is destroyed so that it can complement the actions of a constructor.

- A finally block allows for fail-safe code execution before leaving a try-block, and is independent of exceptions or exception handlers.

9.8 Exercises

1. Consider the CalculateEngine and CalculatorFrame classes to implement the calculator in Chapter 4. Suggest how the framework can take advantage of the exception handling facility in Java so as to maintain modular boundaries and provide better error messages.

2. Implement a Symbol table class so that each symbol may be associated with a numeric value. The two main methods are set() and get():

    ```
    void set(String sym, int value);
    int get(String sym);
    ```

    The set() method associates the int value with the symbol sym, while the get() method performs the complement of retrieving the int value previously associated with sym.

    Define appropriate exceptions so that clients of the Symbol table may respond to conditions appropriately. For example, when retrieve the value of a non-existent symbol, clients can either stop execution, display an error message, or use a default value of 0.

3. Incorporate the Symbol table object into the calculator so that intermediate results may be associated with user-defined symbols.

10 Input and Output Operations

We have covered all the basic mechanisms of Java, but not much have been said about input and output operations like reading from and writing to files. In fact, the Java programming language excludes any description of performing such operations. Instead, this critical functionality is implemented by standard libraries.

In Java, many practical features are not built into the language proper. These functionality are included in libraries known as the Java Application Programming Interface (API), mostly standard across Java platforms. In this chapter, we will briefly view the Java API and its relevance to reading from and writing to files and other generic devices.

10.1 An Introduction to the Java API

Java is an object-oriented programming language. This facilitates the creation of objects and message passing amongst such objects. We have seen too that objects are created from class definitions, and as such, all code written in Java exists within class definitions.

Since the Java API library is merely reusable code, they exist in class definitions too. The Java API is thus a large set of classes to make the task of programming development more productive. Often, our programs need not implement the data-structures it needs. Instead, code within the API may be used, or reused by specialization through inheritance to meet the needs of our custom applications.

The API is used in various generic ways:

- The simplest means of using the API is to create an instance of an API class, for example, to read from a file, we create an instance of FileInputStream. The `read()` method is used on the resultant object to read file contents, and similarly `close()` will perform necessary clean-up to system resources like file descriptors for reuse.

- A new class may be defined based on an API class by inheritance. This facilitates reuse of generic code, for example, to create new threads for specific multi-threaded applications, we define a new class based on the Thread class, but with new definitions relevant to our application.

- Often, class variables of API classes may be used directly without explicit initialization, i.e. `out` is a public class variable in the System class, and may be used directly for the purpose of printing to the standard output stream. This was how `System.out.println()` was used in Chapter 4.

As there are a large number of classes in the Java API, it is fruitful to organize and group them according to their functionality. In JDK 1.0, the Java API was organized into 6 packages: `java.lang`, `java.io`, `java.util`, `java.net`, `java.awt` and `java.applet`.

- The `java.lang` package consists of Java classes which are essential to the execution of Java programs, e.g. the Thread and System classes belong to the `java.lang` package.

- The `java.io` package consists of Java classes which are used for input and output facilities, e.g. the FileInputStream class mentioned earlier belong to the `java.io` package.

- The `java.net` package consists of Java classes which are relevant to networking, e.g. the Socket class belongs to the `java.net` package and is used for network connections to hosts on other machines.

- The `java.util` package consists of Java classes for generic functionality like list collections, date representation, e.g. the Vector and Date classes belong to the `java.util` package.

- The `java.awt` package consists of Java classes which implement the Abstract Windowing Toolkit. These classes are used for creating graphical interfaces for a windows-based environment.

- The `java.applet` package consists of Java classes which are used to support applet execution within the context of a Web browser.

10.2   Reading the Java API Documentation

The Java API is described in the Java API documentation, available in hard copy books, postscript, or HTML. The HTML form is typically preferred in a online environment since it allows for convenient traversal.

From a standard distribution site, the zip or tar file should be downloaded and contents extracted. Viewing local pages using a Web browser is straightforward. In general, there are three navigation strategies when using the API documentation in HTML – browsing by packages, browsing by class hierarchy, and browsing by the variable and method index. With the first method, the package name is selected, followed by the class name, after which the class documentation is available.

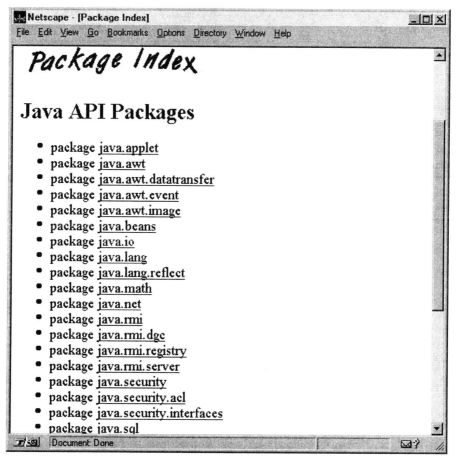

Figure 10-1: Viewing API Documentation by Packages

Browsing the API documentation according to the class hierarchy has classes organized according to their inheritance chain. The link to the root class Object is shown first followed by those classes derived from it.

The following screen snapshot in Figure 10-2 shows the Compiler and Component classes at the same level in the hierarchy. In addition, the classes Button, Canvas, Checkbox, etc. are derived from the class Component, and similarly Applet is derived from Panel, which in turn is derived from Container and then Component.

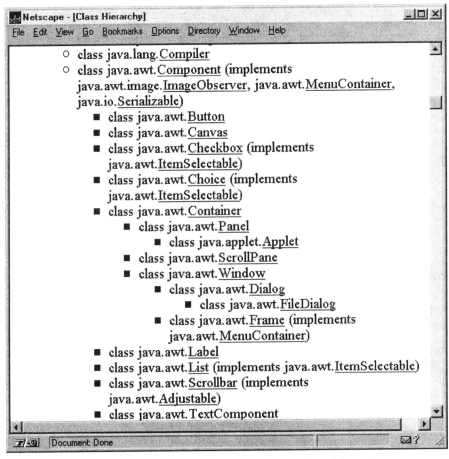

Figure 10-2: Viewing API Documentation by Class Hierarchy

In the last view, the names of all variables and methods have been indexed, as seen in Figure 10-3. Links for these entities ultimately refer back to their class definitions.

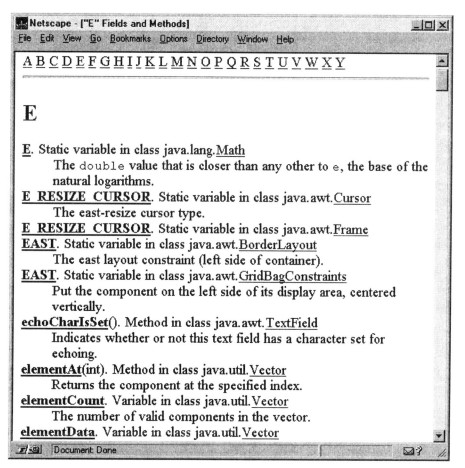

Figure 10-3: Viewing API Documentation by Sorted Names

For each class, the API documentation includes both a brief overview which is hyperlinked to more detailed descriptions. Class entities are color coded, as in Table 10-1, for easy notational convenience.

Entity	Indication in Class Description
Instance Variables	magenta ball
Static Variables	blue ball
Constructors	yellow ball
Instance Methods	red ball
Static Methods	green ball

Table 10-1: Entity Color Coding

10.3 Basic Input and Output

The simplest start to input and output are pre-initialized objects System.in, System.out and System.err. These correspond to the three standard file descriptors stdin, stdout and stderr in UNIX, being bound to the standard input, standard output and standard error streams. Typically for interactive processes, these streams correspond to the keyboard and screen. (While standard output and standard error are bound to the same device, they are logically different and very useful with stream redirection.)

The System class belongs to the java.lang package, but due to heavy use of this package, it is implicitly imported in every Java program unit. in, out and err are class variables of the System class, and they have been pre-initialized with streams for input and output respectively. All this might sound exceedingly strange, but it is fruitful to get the concepts clear at this stage as we begin to probe and use the Java API.

If we look up the System class documentation, out is documented as:

```
public static final PrintStream out;
```

Looking up the PrintStream class documentation will reveal (not exclusive) the following methods for PrintStream instances:

```
print(boolean)
print(char)
print(char[])
print(double)
print(float)
print(int)
print(long)
print(Object)
print(String)
```

This shows that a PrintStream instance (like System.out) can print out boolean, char, char array, double, float, int, long, Object and String values. In addition, the println() method may also accept similar parameters as print() and with similar behavior except that a carriage return is also printed after the value.

Thus, the following statements are legitimate:

```
System.out.print('g');
System.out.print(3.142);
System.out.print(45);
System.out.print("hello there");
System.out.println(23);
System.out.println(3.32123);
System.out.println(23456765432);
System.out.println();
System.out.println(System.out);
```

`println()` without any parameters will just print a carriage return. Note that Object instances are also legitimate parameters to `print()` and `println()`. Since all classes are (directly or indirectly) derived from Object, `println()` will print out any object. In practice, the actual value displayed depends on whether appropriate code is present to provide a suitable textual representation of the object concerned[1].

Since `System.err` is also a static variable initialized as a PrintStream instance, it has the same behavior as `System.out`. It even prints to the same device, i.e. the screen but may be redirected to another via operating system facilities.

The `System.in` stream is quite different because its use is for input. Again, the documentation for the System class will reveal that it is a static variable which is initialized to an InputStream object.

```
public static final InputStream in;
```

Upon further checking of the documentation for the InputStream class, the principal statement of interest is revealed to be reading a byte from the stream.

```
System.in.read()
```

As this method returns the internal representation of the character itself, we typically typecast it to a `char` type by using the ( ) typecast operator.

```
char c = (char) System.in.read();
```

---

[1] The `print()` method relies on the `toString()` method to provide a textual representation of an object. Since `toString()` is defined in the Object class and cannot anticipate properties of future class definitions, it only performs generic text conversion. Of course subclasses are free to override `toString()` with a more appropriate definition to provide more comprehensive details of the object.

Two significant points are noted from the detailed documentation: first, read()
potentially throws an IOException object to indicate an error in the input operation.
As such, it is expected that clients using this method must catch the exception within
a try-block. Next, the method returns an integer value of −1 after it encounters the
last character to be read. Clients must also anticipate against reading past this point.

Putting it all together, we can write a program which reads its input and copies the
contents to the output. We put all this code into the static void main() function.

```
import java.io.*;
class CopyInputToOutput {
  public static void main(String args[]) {
    int x=0, c;
    try {
      while ((c = System.in.read()) != -1) {
        System.out.print((char) c);
        x++;
      }
      System.err.print(x);
      System.err.println(" bytes read");
    } catch (IOException e) {
      System.err.println("I/O Error Exception has occurred");
    }
  }
}
```

The code shows the following points:

• A try-block anticipates the IOException object from read(), as forewarned in
  the signature for read() or its equivalent API documentation.

• A while-statement is used to iteratively read all characters until the end-of-
  stream as indicated by the −1 sentinel.

• The local variable x is initialized to 0, and is incremented each time in the loop
  to count the number of bytes read (and written).

• Output is written into two logical streams. The output stream contains that which
  was read from the input stream, while the error stream is for diagnostic messages
  of byte count, or errors. (If any stream is redirected, the other proceeds with the
  original device binding.)

10.4 File Manipulation

Input and output using the predefined streams has given a preview of how other input and output operations will be performed – via methods such as print() and read().

Input and output involving the standard streams is simple because they have been pre-initialized, and no finalization code is required. This consistently reflects the situation where input and output streams are available when typical programs begin execution and may read from the keyboard or write to the screen, and always remain available.

The situation is different for reading and writing to files which must be opened before use, and subsequently closed when operations are complete. This reflects the dynamic nature of file representation – there may be an instance of a particular file on disk, but it may be at different stages of being read by many other programs. This file representation is encapsulated within a stream object comprising of suitable data-structure to represent how much has been read or written.

10.4.1 File Input

The state of file input, as to how much of the file has been read, is represented by a FileInputStream object. After the file has been opened, reading proceeds similarly with the predefined standard input stream. Finally, the FileInputStream object is closed after use so as to reclaim system resources.

The TestInput code fragment in Listing 10-1 is adapted from the previous one for reading from the standard input stream. In reading from a file, modifications include the instantiation of a FileInputStream object, and catching the FileNotFoundException.

The FileInputStream, FileNotFoundException and IOException classes belong to the java.io package. Due to separate name spaces, we bring the class into scope via the import statement. Instead of just importing specific classes, we have imported the whole package instead.

The documentation of FileInputStream will reveal two important characteristics of TestInput:

- The FileInputStream class is derived from the InputStream class. In other words, instances of FileInputStream are also instances of InputStream, with the behavior of InputStream objects too. This explains why the two code fragments look identical via the read() method.

- The documentation for FileInputStream describes the constructor as potentially throwing a FileNotFoundException object. This explains the extra exception handler.

```
import java.io.*;
class TestInput {
  public static void main(String args[]) {
    int x=0, c;
    FileInputStream f
    try {
      f = new FileInputStream("input.txt");
      while ((c = f.read()) != -1) {
        System.out.print((char) c);
        x++;
      }
      System.err.print(x);
      System.err.println(" bytes read");
      f.close();
    } catch (FileNotFoundException n) {
      System.err.println("File not found");
    } catch (IOException e) {
      System.err.println("I/O Error Exception has occurred");
    }
  }
}
```

Listing 10-1: TestInput class

10.4.2 File Output

The mechanism for file output is intuitively similar to that for file input. Based on the code fragment in TestInput, we can make minor modifications to try out file output, as in Listing 10-2.

The complement of FileInputStream is FileOutputStream. To write to a file, we merely create a FileOutputStream instance by giving an appropriate file name to the constructor. As with previous files, the `close()` method is used to signal the end of file manipulation.

The most significant change in this code fragment is that the `print()` method, used previously with `System.out`, is not used with FileOutputStream. The reason is clear on checking the documentation for FileOutputStream.

```
import java.io.*;
class TestCopy {
  public static void main(String args[]) {
    int x=0, c;
    FileInputStream f;
    FileOutputStream g;
    try {
      f = new FileInputStream("input.txt");
      g = new FileOutputStream("output.txt");
      while ((c = f.read()) != -1) {
        g.write(c);
        x++;
      }
      System.err.print(x);
      System.err.println(" bytes read");
      f.close();
      g.close();
    } catch (FileNotFoundException n) {
      System.err.println("File not found");
    } catch (IOException e) {
      System.err.println("I/O Error Exception has occurred");
    }
  }
}
```

Listing 10-2: TestCopy class

The documentation shows that the write() method is available, but print() method is not. Remember that System.out is an instance of PrintStream, but FileOutputStream is not related to PrintStream. This mystery is cleared in the next section – as to how the print() method may be used with FileOutputStream objects.

10.4.3 Printing using PrintStream

The following two points explain how a PrintStream object may be obtained from an FileOutputStream instance, thereby allowing println() to be used in file output.

*   The FileOutputStream class is derived from OutputStream.

*   The documentation for the PrintStream class reveals that its instance is created from an OutputStream object.

It follows that a FileOutputStream instance may be used (as an OutputStream object) to instantiate a PrintStream class, as indicated in the code example in Listing 10-3.

```
import java.io.*;
class AnotherCopy {
  public static void main(String args[]) {
    int x=0, c;
    try {
      FileInputStream f = new FileInputStream("input.txt");
      FileOutputStream g = new FileOutputStream("output.txt");
      PrintStream p = new PrintStream(g);
      while ((c = f.read()) != -1) {
        p.print((char) c);
        x++;
      }
      System.err.print(x);
      System.err.println(" bytes read");
      f.close();
      p.close();
    } catch (FileNotFoundException n) {
      System.err.println("File not found");
    } catch (IOException e) {
      System.err.println("I/O Error Exception has occurred");
    }
  }
}
```

Listing 10-3: AnotherCopy class

While the previous example shows how a PrintStream object may be obtained, its impact is minimal since the result is a mere change from using write() to using print(). A more significant advantage is that it allows the varied operations of PrintStream to be available.

10.5 Framework for Code Reuse

The use of PrintStream methods for System.out and an instance of FileOutputStream in the previous example shows the paradigm of code reusability in an object-oriented environment.

The following class hierarchy diagram clarifies the scenario which we just observed, that code in the OutputStream class is reused for FileOutputStream objects. A more subtle reuse paradigm is that a PrintStream object may be instantiated from an OutputStream object.

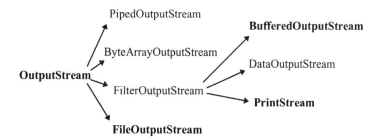

We now move to the bigger picture of the `java.io` package and code reusability. First, besides FileOutputStream, the other classes e.g. PipedOutputStream and ByteArrayOutputStream also benefit from deriving behavior from the OutputStream class. This is the typical scenario of reusing code via inheritance as discussed in Chapter 6.

It could be viewed that PipedOutputStream and ByteArrayIOutputStream, like FileOutputStream are specializations of OutputStream. They all have the same model in that they allow `write()` operations, but whose contents are diverted to a file, a pipe or a byte array.

Note that the ability to create a PrintStream instance comes from FilterOutputStream. The latter provides the framework for adding functionality to an existing OutputStream. In the case of PrintStream, the additional functionality is higher-level output for values of different types, e.g. `int`, `float`, `char`, `char` array, for the existing OutputStream instance used to create it.

In the same way, buffered file output may be achieved by first creating a FileOutputStream and using it for creating a BufferedOutputStream object. Again, it (a superclass of FilterOutputStream) has added functionality to a FileOutputStream object (a superclass of OutputStream):

```
FileOutputStream f = new FileOutputStream("myOutput");
BufferedOutputStream buf = new BufferedOutputStream(f);
```

The combinations are however limitless since BufferedOutputStream is derived from OutputStream. As such, a buffered PrintStream can be obtained using the technique below. More amazing, this code integration technique also copes with code which is yet to be designed (i.e. future superclasses of FilterOutputStream).

```
FileOutputStream f = new FileOutputStream("myOutput");
BufferedOutputStream buf = new BufferedOutputStream(f);
PrintStream p = new PrintStream(buf);
...
p.println(...);
```

The same reuse framework is used for InputStreams, as shown in the class hierarchy diagram below:

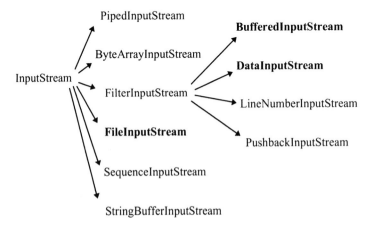

The basic means of file input is via FileInputStream. Just as writing may be diverted, the input stream in this case comes from a file. Similarly, using PipedInputStream, ByteArrayInputStream or StringBufferInputStream, input can be read from a pipe, byte array or string.

Similar to the output case, buffered file input may be achieved by first creating a FileInputStream and using it for creating a BufferedInputStream object:

```
FileInputStream f = new FileInputStream("myInput");
BufferedInputStream buf = new BufferedInputStream(f);
```

Again, the combinations are limitless since the BufferedInputStream class is derived from InputStream. As such, a buffered DataInputStream can be obtained using the same technique below. With a DataInputStream object derived from a BufferedInputStream, the `readLine()` method is implicitly buffered:

```
FileInputStream f = new FileInputStream("myInput");
BufferedInputStream buf = new BufferedInputStream(f);
DataInputStream dis = new DataInputStream(buf);
...
dis.readLine()
```

10.6 Input/Output Classes in JDK 1.1

The standard input/output facilities available via the InputStream and OutputStream classes merely support 8-bit byte streams. The enhancement in JDK 1.1 relating to input and output provides support for *character* streams which allow for 16-bit Unicode characters. The advantage of character streams is that programs can now be independent of specific character encoding, which to some extent, simplify ongoing internationalization efforts.

The new character stream classes have been designed to parallel the byte stream equivalents in JDK 1.0. For example, the abstract input and output byte-stream classes InputStream and OutputStream, together with their subclasses, have new equivalent classes Reader and Writer with correspondingly similar functionality and usage paradigm.

JDK 1.0 byte-stream classes	JDK 1.1 character-stream classes
InputStream	Reader
BufferedInputStream	BuffererdReader
LineNumberInputStream	LineNumberReader
ByteArrayInputStream	CharArrayReader
FileInputStream	FileReader
FilterInputStream	FilterReader
PushbackInputStream	PushbackReader
PipedInputStream	PipedReader
StringBufferInputStream	StringReader
OutputStream	Writer
BufferedOutputStream	BufferedWriter
ByteArrayOutputStream	CharArrayWriter
FilterOutputStream	FilterWriter
PrintStream	PrintWriter
PipedOutputStream	PipedWriter

The InputStreamReader and OutputStreamWriter classes form the bridge between byte and character streams through translation.

10.7 Summary

This chapter has introduced the Java Application Programmer Interface (API). It provides the means by which programmers may code productively by reusing code. The Java API possesses the key success criteria for reusability in that it has a neat reuse framework and is adequately documented.

Code which judiciously use the Java API are shorter and simpler to develop since they effectively build upon the work of others. They have a big user community and it is likely that any bugs discovered will be promptly fixed in future releases.

The `java.io` package is representative of the useful functionalities provided by the Java API. Our discussion has shown:

- the basic input/output functionality may be used via `System.out`, `System.err` and `System.in`; and

- the generic input and output interfaces used in the abstract classes OutputStream and InputStream.

The next usage level of the `java.io` package involves:

- subclasses of OutputStream and InputStream which implement actual I/O operations on suitable medium such as files or pipes via classes FileInputStream and FileOutputStream,

- incorporation of general I/O formats and options as implemented by FilterInputStream and FilterOutputStream classes and corresponding subclasses, and

- the corresponding relationship with Reader and Writer classes in JDK 1.1

10.8 Exercises

1. Check up the HTML-based API documentation to find more details on the
    following:

    *   operations allowable on Strings

    *   constant value of PI

    *   method to return the arc cosine of an angle

    *   `java.util.Dictionary` class (Consider if this class is useful in
        implementing the Symbol table discussed in Chapter 4.)

2. Write a program to read filenames specified in the command-line and copy their
    contents to the standard output.

3. Implement a method to read the contents of the file and write it out to the
    standard output stream, with all lowercase characters converted to uppercase.

4. Suggest how exception handlers may be installed so that input/output errors are
    reported and files appropriately closed after use.

5. Consider the similar code fragments for the solution to Questions 2 and 3, and
    suggest how object-oriented technology may be used to maximize reusability and
    maintainability.

11 Networking and Multi-Threading

In Chapter 10, we previewed the Java API for input and output facilities, especially those associated with files requiring different formatting. The framework used to maximize code reusability was also discussed.

In this chapter, we will go beyond the local machine by looking at networking facilities in the Java API. Since the abstraction for networking primitives turns out to be byte streams, there is indeed much reuse of the classes seen in the previous chapter.

11.1 The Network Model

The networking facility available in Java using TCP/IP involves socket connections. This allows a host to link up with another so that a byte stream which is sent on one machine is received by the partner. A socket connection is symmetric and thus a host also receives what is sent by the partner.

In this model, as illustrated in Figure 11-1, machines may be asymmetrically classified as clients and servers. A client is one which initiates a network connection by naming the corresponding server. A server is one which is ready to receive a connection from a client.

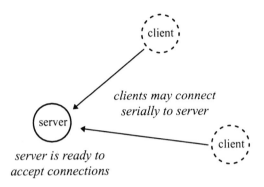

Figure 11-1: Server and Clients

A server host may provide more than one service, and thus a port number is required to distinguish between services. On the Internet, there are well-defined port numbers for the standard services. By UNIX convention, the first 1023 ports are reserved for system privileged services, thereafter other user programs may use the ports on a first-come-first-serve basis.

The following table gives some standard services and their corresponding port numbers:

Service	Port number
telnet	23
ftp	21
mail	25
finger	79
Web (httpd)	80

A socket connection is said to be established when a client successfully connects to a server machine. From this point, as illustrated in Figure 11-2, communication between both parties are symmetric. As such, writing at either end will cause the corresponding partner to receive the contents.

Figure 11-2: Bidirectional Socket Connection

11.2 Sockets in Java

The implementation details of TCP/IP socket connections in Java are encapsulated in the Socket class which exists in the `java.net` package. As before, the Socket class must be brought into scope via an `import java.net.Socket` statement. A socket connection to a server involves instantiating a Socket object with the appropriate connection parameters.

In the typical scenario, we specify the hostname of the server, and the service port at which the server is listening to. A socket connection to the Web server (running at the default port 80) at www.javasoft.com would be made as such:

```
Socket soc = new Socket("www.javasoft.com", 80);
```

Note that the class documentation reveals that this constructor might throw two exceptions. An UnknownHostException is thrown if the hostname is not a valid domain name, while an IOException is thrown if a socket connection with a valid hostname cannot be established. This would be so if the server was not running during the connection attempt, or simply, that the network was not operating.

If a socket object was successfully created, communication may commence by writing to and reading from the other party. These procedures are analogous to what was done in the previous chapter for file input and output. As expected, the streams model is used, as with InputStream and OutputStream.

At this point, we introduce the two methods which are relevant to socket objects. The `getInputStream()` and `getOutputStream()` methods return the InputStream and OutputStream objects associated with a socket. The former allows for reading from, while the latter allows for writing to the other party at the other end of the socket connection.

```
InputStream instream = soc.getInputStream();
OutputStream outstream = soc.getOutputStream();
```

Therefore, the necessary operations and paradigms in Chapter 10 on file input and output apply.

11.2.1 Example Client: Web Page Retriever

In this section, we consider how the Socket class may be used to retrieve content from Web servers. The generic framework for this client is also applicable to many other clients connected to a well-known host for services. (However, different applications might have their own application protocol to request the server for services.)

Section 11.2 gives the basics of how generic clients may connect with their corresponding servers. By following the methods laid out in Chapter 10 on file input and output, information exchange may proceed over the socket connection. The skeleton of the WebRetriever class is revealed in Listing 11-1:

```
import java.io.*;
import java.net.*;

class WebRetriever {

  Socket soc;
  OutputStream os; InputStream is;
  ....

  WebRetriever(String server, int port)
               throws IOException, UnknownHostException {
    soc = new Socket(server, port);
    os = soc.getOutputStream();
    is = soc.getInputStream();
  }
}
```

Listing 11-1: WebRetriever Skeleton

While this has laid the groundwork for clients and server to "talk" over a network, nothing has been discussed about a common language as to what is exchanged. This is also known as the application protocol. In implementing a Web page retriever, we next consider how a Web client works in relation to a Web server.

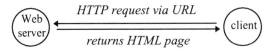

Figure 11-3: Web client/server Communication

A Uniform Resource Locator (URL) is the abstraction of a resource available at a server. (While it is typically a Web server, it is not restricted to Web servers and may include FTP and News servers.) A highlighted anchor in a Web client browser has an underlying URL. Thus, when selecting a HTTP URL, such as http://www.nus.edu.sg:80/NUSinfo/UG/ug.html, the framework of a request issued by the client may be broken into four portions:

`http`	resource is to be retrieved by using the HTTP protocol
`www.nus.edu.sg`	hostname of the server
`80`	port number where service is offered
`/NUSinfo/UG/ug.html`	exact pathname on host root where resource is found

The following table enumerates the interaction between client and server, for the former to obtain a response from the latter.

State	Client Action
A Web server is generally happy to serve out pages to any client, and thus waits for a prospective client.	(server is ready)
Clicking a link on a Web client browser will cause it to initiate a socket connection to the server, and then request the server for a particular page.	Create new Socket
Client requests the server for a particular page.	Write HTTP GET request
On receiving a legitimate request in the form of a URL path, the server would return the contents of the corresponding file.	Read response from server

While there is an Internet RFC document which comprehensively describes the HyperText Transmission Protocol (HTTP), we only need to be aware of two details for the purpose of our example client:

- The GET *path* command requests that the server sends the resource at *path*.

- An empty text line indicates the end of client request to the server.

This basic HTTP request is handled by the `request()` method which packages the requested pathname into a GET command and sends it down the socket:

```
void request(String path) {
   try {
      String message = "GET " + path + "\n\n";
      os.write(message.getBytes());
   } catch (IOException e) {
      System.err.println("Error in HTTP request");
   }
}
```

Following an HTTP request, a response from the server is anticipated. The streams paradigm allows for a familiar code pattern via a `while`-statement in the `getResponse()` method.

```java
void getResponse() {
    int c;
    try {
        while ((c = is.read()) != -1)
            System.out.print((char) c);
    } catch (IOException e) {
        System.err.println("IOException in reading from Web server");
    }
}
```

Tidying after a request is necessary to relinquish networking resources. This is easily achieved via the object finalizer.

```java
public void finalize() {
    try {
        is.close();
        os.close();
        soc.close();
    } catch (IOException e) {
        System.err.println("IOException in closing connection");
    }
}
```

Finally, the `static void main()` method pulls all the work together to implement the retriever.

```java
public static void main(String[] args) {
    try {
        WebRetriever w = new WebRetriever("www.nus.edu.sg", 80);
        w.request("/NUSinfo/UG/ug.html");
        w.getResponse();
    } catch (UnknownHostException h) {
        System.err.println("Hostname Unknown");
    } catch (IOException i) {
        System.err.println("IOException in connecting to Host");
    }
}
```

Note that where the resource from a server is an HTML file, a typical Web browser will render it according to the semantics of HTML. This functionality is not considered here. The complete WebRetriever class is shown in Listing 11-2.

```
import java.io.*;
import java.net.*;

class WebRetriever {
  Socket soc; OutputStream os; InputStream is;

  WebRetriever(String server, int port)
                   throws IOException, UnknownHostException {
    soc = new Socket(server, port);
    os = soc.getOutputStream();
    is = soc.getInputStream();
  }

  void request(String path) {
     try {
       String message = "GET " + path + "\n\n";
       os.write(message.getBytes());
     } catch (IOException e) {
       System.err.println("Error in HTTP request");
     }
  }

  void getResponse() {
     int c;
     try {
       while ((c = is.read()) != -1)
         System.out.print((char) c) ;
     } catch (IOException e) {
       System.err.println("IOException in reading from Web server");
     }
  }

  public void finalize() {
    try {
      is.close(); os.close(); soc.close();
    } catch (IOException e) {
      System.err.println("IOException in closing connection");
    }
  }

  public static void main(String[] args) {
     try {
       WebRetriever w = new WebRetriever("www.nus.edu.sg", 80);
       w.request("/NUSinfo/UG/ug.html");
       w.getResponse();
     } catch (UnknownHostException h) {
       System.err.println("Hostname Unknown");
     } catch (IOException i) {
       System.err.println("IOException in connecting to Host");
     }
  }
}
```

Listing 11-2: WebRetriever class

11.3 Listener Sockets in Java

So far, we have considered Java code to initiate a socket connection to a server. It is time to consider how a server might be implemented in Java to be of service to other clients (which may or may not be implemented in Java). As pointed out earlier in the chapter, the asymmetric nature of clients and servers only occurs initially during match-making. Following that, communication over a socket is symmetric.

In the Java networking model, the additional functionality of listening out for prospective clients is handled by the ServerSocket class. Unlike the Socket class which requires a port number and the host machine which is providing service during object instantiation, a ServerSocket merely needs a port number since it is inviting requests from any machine.

The creation of a ServerSocket reserves a port number for use, and prevents other prospective servers on the host from offering services at the same port:

```
ServerSocket s = new ServerSocket(8080);
```

The `accept()` method waits for the arrival a client. As such, execution of the server suspends until some client arrives, at which time, a socket connection is successfully established. In resuming execution, the `accept()` method also returns a suitable Socket instance to communicate with its client.

```
Socket soc = s.accept();
```

Assuming Java implementations of a server and corresponding client, the following chart illustrates relative progress.

Server Progress	Client Progress
`ServerSocket s =` `new ServerSocket(8080);`	
// Port reserved	*progress of*
`Socket soc1 = s.accept();`	*execution*
// Waiting for prospective client // Server execution suspended	
	`Socket soc2 =` `new Socket(server,7070);`
// Arrival of client // Server execution resumed	

`soc1` and `soc2` are complementary sockets, where one may read the contents written at the other, and vice versa.

11.3.1 Example Server: Simple Web Server

We now proceed to implement a simple Web Server using the new functionality of the ServerSocket class. In comparison, it complements the Web retriever client developed earlier.

The similar framework of socket communication for Web client and server has resulted in a very similar structure in the class skeleton in Listing 11-3.

```
import java.io.*;
import java.net.*;

class WebServe {

  Socket soc;
  OutputStream os; DataInputStream is;
  ....

  public static void main(String args[]) {
     try {
       ServerSocket s = new ServerSocket(8080);
       WebServe w = new WebServe(s.accept());
       w.getRequest();
       w.returnResponse();
     } catch (IOException i) {
       System.err.println("IOException in Server");
     }
  }

  WebServe(Socket s) throws IOException {
    soc = s;
    os = soc.getOutputStream();
    is = new DataInputStream(soc.getInputStream());
  }
}
```

Listing 11-3: WebServe skeleton

The rationale for changes with respect to the client implement are elaborated below:

- The instantiation of the ServerSocket object is done in `main()` so that a WebServe object still contains Socket and Stream objects. It not only preserves the structure, but a more significant reason will be elaborated later in the chapter.

- The input stream is a DataInputStream object so that HTTP request may be easily read on a per line basis. Previously, the retriever client reads data from the server and line structure was not considered.

- While the retriever client sends a request and then waits for a response from the server (via `request()` and `getResponse()`), the server performs the complement of receiving a request and then sending a response back to the client (via `getRequest()` and `returnResponse()` in `main()`).

As seen previously, a Web client makes a request for a resource via a HTTP GET command. However, in a typical Web client, this command is interspersed in a block of other HTTP request, such as:

```
GET /public_html/quick.html HTTP/1.0
Referer: http://sununx.iscs.nus.sg:8080/public_html/ic365/index.html
Connection: Keep-Alive
User-Agent: Mozilla/4.0 [en] (Win95; I)
Host: sununx.iscs.nus.sg:8080
Accept: image/gif, image/x-xbitmap, image/jpeg, image/pjpeg, */*
Accept-Language: en
Accept-Charset: iso-8859-1,*,utf-8
```

Thus, while the `getRequest()` method scans the command block for a GET command, all other commands are ignored. Where a GET word is found it scans for the subsequent pathname of the requested resource. Processing terminates when the end of the block indicated by an empty line is detected.

```
void getRequest() {
   try {
     String message;

     while ((message = is.readLine()) != null) {
       if (message.equals(""))
         break;   // end of command block
       System.err.println(message);
       StringTokenizer t = new StringTokenizer(message);
       String token = t.nextToken();   // get first token
       if (token.equals("GET"))             // if token is "GET"
         resource = t.nextToken();    //   get second token
     }
   } catch (IOException e) {
     System.err.println("Error receiving Web request");
   }
}
```

The `getRequest()` method relies on the StringTokenizer class to strip away unwanted whitespaces to return raw symbols. On instantiating a StringTokenizer with the input string, tokens are returned on each call to `nextToken()`.

It would also be apparent that we need a new instance variable to hold the pathname of the resource requested. The `returnResponse()` method may then use this as a file name to return its contents.

```
void returnResponse() {
    int c;
    try {
      FileInputStream f = new FileInputStream("."+resource);
      while ((c = f.read()) != -1)
        os.write(c) ;
      f.close();
    } catch (IOException e) {
      System.err.println("IOException in reading in Web server");
    }
}
```

Note that "." has been prepended to the pathname of the resource as the Web server is expected to return contents of the current directory. Since the `finalize()` method is unchanged, we have presented all the necessary code for our Web server. Again, the clean up is implicit when the WebServe instance is not accessible.

The complete mini-WebServer is shown in Listing 11-4.

11.3.2 Running the Web Server

We have discussed the workings of Web client and Web server programs written in Java. While the former allows the retrieval of resources across the Internet, the latter can be tested in various scenarios.

- Where networking facilities are available, the Web server can be executed on one machine, and the Web client on another to make requests to the server.

- Where networking facilities are not available, both the Web server and client may be executed on different sessions of the same machine. The client may refer to the server host as the standard name "localhost".

In the same way that the Web client can access another server not written in Java, a typical Web client (such as Netscape or Internet Explorer) may be used to access our Java server.

```java
import java.io.*;
import java.net.*;

class WebServe {
  Socket soc; OutputStream os; DataInputStream is;

  void getRequest() {
    try {
      String message;

      while ((message = is.readLine()) != null) {
        if (message.equals(""))
          break;  // end of command block
        System.err.println(message);
        StringTokenizer t = new StringTokenizer(message);
        String token = t.nextToken();  // get first token
        if (token.equals("GET"))       // if token is "GET"
          resource = t.nextToken();    //   get second token
      }
    } catch (IOException e) {
      System.err.println("Error receiving Web request");
    }
  }
  void returnResponse() {
    int c;
    try {
      FileInputStream f = new FileInputStream("."+resource);
      while ((c = f.read()) != -1)
        os.write(c);
      f.close();
    } catch (IOException e) {
      System.err.println("IOException in reading in Web server");
    }
  }
  public static void main(String args[]) {
    try {
      ServerSocket s = new ServerSocket(8080);
      WebServe w = new WebServe(s.accept());
      w.getRequest();
      w.returnResponse();
    } catch (IOException i) {
      System.err.println("IOException in Server");
    }
  }

  public void finalize() {
    try {
      is.close(); os.close(); soc.close();
    } catch (IOException e) {
      System.err.println("IOException in closing connection");
    }
  }
  WebServe(Socket s) throws IOException {
    soc = s;
    os = soc.getOutputStream();
    is = new DataInputStream(soc.getInputStream());
  }
}
```

Listing 11-4: WebServe class

In practice, the scenario implemented is not practical because the server terminates after serving one resource. Most Web servers continue to run until the machine is rebooted or switched-off. This improvement may be effected by instantiating multiple WebServe objects by using an infinite for-loop. Note that old WebServe instances are garbage collected away. This minor change allows WebServe to work as a more practical Web server, and suitable with standard Web browsers.

```
public static void main(String args[]) {
    try {
      ServerSocket s = new ServerSocket(8080);
      for (;;) {
        WebServe w = new WebServe(s.accept());
        w.getRequest();
        w.returnResponse();
      }
    } catch (IOException i) {
      System.err.println("IOException in Server");
    }
}
```

11.4 Considering Multiple Threads of Execution

Many applications which require networking and graphical user interfaces have fairly complicated internal workings due to complex tasking schedules. For example, while Webserve is processing the bulk of HTTP requests from a Web browser, it cannot perform other tasks such as servicing another Web client. In fact, Webserve currently allows only one socket connection at any time because instructions are executed sequentially. As such, it can only handle retrieval requests serially.

A graphical user interface typically has many concerns. For example, it needs to monitor: mouse activity – in particular if it has moved or over hot areas; keyboard activity – if keys were depressed and special combinations of keys as well as mouse buttons, update screen areas with modified views, or even play an audio clip. If all these activities were to be coalesced into a sequence of serial instructions, it would have been untidy and complex, and possibly error-prone.

Ideally, it would be simpler and neater if concurrent but independent activities be specified separately, yet easily executed concurrently. However, this is impossible with the Java mechanisms because of strict sequential execution, which ultimately imply that one set of instructions are serially executed. This is also known as a *single thread of execution*.

Operating systems like UNIX provide primitives like `fork()` to enable the creation of multiple processes to run multiple jobs. Unfortunately, processes tend to be expensive due to the need to maintain separate address spaces for each instance.

Threads have recently been promoted as a reasonable means for parallel execution, but without the high execution overheads since they share the same address space.

11.5   Creating Multiple Threads of Execution

So far, our code has been executed as a single thread. In this section, we consider the abstraction used in Java programs to initiate multi-threaded execution. There are two specific ways to create threads – using the Thread class or using the Runnable Interface.

11.5.1   Thread Creation using the Thread Class

As we have seen with other mechanisms, the thread abstraction in Java is also encapsulated in an object. The basic functionality of threads is implemented by the Thread class in the `java.lang` package.

The following three properties about this Thread class allow for easy creation and execution of threads in Java:

(i)   A new thread of execution may be created by instantiating a Thread object.

(ii) A newly-created thread does not begin execution explicitly. Execution starts by invoking the method `start()`.

(iii) Execution of a thread involves invoking the `run()` method. An application specific thread would typically be a class which extends from the Thread class, and overriding the `run()` method to run application-specific code.

The following class definition in Listing 11-5 exploits the three properties and provides an extra thread for concurrent execution of the `run()` method.

```
class AddAndPrint extends Thread {

  private static final int TIMES = 30;
  private int val;

  AddAndPrint(int x) { val = x; }

  public void run() { // overrides default run()
    for (int i=val+TIMES; i>val; i--)
      System.err.println("run() : " + i);
  }

  public static void main(String arg[]) {
    AddAndPrint a = new AddAndPrint(243); // create thread
    a.start();                            // start thread execution
    for (int i=0; i<TIMES; i++)           // proceed with code
      System.err.println("main() " + i);
  }
}
```

Listing 11-5: Multi-Thread Using the Thread class

```
...
main() 14
main() 15
main() 16
main() 17
main() 18
main() 19
main() 20
main() 21
main() 22
run() 253
run() 252
run() 251
run() 250
run() 249
main() 23
main() 24
main() 25
main() 26
main() 27
main() 28
main() 29
run() 248
run() 247
run() 246
run() 245
run() 244
```

Listing 11-6: Sample Output

A fragment from the execution of AddAndPrint in Listing 11-6 shows output from `main()` and `run()` interspersed. This indicates that execution of the two blocks were appropriately scheduled and proceeded conceptually in parallel.

11.5.2 Thread Creation using the Runnable Interface

The class derivation method in the previous section has demonstrated a convenient means to creating new threads of execution, but it assumes that such classes must always be derived from the class Thread. This is a limitation for single inheritance languages such as Java, where very often a class should be derived from another class.

Fortunately, there is a second method of creating threads within classes which are not derived from the Thread class. Here, thread functionality involves implementing the Runnable interface, as illustrated in Listing 11-7.

```
class Special extends X implements Runnable {

    private final int TIMES = 30;
    private int val;

    AddAndPrint(int x) { val = x; }

    public void run() {  // necessary for Runnable
      for (int i=val+TIMES; i>val; i--)
        System.err.println("AddAndPrint value: " + i);
    }

    public static void main(String arg[]) {
      Special a = new Special(243);          // create non-thread object
      Thread thr = new Thread(a);            // create thread
      thr.start();                           // start thread execution
      for (int i=0; i<TIMES; i++)            // proceed with code
        System.err.println("main() " + i);
    }
}
```

Listing 11-7: Multi-Threading using the Runnable Interface

While this method may initially seem different from the previous, it does have some similarities:

(i) The side-effect of a thread is still encoded within the `run()` method which becomes mandatory for classes which implement Runnable.

(ii) Thread creation is still effected via a thread object. This time however, an instance of the class which implements the Runnable interface (with a specific `run()`) method is passed as a parameter to the constructor.

(iii) The `start()` method begins thread execution.

11.6 Improvement of Web Server Example

As noted earlier, the simple Web server developed earlier processes requests from Web clients serially. As such, unless an HTTP request is processed and the specified resource chosen to be returned to the Web client, the next request cannot even be accepted.

The brief modifications shown in Listing 11-8 improves the Web server so that instead of proceeding with `getRequest()` and `returnResponse()`, a thread object is created to execute these methods within the `run()` method. In effect, while the new thread executes these methods, control in `static void main()` continues with another loop iteration to accept any new clients.

```
class WebServe implements Runnable {
  ....

  public void run() {
    getRequest();
    returnResponse();
  }

  public static void main(String args[]) {
    try {
      ServerSocket s = new ServerSocket(8080);
      for (;;) {
        WebServe w = new WebServe(s.accept());
        Thread thr = new Thread(w);
        thr.start();
      }
    } catch (IOException i) {
      System.err.println("IOException in Server");
    }
  }
}
```

Listing 11-8: Multi-Threading in WebServe

The fact that other methods in the class definition remains unchanged shows how unintrusively multi-threading can be introduced into Java code.

11.7 Thread Synchronization and Shared Resources

Concurrent execution in the form of multiple threads of execution can allow for simpler code structures, but can also lead to intricate situations where resource sharing must be carefully considered. An example of a shared resource could be a common variable.

While the relative progress of **independent** threads have no bearing to the end result (e.g. threads in our Web server are independent as they proceed on their own and do not depend on each other for more inputs), concurrent threads which interact (i.e. dependent) must be appropriately synchronized. The objective of synchronization ensures that the end result is deterministic, and does not vary depending on the relative execution speeds of each thread.

We first consider the issue of concurrent access/updates on shared variables. For simple expressions involving atomic variables, unexpected interactions will give non-deterministic results.

```
class JustAdd extends Thread {

  private final int N = 100000;
  private int val;

  JustAdd() { val = 0; }
  int value() { return val; }

  public void operate() {
    for (int i=0; i<N; i++) val = val+1;
  }
  public void run() {
    for (int i=0; i<N; i++) val = val+1;
  }
  public static void main(String arg[]) {
    JustAdd a = new JustAdd();     // create thread
    a.start();                     // start run()
    a.operate();                   // add using operate()
    System.out.println(a.value());
  }
}
```

Listing 11-9: Dependent Threads

The objective of JustAdd in Listing 11-9 is to create a thread to increment val (via run()) while the original thread increments val (via operate()). Depending on the Java implementation, the result printed might not be 200000. That was the expected value since val would have been incremented 2*N times, N being 100000.

Now, consider the circumstance where the execution of the assignment statements val = val+1 in both threads were interleaved. Overwriting results if *both* expressions val+1 were evaluated before val was reassigned. This scenario is possible if after evaluating val+1, the thread's time-slice ran out, thus allowing the other thread to evaluate using "old" value of val. Here, the expected result of 200000 will not be obtained.

Java provides the language keyword synchronized to demarcate code and data such that access of these regions by concurrent threads is serialized. This restriction allows shared data to be updated in mutual exclusion, and removes the possibility of interleaved execution.

Each Java object has an associated *use* lock, and a synchronized statement must acquire that lock before execution of its body. In the code fragment below, the lock associated with g is first obtained before h.carefully() is executed. Similarly, the lock is implicitly released on leaving the block.

```
synchronized (g) {
    h.carefully();
}
```

An instance method may also be specified as synchronized – such as workAlone() below. It is equivalent to its whole statement block being synchronized with respect to the current object as indicated by this. As such, the synchronized method workAlone():

```
class X {
    ...
    synchronized void workAlone() {
        p();
        q();
    }
}
```

is equivalent to

```
class X {
    ...
    void workAlone() {
        synchronized (this) {
            p();
            q();
        }
    }
}
```

To enable consistent increments, the JustAdd class could be modified as in Listing 11-10:

```
class JustAdd extends Thread {

  private final int N = 100000;
  private int val;

  JustAdd() { val = 0; }
  int value() { return val; }

  synchronized void increment () { val = val+1; }

  public void operate() {
    for (int i=0; i<N; i++) increment();
  }

  public void run() {
    for (int i=0; i<N; i++) increment();
  }

  public static void main(String arg[]) {
    JustAdd a = new JustAdd();        // create thread
    a.start();                         // start run()
    a.operate();                       // add using operate()
    System.out.println(a.value());
  }
}
```

Listing 11-10: Synchronized Threads

We next consider the traditional consumer-producer synchronization problem by taking the example of two threads: an input thread which reads file contents into a buffer, and its partner output thread which writes buffer contents to the printer. The progress of each thread is dictate by the other: if the output thread proceeds faster, it must ultimately suspend when the buffer is empty. Similarly, if the input thread proceeds faster, it must ultimately suspend when the buffer is full.

The buffer is jointly used by both input and output threads, and is referred to as a shared resource. While it is accessible to both threads, but for correct operation, a thread must be delayed if it is progressing too fast.

Such longer term synchronization involving resource scheduling may be effected by using an object's lock as a monitor and the following methods for waiting and notification:

wait()   The wait() method causes the thread which holds the lock to wait indefinitely (so that it makes no progress in its execution) until notified by another about a change in the lock condition.

notify()   The notify() method wakes up a thread from amongst those waiting on the object's lock.

Let us consider a Writer thread which adds items to a buffer, and a partner Reader thread which removes items from the same. To simplify item generation in the Writer class (as illustrated in Listing 11-11), it will add the contents of a file.

```
class Writer extends Thread {
    Buffer b;
    FileInputStream fs;

    public void run() {
      int x;
      try {
        while ((x = fs.read()) != -1)
          b.put((char) x);
        b.put('\032');
      } catch (Exception e) {
        System.err.println("Cannot read");
        System.exit(1);
      }
    }

    Writer(String fname, Buffer b) {
      this.b = b;
      try {
        fs = new FileInputStream(fname);
      } catch (Exception e) {
        fs = null;
        System.err.println("Cannot open "+fname);
        System.exit(1);
      }
    }
}
```

Listing 11-11: Writer Thread

Similarly, the Reader class will read from the buffer and confirm the contents by writing to the standard output stream, as shown below in Listing 11-12.

```
class Reader extends Thread {
   Buffer b;
   public void run() {
      char x;
      while ((x = b.get()) != '\032')
         System.out.print(x);
   }
   Reader(Buffer b) {
      this.b = b;
   }
}
```

Listing 11-12: Reader Thread

The following are some points concerning the Writer and Reader classes:

- The Buffer object is shared amongst the Reader object which reads from it, and the Writer object which writes to it. It must be accessible to both objects, and is achieved via passing it through the constructor method.

- Unless the Reader object is notified about the end of stream, it will wait indefinitely when no more items from the Writer object is forthcoming. To avoid this situation, the Writer thread puts out the character ^Z to signal the end of the stream. As such, the Reader terminates on receiving this item.

We now consider how the Buffer class, with put() and get() methods may be implemented to work consistently despite concurrent accesses and different rates of thread execution.

Firstly, the basic requirement of a buffer is to keep items placed by put() in its internal state until they are retrieved by get(). This is illustrated in Listing 11-13. To ensure smooth execution of Reader and Writer threads, we allow the buffer to hold more than one item via a circular queue indicated by front and rear indexes.

Note that front and rear moves down the array and wraps around from the last item to the first via the remainder operation %. The distance between the two indexes indicates the number of buffered items.

```
class Buffer {

    final int MAXSIZE = 512;
    char keep[];
    int count, front, rear;

    public char get() {
        char x = keep[rear];
        rear = (rear+1) % MAXSIZE;
        count--;
        return x;
    }

    public void put(char x) {
        keep[front] = x;
        front = (front+1) % MAXSIZE;
        count++;
    }

    Buffer() {
        keep[] = new char [MAXSIZE];
        count = 0;
        front = rear = 0;
    }
}
```

Listing 11-13: Shared Buffer

Secondly, concurrent access of the Buffer object from Writer and Reader threads dictate that calls to get() and put() should not overlap so that the integrity of the internal state is preserved during updates. This may be achieved by tagging these methods as synchronized, so that access to Buffer instances must be implicitly preceded by acquiring the access lock. Subsequently, the access lock is released following access.

Thirdly, the get() method should cause the calling thread to wait when the Buffer object is already empty. Correspondingly, the put() method should notify a thread waiting to access the Buffer object that an item is available. However, the put() method should also cause the calling thread to wait when the Buffer object is already full. Similarly, the get() method must notify a thread waiting to access the Buffer object that a slot is now available for an item. This is illustrated in the improved Buffer class in Listing 11-14.

```
class Buffer {

  final int MAXSIZE = 512;
  char keep[];
  int count, front, rear;

  public synchronized char get() {
    while (count == 0)
      wait();
    char x = keep[rear];
    rear = (rear+1) % MAXSIZE;
    count--;
    notify();   // that a space is now available
    return x;
  }

  public synchronized void put(char x) {
    while (count == MAXSIZE)
      wait();
    keep[front] = x;
    front = (front+1) % MAXSIZE;
    count++;
    notify(); // that an item is now available
  }

  Buffer() {
    keep[] = new char [MAXSIZE];
    count = 0;
    front = rear = 0;
  }
}
```

Listing 11-14: Synchronized Buffer

To summarize, the additional code for thread synchronization includes the
synchronized tag together with wait() and notify() method calls. The former
involves object access locks for short-term synchronization to solve the problem of
concurrent access to object attributes. The latter concerns long-term synchronization
to solve the problem of resource allocation.

Note that our Java Buffer solution is slightly different from other languages.
Firstly, waiting for a resource (either for an item in the buffer to retrieve or a slot in
the buffer to receive a new item) involves repeated testing of the condition in a
while-loop, for example:

```
while (count == 0)        instead of        if (count == 0)
  wait();                                     wait();
```

Secondly, the method call to `notify()` does not specify explicitly which thread should be alerted. In fact, this seems more dubious when we consider that there are two conditions for which threads look out for – that of a empty buffer, and that of a full buffer.

To explain these observations, we recall the nature of the `wait()` and `notify()` methods. The `notify()` method awakes one of the threads waiting on the object's lock queue. This thread might be waiting for a buffer item or an empty buffer slot. Since the `notify()` method does not allow the specification of a condition, awaking from a `wait()` call does not guarantee that the condition for it is fulfilled. As such, the `while`-loop ensures that an anticipated condition be confirmed when waking up from `wait()`. Therefore, the thread continues to wait if the condition is not yet fulfilled.

11.8 Summary

This chapter has discussed the basics of two important areas in Java programming: networking and multi-threading. While implementing these functionality in other languages might be non-trivial, Java has the advantage in that these functionalities are well-encapsulated into objects, and supplied with appropriate APIs. Any additional functionality is thus well-integrated into the language framework.

Network socket connections in Java depend on:

- Socket; and

- ServerSocket classes

as found in the `java.net` package. The Socket class enables Java applications to initiate client connections to other machines with a listening server. The complementary role of implementing a listening server is provided by the ServerSocket class. Successful connections return InputStream and OutputStream objects (via the `getInputStream()` and `getOutputStream()` methods), with subsequent operations similar to that seen for input/output operations on streams and files.

Multiple socket connections (involving multiple hosts) provide a real example when multi-threading is very useful in easing processing logic. Without this means of specifying parallel tasks, these tasks must be serialized, or additional logic might be used to multiplex multiple tasks into a single subroutine via state save/restore operations. However, this is error-prone and an additional chore which many programmers would gladly avoid.

The Java API facilitates thread creation and execution via:

- Thread class; and

- Runnable interface.

Both are almost identical in that thread execution is initiated by the `start()` method, which causes the user-defined `run()` method to execute but does not wait for its termination.

11.9 Exercises

1. A telnet client may be used to simulate a finger request to obtain user information from a finger server (which typically listens to port 79). The username is entered after connection to the finger server is established:

    ```
    $ telnet leonis.nus.edu.sg 79
    Trying 137.132.1.18...
    Connected to leonis.nus.edu.sg.
    Escape character is '^]'.
    isckbk
    Login name: isckbk                     In real life: Kiong Beng Kee
    Directory: /staff/isckbk               Shell: /usr/bin/ksh
    Last login Fri Feb 13 14:56 on ttym4 from dkiong.iscs.nus.
    No Plan.
    Connection closed by foreign host.
    ```

    Simplify the procedure by implementing a finger client in Java which will obtain the username and server from the command-line, and print out details obtained from the finger server via a socket connection.

2. Implement a reverse server in Java. It works by listening for clients on port 1488. For each client socket connection, it reads the first line and returns the reversed string to the client.

3. Many sites with a firewall implement a proxy server as a legitimate means to go through the network barrier. The Web proxy thus sits between server and clients. It forwards a client's request to the server, and thereafter, relays the server's reply to the original client.

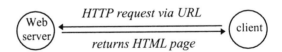

Compared with the proxyless framework shown above, the proxy application has two socket connections. It listens for clients at one end, and then launches the request to the server proper via the other, as shown graphically.

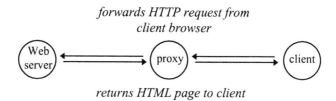

Implement a proxy application to eavesdrop on how a standard Web browser requests for HTML pages as well as submit forms.

4. Suggest a suitable representation for matrices. Discuss sequential and threaded solutions for matrix multiplication.

12 Graphical Interfaces and Windows

In the earlier chapters, we previewed the Java API for input and output mechanisms, networking and multi-threading. In this chapter, we proceed to look at the facilities for incorporating graphical user-interfaces. With the availability of powerful and cheap hardware, and widespread and diverse use of computers, easy and intuitive interfaces have become an important aspect to developers.

To reduce software costs, developers must be able to easily create and modify code which implement these interfaces. The Abstract Windowing Toolkit (AWT) in Java provides a simple yet flexible object-oriented model for building applications which use graphical user-interfaces.

12.1 The AWT Model

Consistent with the principles of abstraction, the AWT model for graphical user-interfaces in Java is broken into several constituents with its own concerns and functionality. Briefly, AWT constituents include:

- Frames

- Components

- Panels

- Layout Managers

- Events

The frame abstraction allows for independent windows in the Java host. While a Java application typically runs in a window, it may also create more graphical windows to provide alternative or complementary views.

The AWT components consist of a custom set of widgets for various styles of user interaction. The range of widgets include:

- text labels

- buttons

- choice and list selections

- scrollbars

- text fields and editing areas

- canvas painting areas

The AWT panels are used to contain a set of logically related AWT components. For example, user authentication by a user name and password may be presented by two text field components together with two buttons. One button allows the user to proceed with authentication, while the other cancels the request. These components may be logically included in an AWT Panel.

The layout manager constituent of the AWT model allow for layout control of components within panels.

Panels are also components, and thus the containment relationship is hierarchical. Where there are two logical groups of components, these could be placed and arranged in two separate panels. These panels are in turn placed into the parent panel, and may be arranged collectively.

Finally, most implementations of graphical user-interfaces typically adopt an event-based approach over polling. It is tedious to anticipate and poll for every input which a user can make: mouse clicks, keyboard input, audio command/feedback, etc. It is more difficult to determine when sub-combinations of these are legitimate.

The event-based model allows for suitable code to be associated with significant events, and be invoked implicitly. We will cover the containment model used in JDK 1.0, as well as the delegation model in JDK 1.1 which is based on Java Beans.

The object-oriented features in Java allow the AWT library to be modular for maintainability. This is evident by the constituents described earlier. Yet they must ultimately be integrated to allow the intended user interaction at run-time. In addition, while basic behavior is in-built for easy usage, it is also highly configurable and many combinations with custom-built components are easily achieved. The implementation highly relies on Java features such as inheritance and polymorphism.

12.2 Basic AWT Constituents

We will first discuss about the AWT through incremental incorporation of its constituents. Following that, we will incorporate event handlers to complete the functionality of an interface by binding it to application level code.

As with other abstractions in Java, the functionality of the AWT constituents are encoded in class definitions, and ultimately its usage manifested in object instances.

12.2.1 Frames

An application window is created by instantiating a Frame object. A program which merely creates a Frame object is shown in Listing 12-1. Since a Frame object is initially invisible, the show() method is used to bring it to the top of the desktop.

```
import java.awt.Frame;

class ExampleFrame {
  public static void main(String arg[]) {
    Frame f = new Frame("Example");
    f.show();
  }
}
```

Listing 12-1: ExampleFrame class

Two observations deserve comment when the class ExampleFrame is executed.

Figure 12-1: Empty Frame

- The Frame instance is considered empty because it does not contain any components. As such, there is no view of interest, and the corresponding window is displayed with its title but no viewable area, as in Figure 12-1.

- While the window may be minimized and maximized, it cannot be closed as the expected custom event-handler has yet to be installed. We will return to this issue in subsequent sections. For the moment, the new window is destroyed by aborting the execution of the ExampleFrame class.

Besides creating a window by instantiating a Frame object, we may also define a new class by inheriting from the Frame class. This is the means for defining a new Frame-like abstraction, but with new default settings or specific behavior. The class skeleton in Figure 12-2 with a default size of 150×100 pixel window is one such example.

```
import java.awt.Frame;

class ExampleFrame2 extends Frame {
  ExampleFrame2(String m) {
    super("Example2: "+m);
    setSize(150,100);
  }
  // new functionality
  public static void main(String arg[]) {
    new ExampleFrame2("Subclassing").show();
  }
}
```

Listing 12-2: ExampleFrame2 class

Figure 12-2: Viewable Empty Frame

12.2.2 Components

The Component class defines the generic behavior of GUI components which may appear in a frame. Specific components, such as those mentioned in the previous section, are defined as subclasses of this generic Component class.

The insertion of a component into a Frame instance proceeds in two steps: first, an instance of the component is created with the appropriate parameters to the constructor method. Subsequently, it is inserted into the Frame via the add() method, with signature:

```
add(Component comp)
```

Thus, any subclass instance of Component may be added into our Frame. We proceed by adding various components to our currently empty Frame. The code in Listing 12-3 is similar to ExampleFrame2 except a Checkbox component has been added.

```
import java.awt.*;

class ExampleFrame3 extends Frame {
  ExampleFrame3(String m) {
    super("Example3: "+m);
    setSize(100,150) ;
    add(new Checkbox("Save settings"));
  }
  public static void main(String arg[]) {
    new ExampleFrame3("Checkbox").show();
  }
}
```

Listing 12-3: ExampleFrame3 class

As before, no event handlers has yet been installed. While the Checkbox provides visual feedback as to its state in response to mouse clicks, there is no code to interrogate that state, nor is any code executed as a result of state changes.

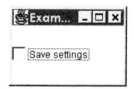

Figure 12-3: Frame with Checkbox Component

A Button component may be similarly placed as shown in Listing 12-4.

```
import java.awt.*;

class ExampleFrame4 extends Frame {
  ExampleFrame4(String m) {
    super("Example4: "+m);
    setSize(100, 150) ;
    add(new Button("Save"));
  }
  public static void main(String arg[]) {
    new ExampleFrame4("Button").show();
  }
}
```

Listing 12-4: ExampleFrame4 class

Since the Frame may currently only contain a single component, the Button component has used the full viewable area for display, and thus looks oversized, as in Figure 12-4. If this is unsightly in appearance, the consolation is that it is improved with Panels.

Figure 12-4: Frame with Button Component

Components will be further discussed in the next section.

12.2.3 Panels

Panels may be succinctly described as components holding other components. As a component, it may be placed in a Frame via add() as already seen with Checkbox and Button. As a container, it will also accept constituent components via the add() method.

This is illustrated in Listing 12-5, with the corresponding view in Figure 12-5.

```
import java.awt.*;

class ExamplePanel extends Frame {
  ExamplePanel(String m) {
    super("ExamplePanel: "+m);
    setSize(100,150) ;
    Panel p = new Panel();                    // create Panel
    add(p) ;                                  // add Panel into Frame
    p.add(new Button ("Save"));               // add Button into Panel
    p.add(new Checkbox ("Save settings"));    // add Checkbox into Panel
  }
  public static void main(String arg[]) {
    new ExamplePanel("Inserting Components").show();
  }
}
```

Listing 12-5: ExamplePanel class

Figure 12-5: Frame with Panel

12.2.4 Layout in Panels

The layout of components in Panels are the responsibility of Layout Managers. The default layout used by Panels is known as FlowLayout. In this layout scheme, components are automatically placed in a left-to-right manner, and down to the next row if the right margin is exceeded. Formatting components within a row may be centered (default), left- or right-justified.

Thus, re-sizing the Frame for more column space will bring the two components (Button and Checkbox) into the same row, as seen in Figure 12-6.

Figure 12-6: Frame with Stretched Panel

Two other layout schemes are commonly used: The GridLayout class implements a table-style layout with fixed rows and columns. Sample code is shown in Listing 12-6, with results visible in Figure 12-7. It is a simple and useful layout scheme when components in a Panel have fairly equal dimensions.

```
import java.awt.*;

class ExampleGridLayout extends Frame {
  ExampleGridLayout(String m) {
    super("ExampleLayout: "+m);
    setSize(240,80);
    Panel p = new Panel();
    add(p) ;
    p.setLayout(new GridLayout(3,2)) ;   // use a 3x2 grid
    p.add(new Checkbox ("Save config"));
    p.add(new Button ("Save"));
    p.add(new Checkbox("Save changes"));
    p.add(new Button("Abort & do not save"));
    p.add(new Checkbox("Ignore colors"));
    p.add(new Button("Quit"));
  }
  public static void main(String arg[]) {
    new ExampleGridLayout("GridLayout").show();
  }
}
```

Listing 12-6: ExampleGridLayout class

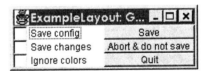

Figure 12-7: Panel with GridLayout

The BorderLayout class allows for even placement of components near borders of containers. The top, left, right and bottom localities of a Panel using this layout scheme are denoted as "North", "West", "East" and "South", as seen in Listing 12-7 and corresponding view in Figure 12-8. This scheme allows for convenient component placement without concern as to absolute coordinates or sizes.

```
import java.awt.*;

class ExampleBorderLayout extends Frame {
  ExampleBorderLayout(String m) {
    super("ExampleLayout2: "+m);
    setSize(340,280) ;
    Panel p = new Panel();
    p.setLayout(new BorderLayout());
    p.add("North", new TextArea(8,40));
    p.add("West", new Checkbox("Save config"));
    p.add("East", new Checkbox("Ignore colors"));
    p.add("South", new Button ("Exit"));
    add(p);
  }
  public static void main(String arg[]) {
    new ExampleBorderLayout("BorderLayout").show();
  }
}
```

Listing 12-7: ExampleBorderLayout class

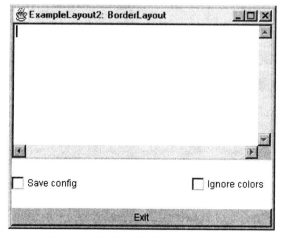

Figure 12-8: Panel with BorderLayout

As in earlier uses of Button components, the Exit button here is stretched too wide. Placing Button within a Panel first, and then the Panel into the outer panel helps, as seen in Figure 12-9.

```
Panel p = new Panel();
p.setLayout(new BorderLayout());
p.add("North", new TextArea());
p.add("West", new Checkbox("Save config"));
p.add("East", new Checkbox("Ignore colors"));
Panel q = new Panel();
q.add(new Button("Exit"));
p.add("South", q);
add(p);
```

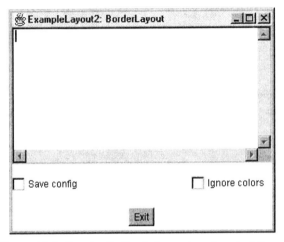

Figure 12-9: Panel with BorderLayout and nested Panel

12.2.5 Events

Currently, the views painted by the application frame with its constituent components are like empty shells with no application processing logic underneath. In a typical scenario, processing logic would involve:

- retrieving the state of switches, such as to determine the states of the "Save config" and "Ignore colors" Checkboxes, or reading input keyed into the top TextArea; or

- reacting to events, such as the click of the Exit Button.

The API documentation for the Checkbox class shows that the getState() method returns the state of a Checkbox object:

```
public boolean getState()
```

Similarly, the API documentation for the TextComponent class shows that the `getText()` method returns the input text of both TextInput and TextField objects (TextComponent being the superclass).

```
public String getText()
```

Event handling is more complex due to the relationships between various handlers. Instead of polling, frames and components wait until events occur, and appropriate predefined code are invoked. The `handleEvent()` method is most significant as it is the main method which is invoked when an event occurs.

The list of events are documented in the API documentation for the Event class. These events may be divided into: action, selection, mouse, keyboard, focus, scroll and window events. Due to the common handling of the first five types of events, `handleEvent()` has channeled the necessary processing to the following handler methods:

`action()`	The `action()` method handles events which request some action by the user, e.g. Button, Checkbox, List, Choice or TextField components.
`mouseEnter()`, `mouseExit()`, `mouseMove()`, `mouseDrag()`, `mouseDown()`, `mouseUp()`	The mouse methods relate to mouse activities – moving a mouse in/out of a component, moving the mouse with/without its button depressed, and mouse button clicks.
`keyDown()`, `keyUp()`	Like mouse events, a keyboard activity also corresponds to two (push/release) events.
`gotFocus()`, `lostFocus()`	Keyboard input for a component in a frame is dictated by whether it has the *keyboard focus*.

We now demonstrate how events may be handled, and will elaborate in subsequent sections.

Since external events ultimately invoke the above methods, custom event handlers may be intuitively installed for components via a new class and inheriting from an existing component. In handling the Exit Button in the previous example, we might use the MyExitButton class which inherits from Button, as seen in Listing 12-8.

```
class MyExitButton extends Button {
  MyExitButton(String label) {
    super(label);
  }
  public boolean action(Event e, Object  what) {
    System.exit(0);
    return true;
  }
}
```

Listing 12-8: New Button with Event Handler

The next example in Listing 12-9 has a responsive Exit button because new
MyExitButton() is used instead of new Button().

```
import java.awt.*;

class ExampleEvent extends Frame {
  ExampleEvent(String m) {
    super("ExampleButton: "+m);
    setSize(340,280) ;
    Panel p = new Panel();
    p.setLayout(new BorderLayout());
    p.add("North", new TextArea());
    p.add("West", new Checkbox("Save config"));
    p.add("East", new Checkbox("Ignore colors"));
    Panel q = new Panel();
    q.add(new MyExitButton("Exit"));
    p.add("South", q);
    add(p);
  }
  publicstatic void main(String arg[]) {
    new ExampleEvent("Event").show();
  }
}
```

Listing 12-9: ExampleEvent class

While this method for installing custom event handlers work, it is tedious in that each
component requires a new class definition to accommodate appropriate
customization. We would thus require two additional class definitions for the two
Checkbox components. Fortunately, the following two design characteristics of
components provide for another means of installing event handlers:

• Just as properties are inherited down the inheritance chain, event handlers which
  are methods are also inherited and are installed for subclass unless redefined.

- The default event handler for an AWT component passes an uncaught event to its parent container.

In our earlier examples, any uncaught events for standard components have been diverted to the containing panel and then the frame that contains them. However, no effort has been made to catch them. The next class example is mostly unchanged from the previous, except for the label of the Button component and two top-level event handler methods to capture events from nested components.

```java
import java.awt.*;

class Example extends Frame {
  TextArea txt;

  public static void main(String arg[]) {
    new Example("Event Handling").show();
  }

  Example(String m) {
    super("Example: "+m);
    setSize(340,280) ;
    Panel p = new Panel();
    p.setLayout(new BorderLayout());
    p.add("North", txt = new TextArea());
    p.add("West", new Checkbox("Save config"));
    p.add("East", new Checkbox("Ignore colors"));
    Panel q = new Panel();
    q.add(new Button("Clear"));
    p.add("South", q);
    add(p);
  }

  public boolean action(Event e, Object target) {
    if (e.target instanceof Button) {
      txt.setText("");
      return true;
    } else if (e.target instanceof Checkbox) {
      Checkbox x = (Checkbox) e.target;
      txt.appendText(x.getLabel()+
                     (x.getState() ? " is on\n" : " is off\n"));
      return true;
    }
    return(super.action(e, target));
  }

  public boolean handleEvent(Event evt) {
    if (evt.id == Event.WINDOW_DESTROY)
      System.exit(0) ;
    return(super.handleEvent(evt));
  }
}
```

Listing 12-10: Event Handling

The WINDOW_DESTROY event is sent following to a request to close a frame. Unlike the common events discussed above, window events are not distributed to other more specialized methods, and we handle this in handleEvent(). We have redefined handleEvent() to be on a lookout for the WINDOW_DESTROY event, but at the same time, rely on the original event handler for normal processing using the super self-reference.

The action() method handles the action group of events. It is invoked when there is a request to perform an action (e.g. Button click or change of Checkbox state). Here, we check the target component where an event was initially directed to, and provide the necessary code to handle it. As an example skeleton code, we substitute code to write to a TextArea component via the setText() and appendText() methods.

This section has provided an overview of the AWT package in JDK 1.0. While it may co-exist with the new event handling model, it is nevertheless discouraged. We thus take a quick look at the delegation based event handling model of JDK 1.1.

12.2.6 Events in JDK 1.1

The containment model in JDK 1.0 has the advantage of requiring minimal effort in understanding and use. However, the associated event handlers tend to be bulky in deciphering which events are relevant, and as a result, becomes untidy in larger applications.

Event handling in JDK 1.1 adopts the delegation model and consist of *event sources* and *event listeners*. One or more event listeners may register to be notified of particular events with a source. Any object may be a listener by implementing the appropriate EventListener interface. Just as in JDK 1.0, where there are various groups of events, there are also various groups of EventListeners in JDK 1.1.

As any object may be delegated the job of event handling, a direct connection may be established between event sources and listeners. Other objects may then be oblivious to this event handling activity.

The following code fragment Listing 12-11 uses components as in previous examples, but using JDK 1.1 styled event handling. Corresponding to Button and Checkbox components and the use of Frames, there are three groups of listeners required – we need EventListeners for action, item and window events. The corresponding listeners are ActionListener, ItemListener and WindowListener.

```
import java.awt.*;
import java.awt.event.*;

class Example1 extends Frame
            implements ActionListener, ItemListener, WindowListener {
  Example1(String m) {
    super("Example1: "+m);
    Button b; Checkbox c;
    setSize(240,140);
    Panel p =new Panel();
    p.add(new Label("Conference Registration"));
    p.add(c =new Checkbox("Attend Tutorial")); c.addItemListener(this);
    p.add(c =new Checkbox("Require Hotel")); c.addItemListener(this);
    p.add(b =new Button("Reset")); b.addActionListener(this);
    p.add(b =new Button("Submit")); b.addActionListener(this);
    addWindowListener(this);
    add(p);
  }

  public static void main(String arg[]) {
    new Example1("Event Handling").show();
  }

  public void actionPerformed(ActionEvent evt) {
    System.out.println("actionPerformed:" +evt.getSource().toString());
  }

  public void itemStateChanged(ItemEvent itm) {
    System.out.println("itemStateChanged: " +itm.getItemSelectable());
  }

  public void windowActivated(WindowEvent we) { }
  public void windowClosed(WindowEvent we)    { }
  public void windowClosing(WindowEvent we) { System.exit(0) ; }
  public void windowDeactivated(WindowEvent we) { }
  public void windowDeiconified(WindowEvent we) { }
  public void windowIconified(WindowEvent we) { }
  public void windowOpened(WindowEvent we) { }
}
```

Listing 12-11: JDK 1.1-style Event Handling

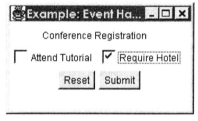

Figure 12-10: Responding to Events

In this example, the Frame subclass instance also implements the listener interfaces and as such, acts as listener for all those events. As such, our example performs two generic actions:

- It registers with the event source that it will handle events.

- It implements the necessary interfaces for a handler.

For the three sources of events, the example application performs the following concrete tasks:

- It registers with the Button components that it will handle action events (via `addActionListener()`), makes itself a listener by implementing the ActionListener interface, and defines `actionPerformed()`.

- It registers with the Checkbox components that it will handle action events (via `addItemListener()`), makes itself a listener by implementing ItemListener interface, and defines `itemStateChanged()`.

- It registers with the Frame that it will handle action events (via `addWindowListener()`), makes itself a listener by implementing WindowListener interface, and defines `windowActivated()`, `windowClosed()`, `windowClosing()`, `windowDeactivated()`, `windowDeiconified()`, `windowIconified()` and `windowOpened()`. (In this case, event source and listener is the same object.)

Judging from the resultant code, the reader may conclude that the delegation model is more complex due to increased code length. This is somewhat true, but this model provides for additional flexibility.

- Our example looks cluttered because it contains all the handlers. However, the delegation model allows for ActionListener and ItemListener to be distinct objects.

- The other complaint is that a WindowListener needs to define seven methods even when six of them have null bodies. This drawback is easily solved by using Adapters. Each EventListener interface which has more than one abstract method has a corresponding Adapter class which implements the interface using standard event-handlers. For example, compare the API documentation for the MouseListener and MouseAdapter classes. Subsequently, we may instantiate new custom Adapters by inheriting from standard Adapters and redefining the necessary methods, instead of implementing all methods necessary in interfaces.

Adaptor classes are further discussed in Section 12.5 with other kinds of class definitions.

12.3 Basic Components

Having seen an overview of creating graphical user-interfaces using basic AWT components in the preview section, we now proceed to study each component more closely. For each component, we will see:

- how it may be created and added to a Panel,

- its corresponding visual layout; and

- how appropriate EventListeners may be created and installed.

12.3.1 Label Component

The Label component allows for the display of fixed text strings in a container such as a Panel.

```
Panel p = new Panel();
p.add(new Label("WEB Search"));
```

12.3.2 Button Component

The Button component allows for clickable buttons in a container.

```
Button b;
Panel p = new Panel();
p.add(b = new Button("Submit query"));
b.addActionListener(actionListener);
```

When clicked, a Button instance invokes the ActionPerformed() method of the ActionListener object which is registered via addActionListener().

12.3.3 Checkbox Component

The Checkbox component allows for a boolean choice in a container.

```
Checkbox c;
Panel p = new Panel();
p.add(c = new Checkbox("Quick query"));
c.addItemListener(itemListener);
```

Corresponding to a modified state, a Checkbox instance invokes the `itemStateChanged()` method of the ItemListener object which was registered via `addItemListener()`.

12.3.4 CheckboxGroup Component

The CheckboxGroup component allows for a group of Checkbox components where only one of them may be on.

```
Checkbox c;
CheckboxGroup cbg = new CheckboxGroup();
Panel p = new Panel();
p.setLayout(new GridLayout(3, 1));
p.add(c = new Checkbox("Birthday", cbg, true));
c.addItemListener(itemListener);
p.add(c = new Checkbox("Engagement", cbg, false));
c.addItemListener(itemListener);
p.add(c = new Checkbox("Wedding", cbg, false));
c.addItemListener(itemListener);
```

Within a CheckboxGroup, a Checkbox object on turning true invokes the `itemStateChanged()` method of the ItemListener object which was registered via `addItemListener()`. The previous Checkbox in the group is implicitly turned false.

12.3.5 TextArea Component

The TextArea component allows for the display and manipulation of text. Its placement within a Panel is similar to other components we have seen so far. In the following example code, contents are placed into a TextArea via `setText()` and `append()`, and after user manipulation, may be retrieved via `getText()`.

```java
import java.awt.*;
import java.awt.event.*;

class MixedComponents extends Frame
              implements ActionListener, ItemListener, WindowListener {
  TextArea txt;
  MixedComponents(String m) {
    super("Mixed Components: "+m);
    Button b; Checkbox c;
    setSize(255,420);
    Panel p = new Panel();
    p.add(new Label("Conference Registration"));

    Panel sub =new Panel(); sub.setLayout(new GridLayout(2,1));
    sub.add(c =new Checkbox("Attend Tutorial"));
      c.addItemListener(this);
    sub.add(c =new Checkbox("Require Hotel"));
      c.addItemListener(this);
    p.add(sub);

    sub = new Panel(); sub.setLayout(new GridLayout(3,1));
    CheckboxGroup g = new CheckboxGroup();
    sub.add(c = new Checkbox("no food restrictions", g, true));
      c.addItemListener(this) ;
    sub.add(c = new Checkbox("no seafood", g, false));
      c.addItemListener(this);
    sub.add(c = new Checkbox("vegetarian food", g, false));
      c.addItemListener(this);
    p.add(sub);

    p.add(txt = new TextArea(10,30));
    p.add(b = new Button("Reset")); b.addActionListener(this) ;
    p.add(b = new Button("Submit")); b.addActionListener(this);
    addWindowListener(this) ;
    add(p) ;
    txt.setText("Events:\n");
  }

  public static void main(String arg[]) {
    new MixedComponents("Event Handling").show();
  }
  public void actionPerformed(ActionEvent evt) {
    txt.append("actionPerformed: " + evt.getSource().toString() +"\n");
  }
  public void itemStateChanged(ItemEvent itm) {
    txt.append("itemStateChanged: " + itm.getItemSelectable() +"\n");
  }

  public void windowActivated(WindowEvent we) { }
  public void windowClosed(WindowEvent we)    { }
  public void windowClosing(WindowEvent we)   {
    System.out.println(txt.getText());
    System.exit(0) ;
  }
  public void windowDeactivated(WindowEvent we)   { }
  public void windowDeiconified(WindowEvent we)   { }
  public void windowIconified(WindowEvent we)   { }
  public void windowOpened(WindowEvent we)   { }
}
```

Listing 12-12: MixedComponents class with Various Handlers

The code in Listing 12-12 shows a slightly cluttered Frame, with subgroups of components in a nested Panel for the benefit of a neat layout in Figure 12-11. Events are logged into the TextArea. The TextField component may be used in place of TextArea when a one-line display suffices.

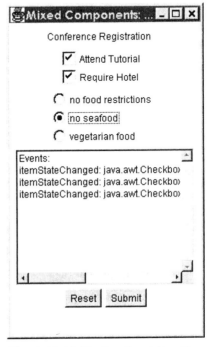

Figure 12-11: Testing Event Handling

12.3.6 Choice Component

The Choice component allows for the selection of items via a pop-up menu. Selectable items are initially specified via the add() method. The current selection is highlighted, and may be interrogated via getSelectedItem().

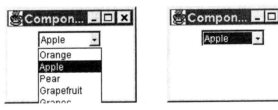

Figure 12-12: Selecting from a Choice Component

```
class ChoiceExample extends Frame
                     implements ItemListener, WindowListener {
    ChoiceExample(String m) {
        super("Components: "+m);
        setSize(170,120);
        Choice c;
        Panel p = new Panel();
        p.add(c = new Choice()); c.addItemListener(this) ;
        c.add("Orange");
        c.add("Apple");
        c.add("Pear");
        c.add("Grapefruit");
        c.add("Grapes");
        c.add("Jackfruit");
        c.add("Apricot");
        add(p) ;
        addWindowListener(this) ;
    }
    public void itemStateChanged(ItemEvent itm) {
        System.out.println("itemStateChanged:"+itm.getItemSelectable());
    }
    public static void main(String arg[]) {
        new ChoiceExample("Event Handling").show();
    }
    public void windowClosing(WindowEvent we) {
        System.out.println(c.getSelectedItem());
        System.exit(0) ;
    }
    // other methods as before ...
}
```

Listing 12-13: Using a Choice Component

12.3.7 List Component

The List component in Figure 12-13 allows for the selection of items via a scrolling list. Clicking on an unselected item selects it, and vice versa. As with the Choice component, its setup and interrogation are via the methods add() and getSelectedItem() respectively.

Figure 12-13: Selecting from a List Component

The List component also allows for multiple selections. In Figure 12-14 this feature may be enabled via the `setMultipleMode()` method, correspondingly illustrated in Listing 12-14. The `getSelectedItems()` method returns a list of selected strings.

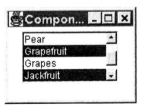

Figure 12-14: Multiple Selections from a List Component

```
class ListExample extends Frame implements WindowListener {
    ListExample(String m) {
        super("Components: "+m);
        setSize(170,120) ;
        List l;
        Panel p = new Panel();
        p.add(l = new List());
        l.setMultipleMode(true); // allow for multiple selections
        l.add("Orange");        l.add("Apple");
        l.add("Pear");          l.add("Grapefruit");
        l.add("Grapes");        l.add("Jackfruit");
        l.add("Apricot");
        add(p);
        addWindowListener(this) ;
    }

    public static void main(String arg[]) {
        new ListExample("Event Handling").show();
    }
    public void windowClosing(WindowEvent we)   {
        String x[] = l.getSelectedItems();
        for (int i=0; i<x.length; i++) System.out.println(x[i]);
        System.exit(0);
    }
    // other methods as before ...
}
```

Listing 12-14: Using a List Component

In making multiple selections, we are never sure whether there are other selections to be made. In this case, it is probably less useful to implement an ItemListener. Instead, a simpler model might rely on an external gesture (e.g. clicking another Button component) to trigger the end of selections.

12.3.8 Menus and Menu Items

The Frame which implements the main window of an application typically includes a
menu bar with various menus and menu items. A typical scenario is seen in Figure
12-15. As with other AWT components, the way in which menu structures are
specified, and how events are handled when menu items are chosen are similar –
appropriate object instances are created and appropriately placed within components.

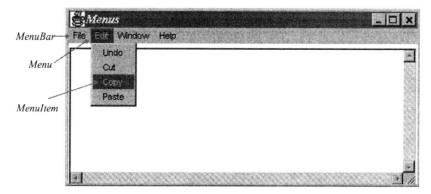

Figure 12-15: Frame with Menu Bar

In this case, the three classes of objects used are MenuBar, Menu and MenuItem.
When seen hierarchically, each menu item is represented by a MenuItem instance,
and all items in the group are collected via the add() method for a menu object.
Similarly, menu instances are collected into the menu bar via the add() method for a
menu bar object. Finally, the single menu bar object is added to the Frame via the
setMenuBar() method. This is shown in the code fragment in Listing 12-15:
Working with Menu Bar which produces the frame in Figure 12-15.

```
class MenuExample extends Frame {
    MenuExample() {
        super("Menus");
        setSize(450,220) ;
        MenuBar mb;
        Menu m;

        mb = new MenuBar();
        setMenuBar(mb) ;

        mb.add(m = new Menu("File"));
        m.add(new MenuItem("Open"));
        m.add(new MenuItem("Save"));
        m.add(new MenuItem("Save as"));
        m.add(new MenuItem("Close"));
```

```
      mb.add(m = new Menu("Edit"));
      m.add(new MenuItem("Undo"));
      m.add(new MenuItem("Cut"));
      m.add(new MenuItem("Copy"));
      m.add(new MenuItem("Paste"));

      mb.add(m = new Menu("Window"));
      m.add(new MenuItem("New Window"));
      m.add(new MenuItem("Arrange"));
      m.add(new MenuItem("Split"));

      mb.add(m = new Menu("Help"));
      m.add(new MenuItem("Index"));
      m.add(new MenuItem("Wizard"));
      m.add(new MenuItem("About"));

      Panel p = new Panel();
      p.add(new TextArea());
      add(p);
   }
   // other methods for event handling ...
}
```

Listing 12-15: Working with Menu Bar

As with Button components, event handling for menu items is effected via a suitable ActionListener by using the addActionListener() method. For brevity, only a skeletal structure for the modified class definition is shown in Listing 12-16.

```
class MenuExample extends Frame
                   implements ActionListener, WindowListener {
   MenuExample() {
      // ... code as before
      MenuItem i;
      mb.add(m = new Menu("File"));
      m.add(i = new MenuItem("Open")); i.addActionListener(this) ;
      m.add(i = new MenuItem("Save")); i.addActionListener(this);
      m.add(i = new MenuItem("Save as")); i.addActionListener(this);
      m.add(i = new MenuItem("Close")); i.addActionListener(this);
      // ... other Menu setup code - similar to above
      addWindowListener(this);
   }
   public static void main(String arg[]) {
      new MenuExample().show();
   }
   public void actionPerformed(ActionEvent evt) {
      System.out.println("menuItem: " + evt.getSource().toString());
   }
   public void windowClosing(WindowEvent we) { System.exit(0); }
}
```

Listing 12-16: Handling Menu Events

12.3.9 Dialog Frames

The Dialog class allows for a dialog window where input is expected from the user. By adding a Label component in a new class, it can be used to deliver a message, as seen in Figure 12-16.

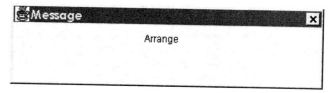

Figure 12-16: Dialog Frame

```
class Message extends Dialog implements WindowListener {
    Message(Frame parent, String message) {
        super(parent, "Message");
        setSize(400,100) ;
        setLayout(new FlowLayout());
        setResizable(false) ;
        add(new Label(message));
        addWindowListener(this) ;
        show();
    }

    public void windowActivated(WindowEvent we)   { }
    public void windowClosed(WindowEvent we)    { }
    public void windowClosing(WindowEvent we)   { dispose(); }
    public void windowDeactivated(WindowEvent we)   { }
    public void windowDeiconified(WindowEvent we)   { }
    public void windowIconified(WindowEvent we)   { }
    public void windowOpened(WindowEvent we)    { }
}
```

Listing 12-17: Implementation of a Dialog Frame

A simple implementation of a Dialog frame may inherit from the basic Frame class, as illustrated in Listing 12-17. The parent parameter in the constructor is passed to the constructor of the superclass. It allows focus to return to the calling parent when the Dialog window is closed. As with other windows, the show() method makes the frame visible while the dispose() method destroys it and reclaims resources to represent it.

In place of printing a string to the standard output, the previous MenuExample class may use the Message class to signal the delivery of an event. This is seen in Listing 12-18.

```
class MenuExample extends Frame
                  implements ActionListener, WindowListener {

    // ... code as before

    public void actionPerformed(ActionEvent evt)  {
        new Message(this, ((MenuItem)evt.getSource()).getLabel());
    }

}
```

Listing 12-18: Invoking a Message Dialog

A Dialog window may also be tagged as Modal via the setModal() method. In this case, it will receive all input from the parent window. The side-effect is that it must be closed before the parent application may proceed.

```
class Message extends Dialog implements WindowListener {
    Message(Frame parent, String message) {
        super(parent, "Message");
        setSize(400,100);
        setLayout(new FlowLayout());
        setResizable(false);
        setModal(true);
        add(new Label(message));
        addWindowListener(this);
        show();
    }
    ...
    public void windowClosing(WindowEvent we) { dispose(); }
}
```

Listing 12-19: A Modal Dialog Frame

12.3.10 File Dialog Frames

A common use of dialog is requesting for an input file to read from, or an output file to write to. An example view is shown in Figure 12-17. The FileDialog class, which is inherited from the Dialog class, easily provides this functionality.

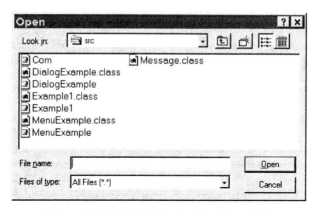

Figure 12-17: File Dialog for Opening a File

```
public FileDialog(Frame parent, String title, int mode)
```

The constructor method allows three parameters to be specified:

- the parent application,

- a title for the window, and

- whether it is the selected file to be loaded or saved.

```
public void actionPerformed(ActionEvent evt)  {
    FileDialog fd;
    String m = ((MenuItem) evt.getSource()).getLabel();
    if (m.equals("Open")) {
        fd = new FileDialog(this, "Open", FileDialog.LOAD);
        fd.show();
        System.out.println(fd.getDirectory()+fd.getFile());
    } else if (m.equals("Save as")) {
        fd = new FileDialog(this, "Save As", FileDialog.SAVE);
        fd.show();
        System.out.println(fd.getDirectory()+fd.getFile());
    } else
        new Message(this, ((MenuItem)evt.getSource()).getLabel());
}
```

12.4 Custom Components

Having seen the basic components provided in AWT, we will next see how custom components might be built. Here, it is easiest to reuse the framework set out by the Component class via inheritance.

For example, referring to the API documentation for Component, we determine that the paint() method is significant as it allows for a component to show itself. As such, in building a custom component, this method is redefined to give an appropriate graphical view of itself.

We consider building a Puzzle component which plays the 15-tile game, as shown in Figure 12-18. The object of the game is to maneuver the tiles via the single empty slot such that they are appropriately ordered.

Figure 12-18: Puzzle Board

First, a component must maintain its state (in terms of board position) so that it can always paint itself – whether the window was restored after being minimized, or brought to view after being hidden. In the case of the Puzzle component, we maintain the board with tiles at their current positions. We thus arrive at a skeletal structure as follows:

```
import java.awt.*;
class Puzzle extends Component {
    final int squares = 4;        // size of board
    int tileSize;                 // pixels per tile
    int state [] [];              // board
    int emptySlotX, emptySlotY;   // position of empty slot
    int moveX, moveY;             // current move
}
```

It is usual to have the constructor method provide the appropriate initialization, consisting of setting up the board and marking the empty slot.

```
Puzzle(int size) {
  tileSize = size / squares;
  state = new int[squares][squares];    // make the board
  for (int i=0;i<squares;i++)           // mess up the tiles
    for (int j=0;j<squares;j++)
        state[squares-j-1][squares-i-1] = i*squares+j+1;
  moveX = moveY = 0;                     // position of empty space
  state[moveX][moveY]=0;                 // mark the empty space
  addMouseListener(mouseListener) ;
}
```

The first of two important tasks which the Puzzle must fulfill is provide visual feedback in response to a changed board. This is done by overriding the paint() method originally defined in the superclass. As shown below, displaying the Puzzle is achieved by displaying each of the 15 tiles.

```
public void paint(Graphics g) {
  // clear board
  g.fillRect(0, 0, tileSize*squares, tileSize*squares) ;
  for (int i=0;i<squares;i++)  // print all tiles
    for (int j=0;j<squares;j++)
        square(g,i,j);
}
```

Each square is displayed by clearing a rectangle at the appropriate *x-y* coordinate which is extrapolated from multiplying row/column with tileSize.

```
void square(Graphics g, int x, int y) {
  if (state[y][x] != 0) {                 // paint a tile
    g.clearRect(x*tileSize+1, y*tileSize+1, tileSize-2, tileSize-2) ;
    g.drawString(new Integer(state[y][x]).toString(),
              x*tileSize+tileSize/2-4, y*tileSize+tileSize/2+4) ;
  }
}
```

The second task is to receive input as to where the user is playing the next move. Mouse activity is obtained by installing a MouseListener in about the same way as what we have done with ActionListener and ItemListener previously.

A MouseListener must implement five methods to track basic mouse activity: mouseClicked(), mouseEntered(), mouseExited(), mousePressed() and mouseReleased(). Two options are available here: the Puzzle component could implement these methods and thus become a legitimate MouseListener. However, as only `mouseReleased()` is significant, the other four methods might be considered extra baggage.

A MouseAdapter is useful here. It is basically a class which provides a basic implementation for the five mouse activity methods. An appropriate MouseAdapter object merely inherits from MouseAdapter but redefines `mouseReleased()`. For the moment, we just provide the method:

```
public void mouseReleased(MouseEvent e)   {
  int newX = e.getX() / tileSize;
  int newY = e.getY() / tileSize;
  if (newX < squares && newY < squares &&
        emptySlotX == newX && (Math.abs(emptySlotY-newY) == 1) ||
        emptySlotY == newY && (Math.abs(emptySlotX-newX) == 1)) {
    //update board
    state [moveY=emptySlotY] [moveX=emptySlotX] = state[newY] [newX];
    state[emptySlotY=newY] [emptySlotX=newX] = 0;
    repaint();
  }
}
```

Updates of the Puzzle state corresponding to tile movement as indicated by a mouse click must translate to update of the screen display. This is signaled by the method `repaint()` which schedules a display refresh by the `paint()` method.

We have now seen most of the code for our Puzzle component. However, we pause to consider, in the next section, an elegant means of including an Adapter object.

12.5 Other Kinds of Class Definitions

The delegation approach to event handling using listener objects is useful in that role of event handling may be distributed to various objects. Where event handling is minimal event handling is neater if it is handled by one object. In our Puzzle example, while we need to redefine `mouseReleased()`, redefining the other methods with null bodies becomes clumsy.

An example MouseAdapter class with null handlers for mouse events might be:

```
class MouseAdapter implements MouseListener {
    public void mouseClicked(MouseEvent e) { }
    public void mouseEntered(MouseEvent e) { }
    public void mouseExited(MouseEvent e) { }
    public void mousePressed(MouseEvent e) { }
    public void mouseReleased(MouseEvent e) { }
}
```

From this standard MouseAdapter class, we may derive a PuzzleMouseListener and redefine the `mouseReleased()` method:

```
class PuzzleMouseListener extends MouseAdapter {
    public void mouseReleased(MouseEvent e)   {
      // check move and update Puzzle board
    }
}
```

However, we encounter a scope problem in PuzzleMouseListener where its method `mouseReleased()` is expected to access instance variables of Puzzle. Even if this was done via proper accessor methods, the problem remains as to how two object instances of different classes may be logically associated.

12.5.1 Inner Classes

The revision of Java in JDK 1.1 allows for inner class, local class and anonymous class definitions to solve this problem. While all classes in Java JDK 1.0 may only be declared at the top level, an inner class is one which is declared in another class. An example is given in Listing 12-20.

Such classes are unknown outside the enclosing class because its instances are implicitly used within instances of the enclosing class.

```
class Puzzle extends Component {
  ...
  int state [] [];                     // board
  ...

  class PuzzleMouseListener extends MouseAdapter {
    public void mouseReleased(MouseEvent e)   {
      // check move and update Puzzle board
      // has access to state
    }
  }
  PuzzleMouseListener listener = new PuzzleMouseListener();

  Puzzle() {
    ...
    addMouseListener(listener) ;
  }
}
```

Listing 12-20: Inner Class Definition

As such, this solves the scope problem in that PuzzleMouseListener may be instantiated within Puzzle, and yet the resultant instance has easy access to instance variables such as state.

12.5.2 Anonymous Classes

While the inner class facility is convenient in terms of overcoming scoping restrictions, they are useful within the enclosing class and unlikely to be reused outside the scope.

When there is to be only one instance of an inner class, the creation of an anonymous class instance provides the syntactic sugar for more succinct code. The example code in Listing 12-21 provides identical functionality to the previous fragment in Listing 12-20.

```
class Puzzle extends Component {
  ...
  int state [] [];                     // board
  ...
  MouseAdapter listener = new MouseAdapter() {
    public void mouseReleased(MouseEvent e)   {
      // check move and update Puzzle board
      // has access to state
    }
  };
```

```
Puzzle() {
  ...
  addMouseListener(listener) ;
}
}
```

Listing 12-21: Anonymous Class Definition

The classname PuzzleMouseListener has been omitted since it is used in the definition and only one instantiation. In an anonymous class, the definition occurs with instantiation, i.e. after the new allocator.

12.5.3 Local Classes

While inner class definitions occur within an enclosing class, local classes are even more restricted in that they occur within blocks of method definitions. Listing 12-22 shows an example local class definition.

```
class Puzzle extends Component {
  ...
  int state [] [];                    // board
  ...

  Puzzle() {
    class PuzzleMouseAdapter {
      public void mouseReleased(MouseEvent e)   {
        // check move and update Puzzle board
        // has access to state
      }
    }
    ...
    addMouseListener(new PuzzleMouseAdapter());
  }
}
```

Listing 12-22: Local Class Definition

In fact, if we desire, we could also create an instance of an anonymous class from the Puzzle constructor, as in Listing 12-23, but this does not necessarily improve code readability.

```
class Puzzle extends Component {
  ...
  int state [] [];               // board
  ...

  Puzzle() {
    ...
    addMouseListener(new MouseAdapter() {
      public void mouseReleased(MouseEvent e)   {
        // check move and update Puzzle board
        // has access to state
      }
    });
  }
}
```

Listing 12-23: Another Anonymous Class Definition

Using instances of anonymous MouseAdapter and WindowAdapter (sub)classes, we again present the complete solution for our Puzzle component in Listing 12-24.

```
import java.awt.*;
import java.awt.event.*;

class Puzzle extends Component {

  final int squares = 4;     // size of board
  int tileSize;              // pixels per row
  int state [] [];            // state of board
  int moveX, moveY,
      emptySlotX, emptySlotY; // positions of empty space
  Dimension psize;

  Puzzle(int size) {
    psize = new Dimension(size, size);
    tileSize = size / squares;
    state=new int[squares][squares];     // mess up the tiles
    for (int i=0;i<squares;i++)
      for (int j=0;j<squares;j++)
        state[squares-j-1][squares-i-1] = i*squares+j+1;
    emptySlotX = emptySlotY = 0;         // position of empty space
    state[emptySlotX][emptySlotY]=0;     // mark the empty space
    addMouseListener(mouseListener) ;
  }

  void square(Graphics g, int x, int y)  {
    if (state[y][x] != 0) {                    // paint a tile
      g.clearRect(x*tileSize+1, y*tileSize+1, tileSize-2, tileSize-2) ;
      g.drawString(new Integer(state[y][x]).toString(),
                   x*tileSize+tileSize/2-4, y*tileSize+tileSize/2+4) ;
    }
  }
```

```
public void paint(Graphics g)  {
  // clear board
  g.fillRect(0, 0, tileSize*squares, tileSize*squares) ;
  for (int i=0;i<squares;i++)              // print all tiles
    for (int j=0;j<squares;j++)
      square(g,i,j);
}

public Dimension getPreferredSize() { return psize; }

MouseAdapter mouseListener = new MouseAdapter() {
  public void mouseReleased(MouseEvent e)   {
    int newX = e.getX() / tileSize;
    int newY = e.getY() / tileSize;
    if (newX < squares && newY < squares &&
        emptySlotX == newX && (Math.abs(emptySlotY-newY) == 1) ||
        emptySlotY == newY && (Math.abs(emptySlotX-newX) == 1)) {
      // update
      state [moveY=emptySlotY] [moveX=emptySlotX] = state[newY] [newX];
      state[emptySlotY=newY] [emptySlotX=newX] = 0;
      repaint();
    }
  }
};

public static void main(String arg[]) {
  WindowAdapter windowListener = new WindowAdapter() {
    public void windowClosing(WindowEvent e) { System.exit(0) ; }
  };
  Frame f = new Frame("Puzzle");
  f.setSize(240,240) ;
  f.addWindowListener(windowListener) ;
  Panel p = new Panel();
  p.add(new Puzzle(200)) ;
  f.add(p);
  f.show();
}
}
```

Listing 12-24: Puzzle class Revisited

12.6 Summary

While graphical user-interfaces allow for convenient interaction and intuitive user models, good interfaces still require careful design and much implementation effort in event handling. The AWT package in the Java API allows for a consistent user-interface at a fraction of the typical implementation effort. This is achieved by its convenient object-oriented framework with reusable GUI components and integration mechanisms for attaching event-handlers.

In this chapter, we discussed:

- the constituents of the AWT model and the framework for their integration in an application,

- detailed incremental development of an example user-interface,

- the basic components in AWT available and their control within an application,

- the use of custom components when predefined components are inadequate,

- event handling using both containment and delegation models in JDK 1.0 and JDK 1.1 respectively; and

- JDK 1.1 language extensions relating to inner class, local class and anonymous class definitions.

12.7 Exercises

1. Review the API documentation for the File class. Note that while the File instance is a directory, the `list()` method returns the list of files in it in a String array. Using this feature, implement a directory browser consisting of List and non-editing TextArea components. The former presents the set of files in a directory, while the latter displays the selected file.

2. Implement the following enhancements to the browser application discussed in Question 1:

   - allow for enabling edit-mode in the TextArea component, and subsequently saving the contents back to the original or new file,

   - allow for block-move edit operations via custom pop-up mouse menu,

   - search-and-replace edit operations via menu and dialog frames; and

   - allow for changing into new directories which is reflected by displaying a corresponding new set of files in the List component.

3. Using the `drawRect()` method in the Graphics class, implement a rectangle drawing application which paints rectangles of various colors and positions indicated by pressing and releasing the mouse to denote opposite corners.

- Include a rubber-band effect to indicate rectangle borders between selecting the two opposite corners of the rectangle.

- Are existing rectangles redrawn when the frame is restored after being minimized? Suggest a scheme to implement this requirement.

- Detect the right-hand mouse button to erase rectangles which enclose the mouse position.

13 Applets and Loaders

We have learnt that Java is an interpreted language. A Java compiler (`javac` in JDK) translates source code to Java bytecodes so that it may execute as long as a Java Virtual Machine (`java` in JDK) is implemented to run on the underlying hardware. As such, Java is described as platform independent. In fact, the Java Virtual Machine not only allows Java to be source-code compatible, but object-code compatible as well. Object-code derived from compilation on one machine, will execute unmodified on another.

This characteristic was exploited at the opportune time of exponential Internet growth, to pave the way for Java bytecodes to travel across a network, and subsequently be loaded into a virtual machine elsewhere for execution. A Java applet, which we have heard so much about over the media, is essentially Java bytecode which have traveled from a Web server to execute within an HTML page as displayed by a Web browser with an embedded Java Virtual Machine.

The ease of distributing Java applets over a network has destined this framework to revolutionize Web applications. With good GUI facilities and intuitive interfaces, enthusiasm for the Internet has been further heightened. The promise of Java applets was to turn static HTML pages to dynamic Internet applications.

We have deliberately left the popular subject of Java applets till now, because the applet framework relies on the AWT package, as well as networking and dynamic code loading facilities of Java. We will examine the execution environment of applets, some of its restrictions and how applications can take advantage of dynamically loaded code.

13.1 Applet Characteristics

The API documentation reveals that Java applets are derived from the java.applet.Applet class. This Applet class is in turn derived from the java.awt.Panel class. Thus, an applet may be viewed as a special Panel which runs within the context of a Java-enabled Web browser such as Netscape Communicator or Microsoft's Internet Explorer.

Due to inheritance from its superclasses, operations applicable to a Panel such as placement of predefined or custom components, as discussed in Chapter 12, will also apply to an applet. Additional properties peculiar to an applet, such as how it behaves within the operations of a Web browser and its life-cycle with respect to init(), start() and stop() methods also applies. In addition, the Applet class implements additional interfaces which allow it to easily retrieve related Web resources from its originating server, display images and play audio clips and communicate with other applets in the enclosing HTML document.

Listing 13-1 shows an example applet with a method init() which overrides the one defined in its superclass.

```
import java.applet.Applet;
import java.awt.*;

public class EgApplet extends Applet {
    public void init() {
        add(new TextArea(10, 60));
        add(new TextField(30)) ;
    }
}
```

Listing 13-1: Example Applet

This class definition is unique from those we have seen in that it does not have a static void main() method, as well as does not seem to have code which invokes init(). The significance of such particularities and the overriding method will be discussed in subsequent sections. For the moment, we present the corresponding HTML document in Listing 13-2, which is used to embed an EgApplet object.

```
<HTML>
<HEAD>
<TITLE>Example Applet</TITLE>
</HEAD>

<BODY>
<P>
Example Applet
</P>
<APPLET CODE=EgApplet.class HEIGHT=270 WIDTH=450>
</APPLET>
</BODY>
</HTML>
```

Listing 13-2: Example HTML with Embedded Applet

While most of the HTML tags are common, the <APPLET> tag stands out as one used to embed a Java applet into an HTML document. Here, two additional attributes are mandatory: the code file of the compiled applet proper, and dimensions (in terms of pixel height and width) of the display area within the browser required.

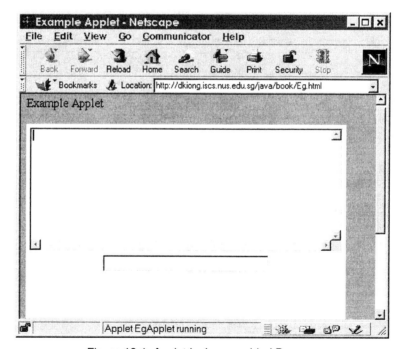

Figure 13-1: Applet in Java-enabled Browser

In placing both HTML document and Java bytecode files in the same directory, and calling a Java-enabled Web browser to load the former (either through a local file load or an HTTPD server) will also load the applet and commence execution as shown in Figure 13-1.

As with panels and components in Chapter 12, we may also attach event handlers for our components. We extend our original applet with an event handler and accessor methods to retrieve other HTML source files as follows:

- The TextArea and TextField components are assigned to instance variables `txt` and `inp` in order that we can interrogate them subsequently (as in `inp.getText()` and `txt.setText()` to retrieve input and write output respectively).

- JDK 1.0 styled event handling is installed via the `action()` method to retrieve input in the TextField component in response to the return key. (This ensures that the applet will still execute on Java-enabled Web browsers without AWT 1.1 libraries.) This is illustrated in Listing 13-3.

- The relative URL specified in TextField is used to retrieve a Web resource, whose contents are displayed in the TextArea. This is implemented by the `display()` method, and it uses the API class in java.io and java.net.

```java
import java.applet.Applet;
import java.awt.*;
import java.io.*;
import java.net.*;

public class EgApplet extends Applet {
    TextArea txt; TextField inp;

    public void init() {
        add(txt = new TextArea(10, 60));
        add(inp = new TextField(30)) ;
    }

    public boolean action(Event evt, Object obj)  {
        if (evt.target instanceof TextField) {
            display(inp.getText());
            return true;
        }
        return(super.action(evt, obj));
    }
}
```

Listing 13-3: Event Handling in an Applet

The EgApplet applet in Listing 13-3 is essentially unchanged from Listing 13-1, except for instance variable declarations and the `action()` event handling method. For the purpose of modular descriptions, the `display()` method is shown in Listing 13-4. It relies on the URL class to construct an URL when given a relative address and the base address of the applet. The `openStream()` method initiates a Web request for the said URL, but relies on InputStream methods to retrieve results.

```
void display(String n) {
   try {
     URL doc = new URL(getDocumentBase(), n);
     InputStream is = doc.openStream();
     StringBuffer b = new StringBuffer();
     int c;
     while ((c = is.read()) != -1)
        b.append((char) c) ;
     is.close();
     txt.setText(b.toString());
   } catch (Exception e) {
     txt.setText("Cannot retrieve "+n);
   }
}
```

Listing 13-4: URL Content Retrieval

As with applications which use predefined AWT components, applets may also be installed with JDK 1.1 styled event-handlers. The restriction here is that such code can only be executed in a Web browser with the JDK 1.1 class libraries.

The EgApplet version in Listing 13-5 uses JDK 1.1 styled event handlers. The applet differs from the JDK 1.0 version in that:

- it implements the interface for an ActionListener by defining the additional method `actionPerformed()`; and

- it installs itself as a listener for the TextField so that input there would subsequently trigger `actionPerformed()`.

```
import java.applet.Applet;
import java.awt.*;
import java.awt.event.*;
import java.io.*;
import java.net.*;

public class EgApplet extends Applet implements ActionListener {
    TextArea txt;
    TextField inp;

    public void init() {
        add(txt = new TextArea(10, 60));
        add(inp = new TextField(30));
        inp.addActionListener(this) ;
    }

    public void actionPerformed(ActionEvent evt)  {
        display(inp.getText());
    }

    ... // void display() remains unchanged
}
```

Listing 13-5: EgApplet using JDK 1.1-styled Event Handling

13.2 Applet Life Cycle

The two versions of the EgApplet applet in the previous section (which uses both JDK 1.0 and JDK 1.1-styled event handling) show that applets are very much like Panels in the java.awt package. This is not surprising since the Panel class occurs in its inheritance chain.

However, because an applet executes within an HTML document of a Web browser, its behavior is in a small way dictated by the browser's operation. For example, after an applet is loaded and is running, provision must be made for when the browser leaves the page, or re-visits the page. In the former case, the applet should be notified so that execution does not continue unproductively. Similarly, when a page containing an applet is re-visited, creating two instances of the same applet is wasteful in terms of computing resources.

A well-behaved applet responds to these state changes via the methods init(), start(), stop() and destroy(), as illustrated in Figure 13-2. The methods init() and start() are invoked for the first time when an applet is loaded and execution commences. After that, stop() and start() are invoked when the browser leaves the HTML page and re-visits it. Finally, the destroy() method is invoked just before the applet is unloaded and disappears into oblivion. Any change in behavior corresponding to this state change should thus be effected by these methods.

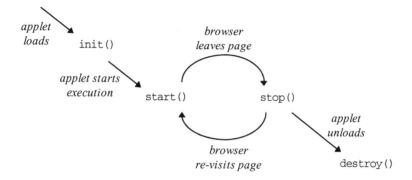

Figure 13-2: Applet Life-Cycle

Consistent with object-oriented programming methodology, applets inherit the standard behavior for these methods init(), start(), stop() and destroy(). Where no additional processing is required for the corresponding states, the standard behavior is adopted. Where required, custom processing is achieved by new method definition.

The EgApplet class in the previous section had a custom init() method, but did not require special processing for start(), stop() or destroy(). In the case of an applet with additional threads, it would be considerate of the applet to stop threads when the browser leaves the HTML page. In this case, the thread would be restarted if the page was re-visited. Thus, the start() and stop() methods would then be defined accordingly.

13.3 Custom Applets

While the use of AWT components continue to be the same for applets, we now compare applets with applications developed in the previous chapter. In re-incarnating the Puzzle application as an applet, we note two major differences:

- Applets are not invoked from the command line, but instead instantiated from a Web browser and with a life-cycle just discussed. As such, static void main() is not useful for applet execution. (However, we might still include it so that the core applet code will run both as an applet and application.) Following from this, applets cannot be terminated via System.exit() because they exist as additional execution threads of the browser.

- While it is natural for an application class to use constructor methods for initialization, this is not the case with applets. In the former case, initialization is implicit at object instantiation. In the latter case, applets cannot always be initialized at instantiation since some properties are derived from its environment which is determined after applet instantiation. As such, applet initialization is thus best via the `init()` method.

```
public class Puzzle extends Applet {

    final int squares = 4;       // size of board
    int tileSize;                // pixels per row
    int state [] [];              // state of board
    int moveX, moveY,
        emptySlotX, emptySlotY; // positions of empty space

    public void init() {
      tileSize = getSize().height / squares;
      state=new int[squares][squares];     // mess up the tiles
      for (int i=0;i<squares;i++)
        for (int j=0;j<squares;j++)
            state[squares-j-1][squares-i-1] = i*squares+j+1;
      emptySlotX = emptySlotY = 0;          // position of empty space
      state[emptySlotX][emptySlotY]=0;      // mark the empty space
      addMouseListener(mouseListener) ;
    }
    ... // other methods unchanged, static void main() now not required
}
```

Listing 13-6: Applet version of Puzzle

13.4 Images and Audio

An applet may easily retrieve images and audio clips from its originating server via the methods

```
public Image getImage(URL url) ;
public Image getImage(URL url, String name);
public AudioClip getAudioClip(URL url);
public AudioClip getAudioClip(URL url, String name);
```

The resultant Image object retrieved by `getImage()` may be displayed via the `drawImage()` method in the Graphics class. The skeletal code for an applet is shown in Listing 13-7.

```
class DrawImage extends Applet {

    Image img;
    ...
    img = getImage(getDocumentBase(), "picture.gif");
    ...
    void paint(Graphics g)  {
        ...
        g.drawImage(img, x, y, this) ;
    }
}
```

Listing 13-7: Skeletal Code for Retrieving and Displaying Images

Similarly, an AudioClip object retrieved via getAudioClip() may commence and stop playback via play() and stop() respectively. The skeletal code for an applet is shown in Listing 13-8.

```
class PlayAudio extends Applet {

    AudioClip song;
    ...
    song = getAudioClip(getDocumentBase(), "sound.au") ;
    ...

    void start() {
        ...
        song.play();
    }

    void stop() {
        ...
        song.stop();
    }
}
```

Listing 13-8: Skeletal Code for Retrieving and Playing an Audio Clip

The Media applet in Listing 13-9 demonstrates how these methods are used: it reads in an image and audio clip via getImage() and getAudioClip() in its init() method. The former is drawn by drawImage() in the paint() method, while the mouse event handler plays and stops the audio clip via play() and stop() corresponding to mouse press and release events.

```
import java.applet.*;
import java.awt.*;
import java.awt.event.*;

public class Media extends Applet {

  Image image;
  AudioClip audio;
  MouseAdapter listener = new MouseAdapter() {
    public void mousePressed(MouseEvent e)  {
      audio.play();
    }
    public void mouseReleased(MouseEvent e) {
      audio.stop();
    }
  };

  public void init() {
    image = getImage(getDocumentBase(),"image.gif");
    audio = getAudioClip(getDocumentBase(),"audio");
    addMouseListener(listener) ;
  }

  public void paint(Graphics g) {
    g.drawImage(image, 0, 0, this) ;
  }
}
```

Listing 13-9: Media Applet

13.5 Animation in Applets

Since the introduction of the Java programming language, animation applets have been a popular means to liven up a Web page. The common technique for animating a Java component is making the paint() method redraw a new image during each time interval.

However, applets themselves should not be making continuous calls to the paint() method, or it will not allow other work to be done such as responding to events. Instead, an extra thread allows the internal state of the applet to be updated transparently. As with other threads, this work is done within the run() method.

The NumberAnim applet in Listing 13-10 creates a thread in the method init(), and starts it running to increment the instance variable count once every 100 milliseconds. In doing so, the display is also scheduled for refresh via repaint() over the same time interval.

```
import java.awt.*;

public class NumberAnim extends java.applet.Applet implements Runnable {
    Thread updateThread;
    int counter=0;

    public void init() {
        updateThread = new Thread(this);
        updateThread.start();
    }

    public void run() {
        for (;;) {
            counter++;
            repaint();
            try {
                Thread.sleep(100);
            } catch (Exception e) {
            }
        }
    }

    public void paint(Graphics g)  {
        g.drawString("counter " + counter, 40, 40) ;
    }
}
```

Listing 13-10: Basic Animation

This version of NumberAnim is inconsiderate as it continues to run even after the HTML page is no longer in view of the Web browser. While the previous EgApplet applet had no housekeeping chores to perform, the NumberAnim applet must however stop the active thread created by init(). This is a good situation where an overriding stop() method should be defined for the NumberAnim class:

```
public void stop() {
    updateThread.stop();
    updateThread = null;
}
```

The applet now prevents a run-away thread in that it stops its execution when it is now longer required. However, the counter does not resume if the applet page was re-visited. Here, we define another method start() to restart thread execution. Since this is similar to the init() method, we no longer need it but instead rely on start().

```
public void start() {
    updateThread = new Thread(this);
    updateThread.start();
}
```

We now attempt something more interesting – instead of a display of incrementing numbers, we will instead display a coordinated series of GIF images to provide the animation effect. Here are the modifications required:

- The initialization method `init()` loads the required set of images `image0.gif`, `image1.gif`, `image2.gif` ... from the applet directory so that it is ready for subsequent display.

- In counting up, the method `run()` applies the `%` modulo operator on `count` so its value rolls over to index the next image to display.

- The `paint()` method draws the appropriate image to the display area.

The resultant Animate applet is shown in Listing 13-11.

```java
import java.awt.*;

public class Animate extends java.applet.Applet implements Runnable {
    Thread updateThread;
    final int MAXIMAGES = 10;
    Image img[]; int counter=0;
    Color background;

    public void init() {
        background = getBackground();
        img = new Image[MAXIMAGES];
        for (int j=0; j<MAXIMAGES; j++)
            img[j] = getImage(getDocumentBase(), "image"+j+".gif");
    }

    public void start() {
        updateThread = new Thread(this); updateThread.start();
    }

    public void stop() {
        updateThread.stop(); updateThread = null;
    }

    public void run() {
        for (;;) {
            repaint();
            counter++; counter = counter % MAXIMAGES;
            try { Thread.sleep(200); } catch (Exception e) { }
        }
    }

    public void paint(Graphics g) {
        g.drawImage(img[counter], 0, 0, background, null) ;
    }
}
```

Listing 13-11: Animate Applet

13.6 Efficient Repainting

While the Animate applet works in the sense that it continuously displays a sequence of images, a slight display flicker is possibly seen due to the way screen updates are performed for AWT components.

So far, we have only seen the `paint()` method which is called in response to a repaint request to refresh the display of an AWT component. In attempting optimum screen updates, we distinguish the two situations in which the `paint()` method is currently invoked.

- We have seen that repainting is necessary due to state changes, e.g. a tile in the Puzzle has moved, or the next image in the animation sequence in Animate is to be displayed.

- The other situation which requires a display update is not caused by state changes within the applet, but instead by its windowing environment, e.g. the applet is visible after being overlapped by another window, or the applet is restored to normal display size after being iconized.

In the second situation, it is likely that a complete refresh is necessary, but incremental updates might suffice in the former case. In the Puzzle applet example, the `paint()` method updates the whole puzzle board, and this is suitable for a formerly iconized or hidden applet. However, in response to movement of a tile, only two positions need to be updated – the original and final position of the tile that has been moved, while the display of all other positions remain unchanged.

The AWT component framework allows such distinctions to be made. In fact, the `paint()` method is invoked for whole updates, whereas the `update()` method is invoked for partial updates. We have thus far ignored the latter because its predefined definition is to clear the background area and rely on `paint()` for repainting. While this is a functionally correct definition and works for all situations, screen flicker in our demonstration applets is caused by erasing the background needlessly just before repainting it again.

A display optimization for the Puzzle applet merely redraws the affected squares may be easily deployed by overriding the `update()` method.

```
public void update(Graphics g) {
    // merely update affected board positions
    square(g, moveX, moveY);
    square(g, emptySlotX, emptySlotY);
}
```

Since the empty position was previously implied by no drawings and relied on the paint() method, using update() for incremental display requires the square() method to now also draw the blank position.

```
void square(Graphics g, int x, int y) {
   if (state[y][x] != 0) {                       // paint a tile
     g.clearRect(x*tileSize+1, y*tileSize+1, tileSize-2, tileSize-2) ;
     g.drawString(new Integer(state[y][x]).toString(),
                    x*tileSize+tileSize/2-4, y*tileSize+tileSize/2+4);
   } else                                        // paint a blank position
     g.fillRect(x*tileSize+1, y*tileSize+1, tileSize-2, tileSize-2) ;
}
```

Display optimization for the Animate applet is also minimal, and consists of placing the body of paint() into update(), and having paint() invoke update(). Clearing the background explicitly is not necessary because drawImage() does so for invisible portions of an image using the selected background color.

```
public void update(Graphics g) {
    g.drawImage(img[counter], 0, 0, background, null) ;
}

public void paint(Graphics g) {
    update(g) ;
}
```

13.7 Applet Parameters

The Animate applet could be more useful if working parameters were not hardwired into code. Currently, the statically determined values include:

- the prefix of image files   image

- the number of images   10

- the delay between 2 images   200 (ms)

- the delay in restarting image sequence   (same as delay between 2 images)

Applet parameters may be specified via the <PARAM> tag within the <APPLET> tag. The associative scheme maps the parameter name in the "name" attribute of a <PARAM> tag to the corresponding value specified by the "value" attribute.

```
<APPLET code=Animate.class height=100 width=100>
   <PARAM name="imagesource" value="image">
   <PARAM name="maximages" value="10">
   <PARAM name="delay" value="200">
   <PARAM name="delaynext" value="1000">
</APPLET>
```

Parameter values are subsequently interrogated from an applet via the getParameter() method. Given the *name* attribute of a <PARAM> tag, it returns the associated *value* attribute. A more flexible version of the Animate applet is shown in Listing 13-12.

```
import java.awt.*;

public class Animate2 extends java.applet.Applet implements Runnable {
    String IMAGESOURCE = "image";
    int MAXIMAGES = 10;
    int DELAY = 200;
    int DELAYNEXT = 200;

    Thread updateThread;
    Image img[]; int counter=0;
    Color background;

    public void init() {
        String val;
        if ((val = getParameter("imagesource")) != null)
          IMAGESOURCE = val;
        if ((val = getParameter("maximages")) != null)
          MAXIMAGES = val;
        if ((val = getParameter("delay")) != null) {
          DELAY = Integer.parseInt(val);
          if (DELAY < 50) DELAY = 50;
        }
        if ((val = getParameter("delaynext") ) != null) {
          DELAYNEXT = Integer.parseInt(val);
          if (DELAYNEXT < 50) DELAYNEXT = 50;
        }
        background = getBackground();
        img = new Image[MAXIMAGES];
        for (int j=0; j<MAXIMAGES; j++)
           img[j] = getImage(getDocumentBase(), IMAGESOURCE+j+".gif") ;
    }

    public void start() {
        updateThread = new Thread(this); updateThread.start();
    }
```

```
public void stop() {
   updateThread.stop(); updateThread = null;
}
public void run() {
   for (;;) {
      repaint();
      counter++; counter = counter % MAXIMAGES;
      try {
         Thread.sleep(counter == 0 ? DELAYNEXT : DELAY);
      } catch (Exception e) {
      }
   }
}
public void paint(Graphics g) {
   g.drawImage(img[counter], 0, 0, background, null) ;
}
}
```

Listing 13-12: Applet Parameters

To aid the documentation process, the redefinition of getAppletInfo() and
getParameterInfo() methods allow an applet to provide information as to itself
and expected parameters.

```
public String getAppletInfo() {
   return("Kiong B.K., Animate Applet, (c) 1998");
}

public String[][] getParameterInfo() {
   String info[][] = {
      {"imagesource","string","prefix name of image files"},
      {"maximages", "int",    "number of images in 1 sequence"},
      {"delay",     "int",    "delay between 2 images (ms)"}
      {"delaynext", "int",    "delay before 2 sequences (ms)"}
   };
   return(info);
}
```

Requesting applet information from Appletviewer returns a window similar to that
shown in Figure 13-3.

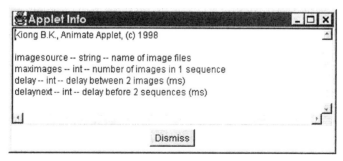

Figure 13-3: Applet Information

13.8 Security Restrictions of Applets

The ease of applet execution over the network makes the Java environment very attractive in terms of reducing code maintenance and distribution costs. Source modifications are merely re-compiled on the Web server, and distribution to the client machines is implied the next time the applet is required.

While this situation works reasonably well on an Intranet with good network bandwidth, there is a potential problem in open and untrusted networks. In making code execution and distribution as easy as clicking a Web hyperlink, virus and trojan horse applets can in principle invade many unsuspecting users.

The Java developers have two main solutions to the problem of running untrusted applets in a secure environment:

- Java applets execute in a restricted sandbox environment where malicious code cannot cause any damage to the client browser machine.

- While the sandbox model keeps malicious code out, it can also at times be too restrictive for legitimate code. For this reason, browsers may be more lenient depending on the origins of the applet. Digitally signed applets allow for users to confirm their originators, and thus clients may choose to provide more access to machine resources.

Applets are generally prevented from:

- reading and writing files on the client machine,

- making network connections except to the host from where the applet originated,

- starting other programs on the client; or

- load library code or call native methods.

Javasoft's Web page on applet security[1] breaks down applet capabilities under four categories:

- Netscape Navigator 4.x loading applets over the network (NN), and from the local file system (NL),

- JDK 1.x appletviewer loading applets over the network (AN), and from local file system (AL).

The JDK appletviewer is flexible in that it allows various levels of restriction, and is less restrictive than Netscape Navigator. In addition, these environments distinguish between applets from a local file system, and applets from the network. The former is assumed to be more trustworthy and thus given slightly more privileges.

On the other hand, Java applications are assumed to be written and installed into a machine by trusted parties. No restrictions are placed on Java applications.

13.8.1   File Access

Applets running within Netscape Navigator do not have access to the local file system – they cannot read, write or delete local files. This might seem to be overly restrictive, but it is a workable situation when seen in the context of network computing. Since users' files are stored in server machines, proponents of this paradigm cite many advantages:

- platform independent access to both data and programs

- location independent access

- minimal file maintenance by the user community.

Network applets running from the JDK Appletviewer have access to portions of the local file system as specified in access-control settings in the properties file (`.hotjava/properties` in the home directory). Read and write access to a file or directory is permitted if its name appears in the `acl.read` and `acl.write` list respectively:

---

[1] `http://www.javasoft.com/sfaq/index.html#summary`

```
acl.read=/tmp:/users/freedom
acl.write=/tmp/log:/users/freedom
```

The above `properties`-file entries permit applets to read files in `/tmp` and `/users/freedom` as well as write files in `/tmp/log` and `/users/freedom`.

Finally, local applet code is assumed to be secure. When the JDK Appletviewer loads such code within CLASSPATH directories, applets are given full access to the client machine regardless of `acl.read` or `acl.write` values.

13.8.2 Network Connections

Applets may participate in network connections, but have restrictions imposed so that the malicious code cannot disrupt the local Intranet. We first consider the categories of network operations.

Applets running under Netscape Navigator are prevented from listening for connections via ServerSocket. This prevents a malicious applet from creating a backdoor in order to gain a foothold of the (applet) host (and ultimately, the local Intranet).

Applets are also prevented from accessing a third-party host (i.e. one other than that from which the HTML page or applet code was downloaded from). This restricts the damage which a malicious applet may cause since other network connections are disallowed.

Instead, applets are only given access to the originating host. An applet may, in principle, rely on its originating host for more resources, e.g. files (via further *httpd* requests), file server space or processor time slices as long as such client/server communication has been built into the application.

13.8.3 File Deletion

An applet is prevented from deleting files via the `delete()` method of File objects in the way a stand alone application would. In addition, an applet is generally prevented from relying on other code to perform the deletion since it cannot create processes to run other code or load additional libraries.

The final exception here is local applet code (which is in the CLASSPATH directories) and are assumed to be secure. Since the JDK Appletviewer loads such code via the file system loader, as opposed to the applet loader, an applet in this category may rely on other processes to perform deletion.

13.9 Dynamically Loaded Code

Static analysis of a program (such as in Pascal, C or C++) spread over a set of files will reveal what subroutines or class definitions are required, and whether sufficient code is available for program execution. This is often the case for Java too, but not always true. Java is said to allow for dynamically loaded code.

The successful compilation of each class definition produces a bytecode file whose name is the name of the class with a ".class" suffix. This scheme allows for code to be loaded on a per class basis and as required.

Consider the case with A.class where A.java makes reference to classes B and C. This would also be apparent in A.class, and loading it will also require loading B.class and C.class. D.class would not be loaded if it was not referenced from A, B or C, even if it existed in the same directory. The MyAppletLoader class in Listing 13-13 reflects this situation. Loading MyAppletLoader.class will cause EgApplet.class to be loaded too. (The MyAppletLoader class does not work properly in that it does not have a DocumentBase, and it does not respond to Window events. These have been intentionally left out for the sake of simplicity. The main issue here is dynamically loading class code.)

```
import java.awt.*;
import java.applet.*;

class MyAppletLoader {
    public static void main(String args[]) {
        Frame host = new Frame("Host");
        Applet a = new EgApplet();
        host.add(a);
        host.setSize(450,270) ;
        a.init();
        a.start();
        host.setVisible(true);
    }
}
```

Listing 13-13: Static Applet Loader

However, the MyAppletLoader class does not reflect the case of applet execution adequately. There are currently two common applet environments for applet execution: a Java-enabled Web browser such as Netscape Communicator, or appletviewer which is bundled in the JDK 1.0 or JDK 1.1 distribution from JavaSoft. In this "real" situation, applet class files cannot be determined prior to the start of execution. Based on the attributes in the <APPLET> tag, the appropriate bytecodes are retrieved over the network, and loaded dynamically for continued execution.

An applet loader functions by anticipating code for an Applet object, by loading code over a network and assembling it into an appropriate class representation. After object instantiation, the applet loader must supports the agreed life-cycle framework for applets involving initialization, execution, suspension and destruction through the methods init(), start(), stop() and destroy() respectively. Regardless of the exact class definition, the framework holds since the object is derived from the Applet class. The framework also holds even if the class was not directly derived from the Applet class, or methods have been overriden. This is consistent with object-oriented programming methodology.

The MyAppletLoader2 class in Listing 13-14 is slightly more realistic as now the applet name is not hardwired. It reads the applet name from the command line, just as a Web browser would determine the applet file from the HTML document.

```
import java.awt.*;
import java.applet.*;

class MyAppletLoader2 {
    public static void main(String args[]) throws Exception {
        Frame host = new Frame("Host");
        Applet a;
        Class c = Class.forName(args[0]) ;
        host.add(a = (Applet) c.newInstance());
        host.setSize(450,270) ;
        a.init();
        a.start();
        host.setVisible(true) ;
    }
}
```

Listing 13-14: Local Applet Loader

Class.forName() is a static method which given a class name, attempts to load its code so as to represent it as a Class object. This is subsequently used to create instances via newInstance().

We now consider the situation where code files are not found in the standard CLASSPATH set of directories, but instead must be retrieved over the network. This framework now approaches that of the JDK appletviewer.

We introduce the new class MyNetworkLoader in Listing 13-15 which inherits from the predefined ClassLoader class. The latter is an abstract class with the ability to process Java bytecodes into Class objects, but no ability to read them. As such, the abstract loadClass() method is concretely defined to differentiate between local and non-local classes, read from the network (an appropriate base URL) where necessary, and obtain the resultant Class object from defineClass().

```
import java.awt.*;
import java.applet.*;
import java.io.*;
import java.net.*;

class MyAppletLoader3 {

    public static void main(String args[]) throws Exception {
        Frame host = new Frame("Host");
        Applet a;
        Class c = new MyNetworkLoader(args[0]).loadClass(args[1]);
        host.add(a = (Applet) c.newInstance());
        host.setSize(450,270) ;
        a.init();
        a.start();
        host.setVisible(true) ;
    }

}

class MyNetworkLoader extends ClassLoader {

    URL base;

    public MyNetworkLoader(String b) {
        try { base = new URL(b) ; } catch (Exception e) { }
    }

    public Class loadClass(String name, boolean resolve)
            throws ClassNotFoundException {
        Class c;
        try {
          c = findSystemClass(name);
          System.err.println("Found class "+name);
        } catch (Exception e) {
           try {
             System.err.println("Loading "+name+" from network...");
             URL f = new URL(base, name+".class");
             InputStream is = f.openStream();
             ByteArrayOutputStream b = new ByteArrayOutputStream();
             int x;
             while ((x = is.read()) != -1) b.write(x) ;
             byte data[] = b.toByteArray();
             c = defineClass(name, data, 0, data.length) ;
           } catch (Exception f) { throw new ClassNotFoundException(); }
        }
        if (resolve) resolveClass(c);
        return c;
    }
}
```

Listing 13-15: Network Applet Loader

Using the MyAppletLoader3 class, an applet (say, `Puzzle.class` from the base location `http://dkiong.iscs.nus.edu.sg/java/demo`) may be retrieved from a Web server and executed via the command line:

```
$ java MyAppletLoader3 http://dkiong.iscs.nus.edu.sg/java/demo Puzzle
```

13.10 Summary

Chapter 13 builds upon AWT components in the previous chapter to show how Java applets may be easily implemented and shipped across the network for execution. We discussed:

- the applet framework and its life-cycle

- JDK 1.0 and 1.1 event handling for applets

- converting between Java applications and applets

- animation in applets

- efficient screen updating via the `update()` method

- applet parameters and security

- dynamic loading of Java code using a custom ClassLoader and the `defineClass()` method

13.11 Exercises

1. The example Puzzle game is functional in that it allows users to rearrange tiles so as to achieve the desired ordering on the puzzle board. However, it does not give a clear indication of the state change because the view is updated instantaneously.

    Animate the display of tiles to give the effect of the selected tile moving to its new board.

2. Extend the Media Applet so that 6 images may be displayed at one time. Prepare 6 different audio clips to be played when the mouse button is depressed over the corresponding image. In addition, allow for different messages when the mouse is over each image.

3. The applet in question 2 could be used as a starting point to build an Internet CD kiosk. Extend it such that different sets of 6 images/audio clips may be selected. Remember the use of <PARAM> tags for customizable parameters.

4. Remote applets are prevented from reading and writing local files on the client browser to prevent malicious applets from reading sensitive files or even damaging the file system. However, applets are allowed to make socket connections back to the originating server.

    Design and implement a means whereby an applet may store and retrieve its data from the server via its network resource.

14 Object Serialization and Remote Method Invocation

Almost every application requires some means of keeping data across program runs. Most applications use a file or database for the storage or *persistence* of data. However, databases are not typically used to store objects, particularly Java objects. On the other hand, flat files alone do not cope well with object structure. What is required is some means to preserve the state of a Java object so that it may be easily stored and subsequently restored to its original state.

Object serialization is a facility that enables objects to be "flattened" out so that they can be stored in a file or sent in a stream across a network. This is accomplished by "writing" the object into an ObjectOutputStream instance, which is then used to resurrect the object from the corresponding flattened representation. The serialization classes convert graph (hierarchies) of objects into bytestreams. Serialized objects may be written to a storage device for persistent retention of their state information or shipped across networks for reconstruction on the other side.

The JDK 1.1 provides the Object Serialization mechanism to tackle this once notorious problem of object persistency. Serialization also allows objects to be easily distributed across various Java Virtual Machines (JVM). As such, we will also discuss Remote Method Invocation (RMI) where a program running on one JVM may invoke methods of objects on another JVM. In this scenario, Java RMI uses the Object Serialization API to pass and return objects during remote method invocation. We will examine RMI and what it brings to Java applications, with an emphasis on understanding the key concepts behind RMI. We will also develop simple applications to illustrate these concepts.

14.1 Object Serialization

The design of object serialization allows for most common cases to be handled easily. The following example code in Listing 14-1 shows:

- a `Serialize` class program which accepts a filename argument, and with methods `write()` and `read()` as representative code for serializing operations,

- an ObjectOutputStream being created from an OutputStream instance (in the form of a FileOutputStream object), and writing out via the method `writeObject()`,

- an ObjectInputStream being created from an InputStream instance (in the form of a FileInputStream object), and reading via the method `readObject()`.

```java
import java.util.*;
import java.io.*;

class Serialize {
   String filename;

   public static void main(String[] args) {
      Serialize a = new Serialize(args);
      a.write("This is a Serialization Test");
      System.out.println(a.read());
   }

   public Serialize(String[] args) {
      if (args.length < 1) {
         System.err.println("Usage: Serialize filename");
         System.exit(0);
      } else
         filename = args[0];
   }

   public void write(String str) {
      try {
         FileOutputStream out = new FileOutputStream(filename);
         ObjectOutputStream outobj = new ObjectOutputStream(out);
         outobj.writeObject(str) ;
         outobj.flush(); outobj.close();
      } catch (Exception e) {
         System.err.println("Failure while writing: "+ e.getMessage());
         e.printStackTrace();
      }
   }
```

```
        public String read() {
            try {
                FileInputStream in = new FileInputStream(filename);
                ObjectInputStream inobj = new ObjectInputStream(in);
                String str = (String) inobj.readObject();
                inobj.close();
                return str;
            } catch (Exception e) {
                e.printStackTrace(); return null;
            }
        }
    }
}
```

Listing 14-1: Serialize.java

14.2 Components in Object Serialization

Object serialization applies to objects such as a String, as in the previous example. Typically, a serialized object is a standard Java object, but it must implement the java.io.Serializable interface to be used with object serialization. The Serializable interface does not have any methods, but instead it is merely used to indicate that the object may be serialized. (There are a few reasons why this empty interface is needed, but more about that later.)

The next concern of serialization is an input/output stream. An output stream is used to save data, as with the file output we saw earlier. Object serialization requires an instance of ObjectOutputStream, which is a subclass of FilterOutputStream. Like all such streams, ObjectOutputStream wraps itself around another output stream to use the output functionality.

On the face of things, serialization is trivial. We could save a serialized string to a file like this:

```
FileOutputStream fos = new FileOutputStream("obj.out");
ObjectOutputStream oos = new ObjectOutputStream(fos);
oos.writeObject("Save me!") ;
```

The writeObject() method can be called any number of times to save any number of objects to the output stream. The only restriction is that each object that is passed to the writeObject() method must implement the Serializable interface.

Not surprisingly, reading a serialized object is equally trivial:

```
FileInputStream fis = new FileInputStream("obj.out");
ObjectInputStream ois = new ObjectInputStream(fis);
Object o = ois.readObject();
```

Once again, the readObject() method may be called unlimitedly to read any number of objects from the input stream. The potential pitfall when reading a stream of serialized data, is knowing what data is expected in the stream. Nothing in the stream identifies the types of objects that are there.

We could use the instanceof operator to determine the class of the object that the readObject() method returned, but that technique is useful only for verification. If we were expecting a String object, it could confirm a String object, but if another type of object was read, there would be no easy way to tell what type of object we actually received. Hence, programs that serialize data streams must be kept in sync with the corresponding programs which de-serialize data, so that the latter may know what type of data to expect.

14.3 Custom Serialization

Since almost all classes in the Java API implement the Serializable interface, why should an empty interface be needed? One reason is due to the way in which these objects are de-serialized from an object stream. De-serialization requires that an object be created, which was created in a special way. Rather than creating the object by calling its constructor, object de-serialization creates the object directly on the heap and then begins to assign the saved values in the stream to the instance variables of the newly-created object.

The JVM will only construct serializable objects in this manner. An interesting case arises when a serializable class extends a non-serializable class. In this case, the JVM will first construct the non-serializable object like any other object, i.e., it creates the non-serializable object by calling its constructor, which must not require any arguments. Hence, a serializable class can only extend a non-serializable class when the latter has a default constructor.

The important benefit of distinguishing serializable objects (from an administrative perspective, the important feature of the Serializable interface) has to do with the security of serialized objects.

Consider the situation with sensitive information, as in the following CreditCard class:

```
public class CreditCard implements Serializable {
   private String acctNo;
   ...
}
```

If this object was serialized into a file, the written data will include the account number too. Although there is other data in the file, the account number string will be readable to anyone with access to the file.

This happens because object serialization has access to all instance variables within a serializable class, which includes private instance variables. The instance variables will be sent in the I/O stream with the rest of the object. Anyone who reads the file where the object is saved will be able to see the private data. Similarly, anyone who is snooping the network, when a serialized object is sent over a SocketOutputStream, will also see the private data.

In a way, then, implementing the Serializable interface can be thought of as a flag to the JVM that says, "Hey JVM, I have thought about the security issues of my object, and it's OK with me if you write the private state of the object out to a data store." This raises the issue of security that requires special consideration, particularly when using sockets. A serialized object traveling across the Internet is subject to the same privacy violations as Email or any other unencrypted communication. It may be read by unintended parties, or it may be tampered with while in transit.

There are two ways to have the best of both worlds whereby the object may still be serialized, but without exposing any sensitive data. The first of these is to mark any sensitive data fields as transient, as in:

```
private transient String acctNo;
```

When it is time for the JVM to serialize an object, it will skip any fields in the object that are marked as transient (including any public or protected fields). In other words, the transient keyword prevents selected fields from being written to a stream.

When an object is read in from a stream, transient data fields are set to their default values, such as 0 for integers, and null for objects such as Strings. The programmer can restore transient data by implementing a readObject() method.

In general, sensitive data in serializable objects, such as file descriptors, or other handles to system resources, should be made both private and transient. This prevents the data from being written when the object is serialized. Furthermore, when the object is read back from a stream, only the originating class can assign a value to the private data field. A validation callback can also be used to check the integrity of a group of objects when they are read from a stream.

On the other hand, if transient data must be serialized together with the rest of the object, this may be achieved by overriding the writeObject() and readObject() methods. These methods provide control over what data is sent (or read) from the data store, and how that data looks while it is in transit. For example, we might redefine our previous CreditCard class as follows:

```
public class CreditCard implements Serializable {
    private transient String AcctNo;
    private int exprYear;

    ...

    public void writeObject(ObjectOutputStream oos) throws IOException {
        oos.defaultWriteObject();
        String s = modify(acctNo);
        oos.writeObject(s);
    }

    public void readObject(ObjectInputStream ois)
                        throws IOException, ClassNotFoundException {
        ois.defaultReadObject();
        String s = (String) ois.readObject();
        acctNo = unModify(s);
    }
}
```

Assuming that we have appropriate implementations of the modify() and unModify() methods, then this technique allows us to save the entire object including potentially sensitive data in a secure way. The defaultWriteObject() method is responsible for writing any non-transient fields (such as exprYear) to the output stream to be subsequently read by the defaultReadObject() method.

The modify() and unModify() methods might work by encrypting the string, or adding a few characters to confuse snoopers. As long as the symmetric operation is available when it is read in, we can take whatever necessary steps to protect such data.

14.3.1 The Externalizable Interface

With the Externalizable interface, the programmer takes full responsibility for reading and writing the object from a stream, including subclass and superclass data. This allows for complete flexibility, such as when a data format has already been defined, or the programmer has a specific format in mind. It also requires more programming, which is beyond the scope of this chapter, but might be an interesting topic for a future book.

14.4 Distributed Computing with Java

So far, we have merely worked with objects represented by one Java Virtual Machine (JVM). In distributed object computing, an object reference may be created locally and bound to a (remote) server object. The local program can then invoke methods on the local reference as if it was a regular local object. The distributed object infrastructure (generally referred to as an Object Request Broker, or ORB) transparently intercepts these method invocations and transmits the method request with its arguments to the server object (via a process known as marshalling), where the work is performed. The return values are then transmitted back to the local invocation.

The ability to pass information from one computer to another is the core of distributed computing. It allows multiple machines (presumably connected by a network) to work cooperatively on a single problem. Java can be treated like any other language in a distributed system where standard connection mechanisms includes Remote Procedure Call systems (Distributed Computing Environment or Open Network Computing) or object request brokers CORBA (Common Object Request Broker Architecture).

In the Java distributed object model, a remote object is one whose methods can be invoked from another Java Virtual Machine, potentially on a different host. An object of this type is described by one or more remote interfaces, which are Java interfaces that declare the methods available on the remote object.

Distributed object computing offers many advantages over traditional approaches such as remote procedure calls (RPC) or socket-based client/server communication:

- The programmer is shielded from the complexity of the underlying communication mechanism. The developer interacts with a remote object via familiar method invocations, just as if the object was local.

- Distributed objects inherit the distinction between interface and implementation imposed by object-oriented programming. By separating the two, developers can work in parallel without concerning themselves about the implementation details of another developer's objects.

The elegance of Java lends itself well to the distributed object paradigm. The Java model boasts all of the object-oriented features necessary to build robust and highly maintainable object-oriented applications. With its rich and continually improving library of network classes, Java is also a network-centric language, as demonstrated by the applet concept. These features beg for an elegant implementation of distributed Java objects. Not surprisingly, several efforts are already underway to add distributed extensions to the Java language.

14.4.1 RMI and CORBA

The Remote Method Invocation (RMI) standard in Java provides a distributed object model that crosses Java Virtual Machines seamlessly. Although RMI is an ORB in the generic sense that it supports making method invocations on remote objects, it is not a CORBA-compliant ORB. RMI is native to Java. It is, in essence, an extension of the core language. RMI depends on many of the other features of Java object serialization. Thus, the inclusion of RMI as a standard part of the JDK 1.1 has caused much controversy, being a direct competitor of the CORBA standard for distributed objects.

One of the major differences between CORBA and RMI is that RMI allows objects to be passed by value. There are of course other differences, from the low-level protocol that each uses (CORBA uses a protocol called IIOP, and RMI uses its own protocol) to the programming interface that each provides (CORBA is programmed via IDL, and RMI is programmed using a normal Java interface).

Over time, many of the differences between the two distributed object systems will disappear, including the most important difference, the different protocols that each uses. This will allow CORBA and RMI to call each other and to coexist to a much greater degree than they do now. However the future directions and unification of CORBA and RMI will not be discussed in this chapter.

Along with Java Database Connectivity (JDBC) and the Java Interface Definition Language (Java IDL) , RMI forms part of the so-called Java Enterprise API. Although it does not address all the issues of deploying objects in a heterogeneous environment, it provides the facilities needed by a wide range of distributed Java applications in a "Java world".

By compromising on some generality, RMI has been assigned to retain the semantics of the Java object model and provide close integration with the rest of the Java system. It allows objects in one JVM to call methods of objects residing in other JVMs, with very little change in either the local or remote code. The main difference from the user's perspective is the need to handle the additional exceptions that may be generated by a remote object, mostly related to issues of communication.

Enterprise Java addresses how network-centric computing is changing the way applications are developed and deployed. It is a huge initiative and consists of a number of Java APIs. RMI addresses the incorporation of the network into a programming language, a key issue in network computing.

14.4.2 Java Limitations

In a distributed application, it is the designer's responsibility to select the protocol used to move data between client and server. Sometimes a well-known and supported protocol may be available, such as FTP for transferring files. More often, with a custom database application, for example, no such protocol exists. It is necessary to both design and build an application-specific protocol to connect to both parts of the system.

In this situation, Java itself offers no advantage over other languages. If performance bottlenecks are discovered when the system is deployed, functionality will have to migrate to rectify the problem. The protocol between client and server might require change, and so must the code which implement the protocol. In fact, code has to change for each different arrangement, making empirical tuning an expensive business. In other words, Java lacks support for location transparency.

14.5 An Overview of Java RMI

Until the release of the RMI API, sockets were the only facility built into Java that provides direct communication between machines. RMI is quite alike RPC (Remote Procedure Call) which is intended for usage in procedural languages such as C. It allows programs to call procedures over a network as if the code was stored and executed locally. Think of RMI as the object equivalent of RPC. Instead of calling a procedure over a network as if it was local, RMI invokes an object's methods. In short, RMI abstracts the socket connectivity and data streaming involved with passing information between the hosts, so that method invocation to remote objects are made no differently than method invocation to local objects.

It is common practice for an object to invoke methods of other objects. This "local" method invocation forms the basis of object interaction in a program. For example, when a button object is clicked, it triggers a message that causes your program to invoke a method in a graphics object that causes it to calculate a 3D-rendered image.

RMI allows us to leverage on the processing power of another computer. This is called *distributed computing*. Clicking the button could cause the program to invoke a method in a graphics object on the server computer. The server then calculates the values needed to render the 3D object locally, and returns those values to the client program.

RMI attempts to make communication over the network as transparent as possible for the programmer. It may be used to inter-link a number of objects that are distributed throughout a network and physically residing on different machines. RMI brings the distributed objects under a virtual umbrella. From the application's point of view, a remote method and a local method are invoked in the same manner following the same semantics. RMI takes care of the details at the lower implementation level.

The end result is that programs enjoy advantages similar to those of client/server database programming without the complexity overhead. With RMI, a client program may invoke methods on the server object as if it was local. The method is then invoked and executed on the server machine (as required), but via a local syntax in the client program. This greatly simplifies the design of the application while leveraging on the processing power of possibly many computers.

14.6   Using Java RMI

The RMI API is a set of classes and interfaces designed to enable the developer to make calls to remote objects that exist in the runtime of a different JVM invocation. This "remote" or "server" JVM may be executing on the same machine or on an entirely different machine from the RMI "client".

14.6.1   Setting up the Environment on your Local Machine

The existing JDK environment may be enhanced to allow RMI via the following steps.

- Get and install the RMI classes according to the directions provided. Make sure you set your CLASSPATH environment variable to include the lib/rmi.zip file in the RMI directory.

- Download and unzip the example files provided. Install these files into a directory and add it to CLASSPATH. Use the appletviewer or the Java Virtual Machine to run the supplied applets.

14.6.2   How RMI works

Writing an RMI application is not inherently complex, but it has to be done in the correct order. The following are the steps to create an RMI application:

- Create an interface

- Create a class that implements the interface

- Create a server that creates an instance of this class

- Create a client that connects to the server object using `Naming.lookup()`

- Compile these classes

- Run the RMI interface compiler (`rmic`) on the .class file of the implementation class to create the stubs. The stub classes provide the actual implementation for the underlying RMI functionality.

- Start the RMI registry (`rmiregistry`)

- Start the server class

- Run the client program

Creating the interface is perhaps the most important portion of the design of a RMI-driven multi-tiered client/server application. It defines the functionality the server will provide to the clients. Since the Java language does not allow multiple inheritance, the interface mechanism is used to allow classes to exhibit multiple types of behavior. An interface contains method declarations, but cannot contain method implementations.

RMI interfaces must extend the java.rmi.Remote interface, and every method declared in the interface must be declared as throwing a java.rmi.RemoteException (a generic exception that is reported when an unexpected network problem occurs). This is because a lot of work goes on behind the scenes to allow remote objects to be used in a seamless manner and any number of problems could occur. For instance, the server could shutdown unexpectedly, or a network cable could be cut.

Each time a method is called, the parameters to that method must be serialized and sent back. The reverse occurs with results from methods. (More information on the topic of argument passing in RMI is available in the JDK 1.1 documentation.)

14.6.3 An RMI Example

Let us now consider a simple example. Say we have two objects: a client and a server. We want the client object to invoke a method on the server object. Since the two objects reside on different machines, we need a mechanism to establish a relationship between the two.

RMI uses a network-based registry to keep track of the distributed objects. The server object makes a method available for remote invocation by binding it to a name in the registry. The client object, in turn, can check for availability of an object by looking up its name in the registry. The registry acts as a limited central management point for RMI and functions as a simple name repository. It does not address the problem of actually invoking the remote method.

Recall that the two objects physically reside on different machines. A mechanism is needed to transmit the client's request to invoke a method on the server object to the server object and provide a response. RMI uses an approach similar to RPC in this regard. The code for the server object must be processed by an RMI compiler called rmic, which is part of the JDK. This is depicted in Figure 14-1.

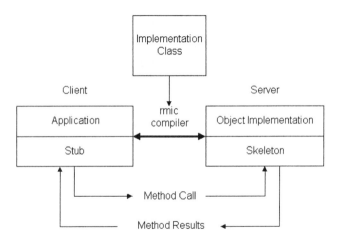

Figure 14-1: Java Remote Method Invocation

The rmic compiler generates two files: a stub which resides on the client machine and a skeleton which resides on the server machine. Both comprise Java code that provides the necessary link between the two objects.

When a client invokes a server method, the JVM looks at the stub to do type checking (since the class defined within the stub is an image of the server class). The request is then routed to the skeleton on the server, which in turn calls the appropriate method on the server object. In other words, the stub acts as a proxy to the skeleton, while the skeleton is a proxy to the actual remote method.

14.7 RMI System Architecture

The RMI system in Figure 14-2 is built in three layers: the stub/skeleton layer, the remote reference layer and the transport layer. These layers are built using specific interfaces and defined by specific protocols in order to make the layers independent of each other. This was done intentionally to make the system flexible and allowing modification of the implementation of any given layer without affecting the other layers. For example, the TCP-based transport could be modified to use a different transport protocol. As mentioned earlier, RMI uses stubs and skeletons to act as surrogate placeholders (proxies) for remote objects. The transport of objects between address spaces is accomplished through the use of object serialization, which converts object graphs to bytestreams for transport.

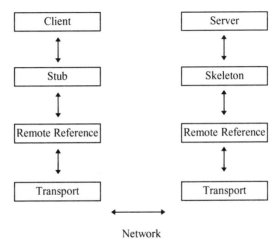

Figure 14-2: Java RMI Architecture

The Stub/Skeleton layer is the interface between the Application layer and the rest of the RMI system. This layer does not deal with any of the specifics of any transport, but transmit data to the Remote Reference Layer (RRL) .

A client invoking a method on a remote server object actually makes use of a stub or proxy for the remote object as a conduit to the remote object. A skeleton for a remote object is a server-side entity that dispatches calls to the actual remote object implementation.

Stubs interact with the client-side RRL in the following ways:

* The stub receives the remote method invocation and initiates a call to the remote object.

- The RRL returns a special type of I/O stream, called a marshal stream, which is used to communicate with the server's RRL.

- The stub makes the remote method call, passing any arguments to the stream.

- The RRL passes the method's return value to the stub.

- The stub acknowledges to the RRL that the method call is complete.

Skeletons interact with the server-side RRL in the following ways:

- The skeleton unmarshals (receives and interprets) any arguments from the I/O stream, established by the RRL.

- The skeleton makes the up-call to the actual remote object implementation.

- The skeleton marshals the return value of the call (or an exception, if one occurred) onto the I/O stream.

The Remote Reference Layer (RRL) is responsible for carrying out the semantics of the method invocation. It manages communication between the stubs/skeletons and the lower-level transport interface using a specific remote reference protocol which is independent of the client stubs and skeletons. The RRL's responsibilities include managing references to remote objects and reconnection strategies if an object should become unavailable.

The RRL has two cooperating components: the client-side and the server-side. The client-side component contains information specific to the remote server, and communicates via the transport layer to the server-side component. The server-side component implements the specific remote reference semantics prior to delivering a remote method invocation to the skeleton.

The reference semantics for the server are also handled by the RRL. It abstracts the different ways of referring to objects that are implemented on servers – those that are always running on some machines, and those that are run only when some method invocation is made on them (activation). These differences are not obvious at the layers above the RRL.

The Transport Layer is a low-level communication layer that provides the actual shipment of marshal streams between different address spaces or virtual machines. It is responsible for setting up and managing connections, listening for incoming calls, passing data to and from the remote reference layer. It also maintains a table of remote objects residing in particular address spaces.

The Transport Layer performs the following tasks:

- Receives a request from the client-side Remote Reference Layer.

- Locates the RMI server for the remote object requested.

- Establishes a socket connection to the server.

- Passes that connection back to the client-side Remote Reference Layer.

- Adds this remote object to a table of remote objects that it knows how to communicate with.

- Monitors connection "liveness".

At the Transport Layer, remote objects are represented by object identifiers and endpoints. An object identifier is used to look up which objects should be the targets of remote calls. Endpoints represent particular address spaces or virtual machines. The transport layer creates channels between endpoints by establishing connections and physically transferring data through input/output.

The RMI system uses a TCP-based transport, but the transport layer supports multiple transports per address space, so it is also capable of supporting UDP-based transport or even TCP and UDP.

14.8 Under the Hood

We have covered enough theory so that we can examine a simple application that uses RMI. Listing 14-2 shows a client application that invokes the doSomething() method of a remote object (of type Server1).

Firstly, all RMI-based applications will need to import java.rmi and java.rmi.server packages. The static void main() method sets the Java security manager and it is the job of the security manager to grant or deny permissions on the operations performed by the application (such as reading and writing a file). If the security manager is not set, RMI will only load classes from local system files as defined by CLASSPATH.

We then create a try/catch block that performs the remote method invocation. Recall that a registry acts as the repository of names for objects whose methods can be invoked remotely. The server object, in our case, has registered itself using the name "ServerObject". The client application must do a lookup in the registry using that name.

```
import java.rmi.*;
import java.rmi.server.*;

public class Client1 {
    public static void main(String[] args) {
        System.setSecurityManager(new RMISecurityManager());
        try {
            Server1 ro = (Server1) Naming.lookup("doSomething") ;
            System.out.println("Location:"+System.getProperty("LOCATION"));
            ro.doSomething();
        } catch (Exception e) {
            e.printStackTrace();
            System.exit(-1);
        }
    }
}
```

Listing 14-2: Client1.java

The returned object from the lookup operation is then assigned to the object ro which is of type Server1. The client can then use this object and invoke its methods as if it was a local object. In particular, the client application invokes the doSomething() method of the object ro, which in turn invokes the method with the same name on the Server1 object.

Server1, which is used in the client application to declare the remote object type, is actually an interface. In fact, all remote objects are referenced through interfaces. Listing 14-3 shows the Server1 interface. However, two points must be made about the Server1 interface:

• Like all RMI interfaces, it extends the Remote interface.

• The method doSomething() throws a RemoteException exception which all remote operations must be able to handle.

```
import java.rmi.*;
public interface Server1 extends Remote {
    public void doSomething() throws RemoteException;
}
```

Listing 14-3: Server1.java

We now have a client and a server application. The last piece is a class which implements the Server1 interface shown above. Such a class is shown in Listing 14-4, which forms the heart of the application.

```java
import java.rmi.*;
import java.rmi.server.*;
import java.rmi.registry.*;

public class Server1Impl extends java.rmi.server.UnicastRemoteObject
                         implements Server1 {
   public static void main(String[] args) {
      System.setSecurityManager(new RMISecurityManager());
      try {
         Server1Impl obj = new Server1Impl();
         Naming.rebind("doSomething", obj) ;
         System.out.println("doSomething bound in registry");
      } catch (Exception e) {
         e.printStackTrace();
         return;
      }
   }

   public Server1Impl() throws RemoteException {}

   public void doSomething() throws RemoteException {
      System.out.println("This is printed by the Server1 object");
      System.out.println("Location: "+System.getProperty("LOCATION"));
   }
}
```

Listing 14-4: Server1Impl.java

The Server1Impl class extends the UnicastRemoteObject class. This class defines a non-replicated remote object whose references are valid only while the server process is alive. It supports point-to-point active object references via TCP streams. Once again, the first thing the main method does is to set the security manager. It then instantiates an object of type Server1Impl. This object is registered in the registry using the name doSomething.

We could have used the bind() method instead of rebind(). The difference is that rebind() will replace the name in the registry if it already exists. Method doSomething() of obj is now available for remote invocation.

Next, the constructor for the Server1Impl is defined. A remote implementation class must have a zero-argument constructor. In addition, the constructor method must throw RemoteException.

Finally, the doSomething() method is defined. Note that since it is a remote method, it throws RemoteException. In our case, the remote method does not really do anything useful. It merely prints a couple of lines to the console. In a more meaningful application, the remote method may perform a query on a database, or read and process data from a file.

14.9 RMI Deployment

Our simple RMI application consist of a client, a server and an implementation of the server interface. We still need two more pieces: the stub and the skeleton. To generate these two, we use the rmic compiler which comes with the JDK. You can generate them by the following command:

```
$ rmic rmi1.Server1Impl
```

This will create the two files: ServerImpl_Stub.class and ServerImpl_Skel.class. Should you want to see the Java source code for these files, use the -keepgenerated option.

One may wonder why rmic is used with the implementation of the server and not the server itself. The answer is that the method to be invoked remotely is defined in the ServerImpl class, and the purpose of rmic is to generate stubs and skeletons for the remote methods.

We now have all the necessary pieces for our application. The following three commands may be executed in separate windows in the order shown:

```
$ rmiregistry &
$ java -DLOCATION=server rmi1.Server1Impl
$ java -DLOCATION=client rmi1.Client1
```

The first command is not going to generate any output. It basically starts the registry in the background.

The second command starts the server, which registers the remote object with the registry. We use the -D option to set a system parameter LOCATION which is used to indicate that the code belongs to the server.

The last command starts the client. Again, we use the -D option to set the value of the system parameter LOCATION to client. Whenever the client starts, a message will be printed on the server window, since the remote method doSomething() simply prints a couple of lines.

The client may be started several times, and the messages would be correspondingly printed. This shows that the client application has started successfully and invoked the method on the server application using RMI.

The above three commands may be executed on three different machines, with the same results. Remember to distribute the skeleton and stub class files appropriately.

The stub goes with the client application while the skeleton goes with the server application.

With very little coding effort, we have created a prototype for a potentially valuable and marketable service that could be deployed on the Internet today. As distributed object computing becomes more viable with time, we should see the rise of a rich library of distributed objects available on the Internet. Entire class libraries could be deployed on the Internet as distributed objects, enabling Java programmers around the world to use them in their own applets and applications.

14.10 Summary

This chapter has introduced Java solutions to key technologies: object serialization for object persistence and distributed objects for effortless client/server communication.

- Object serialization allows objects to be flattened and represented in a bytestream, for subsequent reconstruction to its original state.

- Java RMI provides a framework for communication between Java programs running in different virtual machines.

- Using object serialization, Java RMI allows for parameters in the form of object graphs to be converted into bytestreams for transport across the network and reconstruction on the other side.

The RMI system is unique in that it preserves the full Java object model throughout the distribution, allowing true polymorphism of both remote and local objects. The syntax of a remote method call is exactly the same as the syntax of a local remote call, making distributed programming easy and natural. Any Java object can be passed during remote method calls, including local objects, remote objects and primitive types.

14.11 Exercises

1. Implement an ordered binary tree so that it will accept a list of words. Serialize the tree, and then retrieve it in another program to confirm that the resultant tree structure is unchanged.

2. Using RMI, implement a service to accept a filename and retrieves the contents of the remote file.

15 Java Database Connectivity

It was only a while ago when most Web sites were delivering simple Web pages that amounted to nothing more than fancy billboards. Many organizations that were publishing on the Web have now moved onto more complex features, including Java-based content and navigation tools, document repositories featuring keyword search-engines and online ordering systems. They have also found the need to put relational database management systems behind their Web sites, and have sought flexible, affordable and extensible tools to accomplish this need.

Similarly, organizations which have typically met their internal development needs with front-end tools such as PowerBuilder, FoxPro and Microsoft Access, or other database systems are now looking towards Web-based solutions. In doing so, they build their proverbial Intranet systems.

Java is a big favorite among the user groups mentioned above. It is being integrated into more products and operating systems each day and not just Web browsers. Furthermore, Web servers such as Netscape Enterprise Server integrate Java on the server side. JigSaw[1] is the World Wide Web Consortium's sample implementation of an HTTP/1.1 complaint Web server written in Java. The use of Java allows the server to be dynamically extensible. In addition to the CGI interface (which carries the overhead of process creation), server functionality may be extended by writing new resource objects. This is a cost-effective replacement for CGI processing.

---

[1] Information about Jigsaw is available at the URL http://www.w3.org/Jigsaw/.

Today, many think of Java as a language for building applets that are downloaded and executed within browsers. However, the database API has been designed for larger and more sophisticated applications, but is less known. Java Database Connectivity (JDBC)[2] provides for unified database access in Java such as applets. Apart from distinguishing between trusted and untrusted applets,[3] communications between databases and Java applets also face an unknown latency as requests are routed across an ever-changing network topology to a server that may be in the next room or on the next continent.

JDBC presumes that Java will be used in other application scenarios. As such, the API is designed to manage data access where code is trusted and is permitted to access local or network resources (beyond a specific URL) to read and write files and open network connections. To succeed as a language and as an interface, Java and JDBC must provide a solution to developers of mission-critical database applications. In a typical intranet scenario, developers may use Java to build multiple applications on which access to a single database is both common and essential.

JDBC is also designed to provide a natural implementation platform for N-tier client/server environments. In this scenario, a Java application may make calls to a middleware layer of services, which in turn would access databases. These calls may be made through mechanisms such as a remote procedure call (RPC), an object request broker, or dare we say, OLE. Multi-tier database implementations provide an additional layer of security, performance and management for database administrators by providing mediated access to specific databases where caching or local business rules may be implemented as needed.

15.1 JDBC Demystified

Approximately half of all software development can fall into client/server model and architecture. A great promise of Java has been the ability to build platform independent client/server database applications. Java Database Connectivity in JDK 1.1 makes it possible. Although there is a "standard" database language, Structured Query Language (SQL-92), feature wars have often made it necessary to write vendor-specific code. As JDBC is designed to be platform independent, one need not worry about which database is in use. However, it is still possible to make vendor-specific calls.

---

[2] As a point of interest, JDBC is a trademarked name and not an acronym. JDBC is often thought of as an abbreviation for "Java Database Connectivity".

[3] Untrusted applets are typical in an Internet scenario in which information is transferred across insecure boundaries. Untrusted applets face a particular set of challenges in that they must execute in the restricted "sandbox" of the Java Virtual Machine (JVM). Here, there is no access to the local client's systems resources.

JDBC is a Java API for executing SQL statements. It is designed to insulate a database application developer from a specific database vendor, and consists of a set of classes and interfaces written in the Java programming language. This enables tool/database developers to write database applications using a pure Java API. JDBC enables the developer to concentrate on writing the application, making sure that queries to the database are correct and that the data is manipulated as designed.

Like many other Java APIs, JDBC is designed for simplicity. Method calls correspond to logical database operations, such as connecting to the database, creating a statement and executing the query, and ultimately viewing the result set.

Extracting information from a database and writing it back is done in a language called SQL. SQL has been refined over more than two decades and is the language used to access essentially all modern databases.

With JDBC, it is easy to send SQL statements to virtually any relational database. In other words, with the JDBC API, it is unnecessary to write one program especially to access different database management systems, e.g. Sybase, Oracle, Informix, etc. A single program using the JDBC API suffices and the program will be able to send SQL statements to the appropriate database.

As such, JDBC extends the scope of Java deployment. For example, with Java and the JDBC API, it is possible to publish a Web page containing an applet that uses information obtained from a remote database. Or, an enterprise can use JDBC to connect all its employees (even if they are using a conglomeration of PC, Macintosh, and UNIX machines) to one or more internal databases via its intranet. With more and more programmers using the Java programming language, the need for easy database access from Java continues to grow.

The combination of Java and JDBC makes disseminating information easy and economical. Businesses can continue to use their installed databases and access information easily even if it is stored on different database management systems. Development time for new applications is also shortened, with installation and version control made simplified. A programmer can write an application or an update once, put it on the server, and everybody has access to the latest version. For businesses selling information services, Java and JDBC offer a better way of providing information updates to external customers.

15.2 JDBC and Enterprise Computing

Java has a bright future in enterprise computing. Large enterprises stand or fall by the quality of their corporate databases. MIS departments fell in love with Web browsers because the HTML forms and CGI processing have made it so easy to develop and deploy applications involving database access, compared with traditional client/server techniques. Now Java makes it possible to write even more flexible and more efficient programs by using this same approach. As such, providing database hooks for Java was obvious, precisely because developers saw the value of Web tools in database applications before they saw the light about Java.

The very first library that SUN provided after the Java Development Kit was the JDBC library. SUN designed the JDBC to allow access to any ANSI SQL-92 standard database.

A good understanding of database terms and techniques (like SQL) is essential to fully appreciate this chapter. We will sketch out some of these, but the topic really requires a complete book of its own instead of a chapter.

15.3 What does JDBC do?

Briefly, JDBC is the Java API which facilitates the following three aspects of database processing:

- establish a connection with a database;

- send SQL statements; and

- process the results.

The following code fragment gives a basic example of these three steps :

```
Connection con = DriverManager.getConnection
                    ("jdbc:odbc:wombat", "login", "password") ;
Statement stmt = con.createStatement();
ResultSet rs = stmt.executeQuery("SELECT a, b, c FROM Table1");
while (rs.next()) {
    int x = rs.getInt("a") ;
    String s = rs.getString("b") ;
    float f = rs.getFloat("c") ;
}
```

JDBC code is relatively simple to understand. The confusing part is making it work on a particular system with the appropriate JDBC driver loaded properly and working with a database using a vendor DBMS.

15.4   JDBC is a Low-level API and a Base for Higher-level APIs

JDBC is a "low-level" interface, which means that it is used to invoke (or "call'") SQL commands directly. It works very well in this capacity and is easier to use than other database connectivity APIs. However, JDBC was also designed to be a base upon which higher-level interfaces and tools were built. A higher-level interface is more "user-friendly" and uses a more comprehensible and convenient API to be subsequently translated behind the scenes into a low-level interface such as JDBC. At the time of writing, two kinds of higher-level APIs are under development above JDBC:

- embedded SQL for Java:

  At least one vendor plans to build an embedded SQL for Java. As a database system implements SQL and JDBC requires that the SQL statements be passed as strings to Java methods, an embedded SQL preprocessor allows a programmer to instead mix SQL statements directly with Java. For example, a Java variable can be used in an SQL statement to receive or provide SQL values. The embedded SQL preprocessor then translates this Java/SQL mix into Java with JDBC calls.

- direct mapping of relational database tables to Java classes:

  JavaSoft and others have announced plans to implement a direct mapping of relational database tables to Java classes. In this "object/relational'" mapping, each row of the table becomes an instance of that class, and each column value corresponds to an attribute of that instance. Programmers can then operate directly on Java objects. The required SQL calls to fetch and store data are automatically generated "beneath the covers". More sophisticated mappings are also provided, for example, where rows of multiple tables are combined in a Java class.

JDBC is deliberately a "low-level" API that is intended for application builder tools and as a base for higher-level APIs. It is based on the X/Open SQL CLI (Call Level Interface) standard and Microsoft's ODBC (Open DataBase Connectivity) standard. Choosing ODBC was a pragmatic choice since it is a widely accepted and implemented standard for SQL database access. Virtually all databases support ODBC, and it has recently been extended beyond Microsoft platforms to be supported on most Unix platforms as well.

As interest in JDBC has grown, more developers have been working on JDBC-based tools to make building programs easier. Programmers have also been writing applications that make database access easier for the end-user. For example, an application might present a menu of database tasks from which to choose. After a task is selected, the application presents prompts and blanks for filling in information needed to carry out the selected task. With the requested input typed in, the application then automatically invokes the necessary SQL commands. With the help of such an application, users can perform database tasks even when they have little or no knowledge of SQL syntax.

15.5   JDBC-ODBC Bridge

With the release of JDBC, developers can now tie their Java programs into a database management system. Unfortunately, JDBC has produced a lot of confusion about what it is and is not. Shortly after JDBC was introduced, JavaSoft and InterSolv released a reference implementation of a JDBC-to-ODBC bridge. This allows people to implement Java applications which access data in the ODBC data sources. However, the ODBC driver manager and data sources must be installed on the machine running the Java application.

This may be a suitable situation for deploying applications on a single platform. Since the Java classes for ODBC bridging are implemented in native code and can only be run on Solaris or Win32, it is not supplied for any other platform. Another potential drawback associated with ODBC connectivity is that for typical sites, the only ODBC data sources available are products such as FoxPro, dBase or Access. These products are not really ideal for high-volume ODBC access because they are implemented as single-tier drivers. The ODBC driver manipulates the data directly rather than making requests to a server-side engine, which is typical of a multi-tier environment. A single-tier refers to the direct connection between the driver and the physical data; while multi-tier refers to the ODBC driver's tier and at least one other tier being the data server's connection to the physical layer. The bottom line is this: if you can use a database server for managing your data, you are better off, and if you can use a driver other than the JDBC-ODBC bridge, you are better off.

Until recently, getting a database server, especially on Win32, has been an expensive proposition. Products such as Oracle and Sybase are quite expensive and often require a full-time administrator. Currently, there are no JDBC drivers that talk directly to these data servers without some sort of native code layer, since the APIs for communicating with these servers have not been implemented in 100% Java code.

15.6   JDBC versus ODBC and other APIs

At this point, Microsoft's ODBC (Open DataBase Connectivity) API is probably the most widely-used programming interface for accessing relational databases. It offers the ability to connect to almost all databases on almost all platforms. So why not just use ODBC from Java?

While ODBC is usable from Java, this is best done via JDBC in the form of the JDBC-ODBC Bridge, which will be covered shortly. The following are reasons for using JDBC:

- ODBC is not appropriate for direct use from Java because it uses a C interface. Calls from Java to native C code have a number of drawbacks in the security, implementation, robustness and implied portability issues of applications.

- A literal translation of the ODBC C API into a Java API would not be desirable. For example, while Java has no explicit pointers, ODBC makes copious use of them, including the notoriously error-prone generic pointer void *. JDBC may be thought of as ODBC translated into an object-oriented interface which is more natural for Java programmers.

- ODBC has a fairly steep learning curve. It mixes simple and advanced features together, and it has complex options even for simple queries. JDBC, on the other hand, was designed to keep simple things simple while allowing more advanced capabilities where required.

- A Java API like JDBC is needed in order to enable a "pure Java'" solution. When ODBC is used, the ODBC driver manager and drivers must be manually installed on every client machine. When the JDBC driver is written completely in Java, however, JDBC code is automatically installable, portable and secure on all Java platforms from network computers to mainframes.

In summary, the JDBC API is a natural Java interface to the basic SQL abstractions and concepts. Rather than start from scratch, it builds on ODBC so programmers already familiar with ODBC will find it very easy to learn JDBC. JDBC retains the basic design features of ODBC. In fact, both interfaces are based on the X/Open SQL CLI (Call Level Interface) . The significant difference is that JDBC builds on and reinforces the style and virtues of Java and is easy to use.

Recently, Microsoft introduced new APIs beyond ODBC: RDO, ADO, DAO, and OLE DB. These designs move in the same direction as JDBC in many ways. For example, the object-oriented interfaces to databases is based on classes that can be implemented on ODBC. However, whether the functionality in any of these interfaces is sufficiently compelling to make them alternatives to ODBC remains to be seen, especially with the ODBC driver market well-established.

15.7 Two-tier and Three-tier Models

The JDBC API supports two-tier and three-tier models for database access. In the two-tier model, a Java applet or application talks directly to the database. This requires a JDBC driver that can communicate with the particular database management system being accessed. SQL statements are delivered to the database, and the results are sent back to the user. The database may be located on another machine which is distinct from the user's machine on the network. This is referred to as a client/server configuration, with the user's machine acting as the client and housing the database as the server. The network can be an intranet, which, for example, connects employees within a corporation, or it can be the Internet.

In the three-tier model, commands are sent to a "middle-tier" of services, which then sends SQL statements to the database. The database processes the SQL statements and returns the results back to the middle-tier, which then returns them to the user. MIS directors find the three-tier model very attractive because the middle-tier makes it possible to maintain control over access and the kinds of updates that can be made to corporate data. Another advantage is that when there is a middle-tier, the user can employ an easy-to-use higher-level API which is translated by the middle-tier into the appropriate low-level calls. Finally, in most cases, the three-tier architecture can provide performance advantages.

Until now, the middle-tier has been written in languages such as C or C++, which offer fast performance. However, with the introduction of optimizing compilers that translate Java bytecode into efficient machine-specific code, it is becoming practical to implement the middle-tier in Java. This option to take advantage of Java's robustness, multi-threading and security features is certainly attractive. Of course, JDBC is important in allowing database access from a Java middle-tier.

15.8 SQL Conformance

Structured Query Language (SQL) is the standard language for accessing relational databases. Unfortunately, SQL is not yet as standard as one would like.

One area of difficulty is the variation of data types used by different database systems. JDBC deals with this by defining a set of generic SQL type identifiers in the class java.sql.Types. Note that the terms "JDBC SQL type", "JDBC type", and "SQL type" are interchangeable and refer to the generic SQL type identifiers defined in java.sql.Types.

Another area of difficulty is the varying degree of SQL conformance to more recently-defined standard SQL syntax or semantics for more advanced functionality. For example, not all databases support stored procedures or outer joins, and those that are not consistent with each other. It is hoped that the portion of SQL that is truly standard will expand to include more and more functionality. In the meantime, the JDBC API must support SQL as it is.

One way the JDBC API deals with this problem is to allow any query string to be passed through to an underlying DBMS driver. This means that an application is free to use as much SQL functionality as desired, but it runs the risk of receiving an error on some database systems. In fact, an application query need not even be SQL, or it may be a specialized derivative of SQL designed for specific database systems (e.g. document or image queries).

Another way JDBC deals with problems of SQL conformance is to provide ODBC-style escape clauses. The escape syntax provides a standard JDBC syntax for several of the more common areas of SQL divergence. For example, there are escapes for date literals and for stored procedure calls. Readers may refer to more details in the "Statements" section in the JDBC overview of the JDK 1.1 documentation.

For complex applications, JDBC deals with SQL conformance in a third way. It provides descriptive information about the database system by means of the interface DatabaseMetaData so that applications can adapt to the requirements and capabilities of each DBMS. Typical end users need not worry about metadata, but experts may want to refer to the overview in "DatabaseMetaData" in the API documentation.

Since the JDBC API will be used as a base API for developing higher-level database access tools and APIs, it has to address the problem of conformance for anything built on it. The designation JDBC Compliant^{TM} was created to set a standard level of JDBC functionality on which users can rely. To use this designation, a driver must support at least ANSI SQL-2 Entry Level.[4] Driver developers can ascertain that their drivers meet these standards by using the test suite available with the JDBC API.

The JDBC Compliant designation indicates that a vendor's JDBC implementation has passed the tests provided by JavaSoft ^{TM}. These conformance tests check for the existence of all of the classes and methods defined in the JDBC API are ascertained that the SQL Entry Level functionality is available. Such tests are not exhaustive, of course, and JavaSoft is currently not branding vendor implementations. However, this compliance definition provides some degree of confidence in a JDBC implementation. With wider acceptance of the JDBC API by database vendors, connectivity vendors, Internet service vendors and application writers, JDBC is quickly becoming the standard for Java database access.

---

[4] ANSI SQL-2 refers to the standards adopted by the American National Standards Institute in 1992. Entry Level refers to a specific list of SQL capabilities.

15.9 Design Perspective

Although Java is an object-oriented language, the java.sql package provides something close to a *call level interface* to the database. Thus, it is not very object-oriented and inclusion of JDBC calls in the client code can be a serious impediment to re-use. Further, the spreadsheet-like data layout provided by the relational database is unlikely to fit the user's real view of the data.

For example, suppose that we are writing an employee benefit application to provide feedback to the employee on pension plans in order to feel confident about his ultimate retirement. From the design perspective, your problem space might include the following objects among others:

- Employee
     Beneficiary
     Salary History
     Savings Transaction History
     Set of Savings Account Objects

The employee object would have properties like a *date of birth* and *date of employment*. It would also contain the other objects listed above. Some of these objects will have a single instance, while others, like the savings account objects, may have multiple instances which form a set. The employee will also have methods to provide various calculated results like his average salary over the last five years.

The properties and contained objects are most likely spread across multiple database tables and multiple rows within these tables. From the perspective of working with the data, it needs to be gathered in a logical way. This assembly process is best fulfilled by the business logic tier. This approach has the following advantages:

- Insulates the client code from changes in the underlying database.

- Simplifies the coding at the client level by reducing it to the problem of how best to communicate the information.

- Enhances the possibility of re-use. For example, the same employee object could be used to provide the data to a GUI application as well as to a batch application for printing employee statements.

15.10 JDBC Architecture

Before we look at the JDBC API, let us see how JDBC is implemented. Figure 15.1 shows the major architectural components of JDBC.

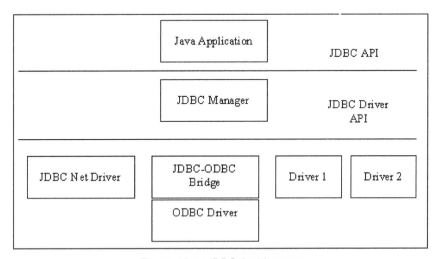

Figure 15-1: JDBC Architecture

JDBC consists of two main layers: the JDBC API, which supports Java application-to-JDBC Driver Manager communications; and, the JDBC Driver API which supports JDBC Driver Manager-to-ODBC Driver communications. The JDBC Driver Manager is designed to handle communication with multiple drivers of different types. All three drivers are depicted in Figure 15.1.

The first is the JDBC-ODBC bridge driver which translates JDBC method calls into ODBC function calls. This allows off-the-shelf ODBC drivers to be used, enabling JDBC to leverage the database connectivity provided by the existing array of native ODBC drivers. The JDBC-ODBC bridge is offered by JavaSoft as part of the JDBC package as discussed in the previous section.

The second driver is the JDBC-Net Bridge which uses a published protocol to communicate with a remote database listener and front ends with the ODBC Driver Manager. With this configuration, the client-side is completely written in Java, enhancing portability and removing the need to have drivers for different databases installed on the client.

The last type of bridge is a direct JDBC driver that communicates directly with a specific database system, bypassing the ODBC layer. The advantage of supporting this style of bridge is the performance benefit gained from eliminating the ODBC layer.

The JDBC API defines Java classes to represent database connections, SQL statements, result sets and database metadata. In terms of Java classes, the JDBC API consists of:

- java.sql.Connection

- java.sql.Statement

- java.sql.PreparedStatement

- java.sql.CallableStatement

- java.sql.ResultSet

A Connection represents a session with a specific database. Within the context of a Connection, SQL statements are executed and results are returned.

A Statement object is used for executing a static SQL statement and obtaining the results produced by it. The executeQuery() method is used for SELECT statements that return a single ResultSet. The executeUpdate() method is used for INSERT, UPDATE, DELETE and other simple statements that do not return results. The execute () method is used to handle more esoteric variations (for example, queries that return multiple results).

An SQL statement can be pre-compiled and stored in a PreparedStatement object. This object can then be used to efficiently excute the statement multiple times. PreparedStatement also adds support for IN parameters. There are a series of setXXX() methods (where XXX is one of the JDBC supported data types) that allow assigned parameters.

CallableStatement extends PreparedStatement for use with stored procedures. It adds support for OUT parameters. You have to first register OUTs using the registerOutParameter() method and then retrieve the value after the call execution using one of the getXXX() methods.

ResultSet provides access to a table of data generated by executing a SELECT statement. A ResultSet maintains a cursor pointing to its current row of data. Initially the cursor is positioned before the first row. The next () method moves the cursor to the next row. The getXXX() method retrieves column values for the current row. You can retrieve values by either using the index number of the column, or by using the name of the column.

The API also contains two classes, java.sql.DatabaseMetaData and java.sql.ResultSetMetaData, that are used for metadata interfaces.

15.10.1 JDBC Data Types

The following table shows the data types supported in JDBC:

SQL Type	Java Type	Description
CHAR	`String`	Single Character
VARCHAR	`String`	Variable length string of characters
LONGVARCHAR	`java.io.InputStream`	Very long (multi-megabyte) strings
NUMERIC	`java.sql.Numeric`	Absolute precision fixed-point values
DECIMAL	`java.sql.Numeric`	Absolute precision Decimal value
BIT	`boolean`	Single bit/binary value (on or off)
TINYINT	`byte`	8-bit integer
SMALLINT	`short`	16-bit integer
INTEGER	`int`	signed 32-bit integer
BIGINT	`long`	signed 64-bit integer
REAL	`float`	Floating-point value
FLOAT	`float`	Floating-point value
DOUBLE	`double`	Large floating-point value
BINARY	`byte[]`	Array of binary values
VARBINARY	`byte[]`	Variable length array of binary values
LONGVARBINARY	`java.io.InputStream`	Very large (multi-megabyte) array of binary values
DATE	`java.sql.Date`	Date value
TIME	`java.sql.Time`	Time value (GMT)
TIMESTAMP	`java.sql.Timestamp`	Time value with additional nanosecond field

15.11 A JDBC Example

Let us look at a how a simple example query can be performed using Java JDBC classes. The extremely small database in Table 15-1 suffices to demonstrate the basic principles. The code in Listing 15-1 is about the smallest possible piece of Java code that allows you to execute a single SQL query against a relational database.

Person#	First name	Last name
43674	Sandor	Spruit
90329	John	Doe
65435	Donald	Duck

Table 15-1: Sample Database with 3 rows and 3 columns from a "Person" Table

```
String url = "jdbc:odbc:sample";
String query = "SELECT * FROM PERSON";
boolean more;

try {
   Class.forName("sun.jdbc.odbc.JdbcOdbcDriver");
   Connection con = DriverManager.getConnection(url, "sandor", "guest") ;
   Statement stmt = con.createStatement();
   ResultSet rs = stmt.executeQuery(query);
   while (more = rs.next()) {
      int number = rs.getInt("PERSON#");
      String firstName = rs.getString("FIRST_NAME") ;
      String lastName = rs.getString("LAST_NAME");
      System.out.println(number + " " + firstName + " " + lastName);
   }
   rs.close();
   stmt.close();
   con.close();
} catch (SQLException ex) {
   ex.printStackTrace();
}
```

Listing 15-1: JDBC Example

The code in Listing 15-1 loads Sun's JDBC/ODBC driver via the method forName(), establishes a connection to the database pointed to by jdbc:odbc:sample, and executes the simple SELECT query against it. Unless an SQLException is caught, it loops through the ResultSet to extract the rows from the database one field at a time and prints out the results.

Now, what is untidy with this code in Listing 15-1? All programmers with an urge to produce elegant code will feel very uncomfortable writing this sort of code. There are two things that are undesirable with the code presented.

- This code can only be written using a considerable amount of database meta-information and this information is all hard-coded into the program. Fetching a number, for example, requires advance knowledge as to whether an integer, a float, or a double would be received. It is difficult, if not impossible, to write a class that can handle any database. Each minor adjustment to the database forces you to carefully check and modify the code.

- The database information is always delivered as a single RecordSet instance, which is not a real object. The RecordSet class, like other database class wrappers, is more like a pointer or a cursor, providing access to database information via methods. The instances of RecordSet do not actually contain information, but merely represent the means to get to it. This is why you have to work your way through the RecordSet by advancing a cursor using

`ResultSet.next()` when calling other RecordSet methods to get to some real information. In fact, the JDBC classes only deliver such sets of loosely coupled fields. These are of little use, when even inner details of the database's structure is known, because in Java, real objects provide the pre-dominant way to store and process information.

Ideally, an elegant solution extracts the records and fields from a database one by one (via a RecordSet) and transforms the information into fresh objects. The key to such a solution lies in the similarity between relational and object-oriented models of a certain data set. The definitions of classes and tables partially serve similar purposes, while objects and records share some properties too. You can readily think of records as sets of values to initialize an object's data members. However, an appropriate class constructor to create the fresh objects from an arbitrary record in an arbitrary table is required.

When developing a small application, it is possible to deliver each record to some constructor that creates an object from it. An Object reference may be used to manipulate any value extracted from the database since any object obtained using a RecordSet is an extended java.lang.Object. It may be possible to define a BigClass with the features would otherwise be placed into separate classes.

BigClass might also contain several constructors, each having a slightly different signature. Thus, `BigClass(int,int)`, `BigClass(int,float)`, and so on are used depending on the sort of information obtained while looping through the RecordSet. (This implementation would undoubtedly include much nasty casting.) However, neither of these suggestions would really solve anything, because the relations between the records and constructors would still be hard-coded into the program. For generic database code to work with anything but toy applications, we require some different way to automatically connect tables and constructors.

This is where a nice Java feature comes to our rescue. The code fragment in Listing 15-2 creates a new instance of any Java class, given nothing but a class name as a String. This means we can use names of classes and tables to find out which constructor can handle a record fetched from a table. It is easy to obtain a complete list of table names from a database using standard JDBC classes, so we can put this little Java trick to good use! Here, Java classes are defined, one per database table, where the class name matches the table name. Whenever a record is read from a table, it creates an object by passing the table name to `Class.forName()`.

```
Class c = Class.forName("Person");
Object p = c.newInstance();
System.out.println("... just created a " + c.getName());
```

Listing 15-2: A Simple `Class.forName()` Example

However, there is a slight complication. As the `forName()` method calls the `void` constructor for the given class, the RecordSet variable cannot be directly given to the constructor. Instead, an initialization method with a ResultSet parameter that extracts one record from it, and uses it to assign the values to the object's data members is required. It may be wise to introduce a superclass as the common ancestor to all the classes linked to a table, because they all need it. In fact, this class plays a key role in querying the database, as will be demonstrated shortly.

It is fine to create objects from records, but you still need SQL statements to query a database. These statements cannot be constructed without having some insight into the database structure. So it seems we are back where we started: the SQL statements would still have to be hand-coded, even if we can automatically match table and class names. This implies manually editing statements each time the database structure is modified. Notice, however, that we can overcome this hurdle using the approach outlined above once more. After all, there is little to know to query a database table. A database table is typically queried using names and values for those fields that are part of either the primary key or an index. In other words, records (or objects) may be extracted from a table as long as suitable values for all the right fields are provided. A quick look at the JDBC specification reveals that DatabaseMetaData objects can be used just to retrieve not only lists of table names, but lists of primary key and index fields.

A relational database can be queried using a relatively small piece of code, by feeding it a series of proper (name, value) pairs. We match all the names in the pairs with the field names of the primary keys and the indices. Whenever a complete primary key or an index in the list of names is found, the corresponding values are used to build an SQL statement, executed to obtain a RecordSet and transformed to objects via the `Class.forName()` construct.

This idea requires instances of any class associated with a database table to have methods that allow access to its data members as (name, value) pairs, but such methods can be implemented perfectly well by the common ancestor we introduced in the previous section. Listing 15-3 and Listing 15-4 present this method in pseudo-code.

```
Open the database connection;
Retrieve a list of user defined tables;
For each table {
   Check whether there is a corresponding class file;
   if (it is available) {
      load the class file;
      Retrieve lists of key fields and indices for this table;
      Store these lists in hashtables for easy access;
   } else throw an exception;
}
```

Listing 15-3: Pseudocode to initialize a Database Connection

```
        Take an object A containing a series of (name, value) pairs;
        For each table T {
            For each (name, value) pair {
                if (name matches primary_key_field or index_field)
                    store a reference to both name and value;
            }

            if all key_fields were found
                create a query string using key names and values;
            else if all index_fields were found
                create a query string using index names and values;

            execute the query to obtain a ResultSet;

            For each record in the ResultSet {
                Create an object of the class associated with table T;
                Initialize the object using the record's contents;
                Add the object to the results, e.g., attach it to A
            }
        }
```

Listing 15-4: Pseudocode Describing a Database Query

15.12 Using Beans and Reflection

Now that we can relate database table to classes and create objects from records, let us consider an alternative.

The introduction of the JDK 1.1 brought us many powerful new features, such as new user interface classes. Two of the new JDK 1.1 APIs in particular deserve our special attention: the reflection facility (the java.lang.reflect package) and the JavaBeans component API (the java.beans package). These APIs will help us build a sophisticated database class as they allow us to work with meta-information about classes. They are the "heavy artillery" that help in solving the problems of developing a generic database class.

The class Class, with its forName() and newInstance() methods, is a simple example of the power of reflection. The point is that the String parameter for the forName() method is not necessarily some character sequence appearing in your source code. Given its name as any character sequence, *any* class may be loaded and instantiated. In the case of our database class, we can derive the class name *directly* from the table name obtained from the database itself. This means the name of the Java class associated with a database table does not have to appear anywhere in our source code. Consequently, you will not have to update your source code when a table's name changes or when a table is added. You will just have to ensure a class with the new name is available on your system.

The idea of using meta-information about classes can be exploited further. The reflection classes allow information about the classes in Java code to be obtained, stored and processed *at runtime*. Their instances can be used like any object in Java, allowing one to tinker with classes, types, return types, method references and arguments as easily as with strings and integers. This reflection concept with immediate access to all the information on classes, methods, and parameters in your own code may seem quite useless at first. After all, the one who wrote the source code already has all such information.

The answer is that reflection will work on *compiled* code in Java class files, not at the source code level. It does not matter whether source files are accessible, because useful information is directly obtained from compiled classes. Reflection easily applies for code which has been imported into one's applications, allowing the inner workings of such imported (and compiled) code to be examined. The JavaBeans API is, in fact, meant to do just that: allow for the construction of applications using classes from completely different programmers and vendors.

The JavaBeans specification prescribes a set of conventions for the names of class members, to make sure the name of the methods systematically describe their function. Any Java class that adheres to the rules can be interrogated by a Bean Introspector instance (using reflection) to reveal important aspects of its behavior, such as like the sort of events the class will respond to and the events it may generate. Any class that adheres to these rules is effectively a Bean, and thus a component. In theory, this means that a set of Beans may be collected from various sources and bound them together at runtime, so that they appear to trigger and consume the same sort of events.

But how is reflection and Beans related with querying databases? Apart from naming conventions on event handling, there is another series which apply to the data members of a class. These conventions are crucial to our database endeavors. Let us consider a Bean example to illustrate how these features can serve our purposes.

The example Translation Bean in Listing 15-5 has one constructor and two methods to manipulate a single property named "language". Remember that a Bean Introspector is merely capable of checking out the code of a class to learn about its constructors, methods and properties.

```
public class Translation extends Object {
    int language;

    public Translation() {}

    public int getLanguage() {
        return(language);
    }

    public void setLanguage(int language) {
        this.language = language;
    }
}
```

Listing 15-5: Translation Bean

A Bean Introspector can supply arrays of PropertyDescriptor instances containing type information for any Bean's properties, defined by the very presence of the sort of getXXX()/setXXX() methods shown in the example.

Reflection facilities provide the means to check the integrity of an otherwise loose connection between classes and database tables. The fact that some class is available with a name matching the name of a table does not guarantee that its internals are consistent. A class associated with a table obviously should have members so that its instances store all the table's columns. For all we know, a class may have the right name, but the initialization code could be missing. It may have the right name, but have members with either the wrong name or the wrong type. A good combination is the combined use of of JDBC's DatabaseMetaData and the reflection facilities to check whether they all match.

To sum up, the combination of JDBC, reflection and JavaBeans technology make it possible to fetch records from a relational database and use them to initialize complete components – not just objects. Databases need not be modified for this to work, instead, classes must adhere to the Bean specification and that their properties match those of tables. Other Beans facilities such as their own user-interface components and Customizers enrich this framework.

15.13 Summary

JDBC has ushered in an era of simple but powerful database access for Java programs. It is an important step in the right direction to elevate the Java language to the Java platform. The Java APIs including the Enterprise APIs (JDBC, RMI, Serialization, and IDL), Security APIs, and the Server APIs are the essential ingredients for developing enterprise-level, distributed, multi-tier client/server applications.

One factor in favor of JDBC is its similarity to ODBC. JavaSoft made the right decisions to follow ODBC philosophy and abstractions, thus making it easy for ISVs and users to leverage their ODBC experience and existing ODBC drivers.

By making JDBC a part of the Java language, we gain the advantages of the Java language concepts for database access. As all implementations have to support the Java APIs, JDBC has become a universal standard. This philosophy, stated in the JDBC specification as "provide a Java interface that is consistent with the rest of the Java system", makes JDBC an ideal candidate for use in Java-based database development.

Another good design philosophy is the driver independence of the JDBC. The underlying database drivers can either be native libraries, such as a dynamic link library (.dll) for the Windows system, or Java routines connecting to listeners. The full Java implementation of JDBC is suitable for a variety of Network and other Java OS computers, thus making JDBC a versatile set of APIs.

Bibliography

Allen, M. 1997. Hands-On JavaBeans, Prima Pub.

Appel, A. 1998. Modern Compiler Implementation in Java, Cambridge University press.

Arnold, K, and Gosling, J. 1998. The Java Programming Language (Java Series), Addison-Wesley.

Beck, K., and Cunningham, W. 1989. A Laboratory for Object-Oriented Thinking. Proceedings of OOPSLA 89. SIGPLAN Notices, Vol. 24, No. 10.

Bell, D. 1997. Java for Students, Prentice Hall.

Ben-Natan, R. 1998. Corba on the Web, McGraw-Hill.

Booch, G. 1994. Object-Oriented Analysis and Design, Benjamin/Cummings.

Booch, G., Jacobson, I., and Rumbaugh, J. 1997. The Unified Modelling Language specification documents, Rational Software Corp., available at http://www.rational.com.

Boone, B. 1997. Java Certification for Programmers and Developers, McGraw-Hill.

Budd, T. 1998. Understanding Object-oriented Programming with Java, Addison-Wesley.

Cameron, D. 1998. Java strategies, Computer Technology Research.

Campione, M., and Walrath, K. 1998. The Java Tutorial: Object-Oriented Programming for the Internet (Java Series), 2nd Edition, Addison-Wesley.

Chan, M. C. 1997. 1001 Java Programmer's Tips, Jamsa Press.

Chan, P., and Lee R., 1997. The Java Class Libraries: java.applet, java.awt, java.beans (Java Series), Vol. 2, 2nd Edition, Addison-Wesley.

Chan, P., Lee R., Kramer, D., and Kramer, D. 1998. The Java Class Libraries: java.io, java.lang, java.math, java.net, java.security, java.text, java.util (Java Series), Vol. 1, 2nd Edition, Addison-Wesley.

Chang, D. 1998. Client/Server Data Access with Java, Wiley.

Chew, F. F. 1997. The Java/C++ Cross-reference Handbook, Prentice Hall.

Coad, P. 1995. Object Models: Strategies, Patterns and Applications, Prentice-Hall.

Coleman, D. et al. 1994. Object-Oriented Development: The Fusion Method, Prentice-Hall.

Cornell, G. 1997. Core Java , SunSoft Press.

Courtois, T. 1998. Java Networking and Communications, Prentice Hall PTR.

Englander, R. 1997. Developing JavaBeans, O'Reilly.

Fawcett, N. 1997. Java, Butterworth-Heinemann.

Feghhi, J. 1997. Web Developer's Guide to JavaBeans, Coriolis Group Books.

Felleisen, M. 1998. A Little Java, a Few Patterns, MIT Press.

Geary, D. M. 1997. Graphic Java, SunSoft Press.

Gilbert, S. 1998. Object-oriented Design in Java, Waite Group Press.

Goodrich, M. T. 1997. Data Structures and Algorithms in Java, Wiley.

Grand, M. 1997. Java Fundamental Classes Reference, O'Reilly.

Grand, M. 1997. Java Language Reference, O'Reilly.

Hall, M. 1998. Core Web Programming, Prentice Hall PTR.

Hamilton, G. 1997. JDBC Database Access with Java, Addison-Wesley.

Hamilton, G., Cattell, R., and Fisher, M. 1997. JDBC Database Access With Java: A Tutorial and Annotated Reference (Java Series), Addison-Wesley.

Harold, E. R. 1998. JavaBeans, IDG Books Worldwide.

Hoque, R. 1998. Programming Web components, McGraw-Hill.

Horstmann, C. S. 1997. Practical Object-oriented Development in C++ and Java, Wiley Computer Pub.

Hunt, J. 1998. Key Java, Springer.

Hunt, J. 1998. Java and Object Orientation, Springer-Verlag.

Ince, D. 1997. Programming the Internet with Java, Addison-Wesley.

Jacobson, I. 1992. Object-Oriented Software Engineering: A Use Case Driven Approach, Addison-Wesley.

Jenkins, M. S. 1998. Abstract Data Types in Java, McGraw-Hill.

Joshi, D. I. 1997. The Comprehensive Guide to the JDBC SQL API, Ventana.

Jubin, H. 1998. JavaBeans by Example, Prentice Hall PTR.

Kamin, S. N. 1998. An Introduction to Computer Science using Java, WCB/McGraw-Hill.

Koenig, A. 1989. Objects, Values, and Assignment, Journal of Object-Oriented Programming, Vol. 2, No. 2, pp 37-38.

Lea, D. 1996. Concurrent Programming in Java : Design Principles and Patterns, Addison-Wesley.

Lewis, G. 1998. Programming with Java IDL, Wiley Computer Pub.

McCarthy, M. 1998. Building 3D worlds in Java and VRML, Prentice Hall.

McCarty, B. 1998. SQL Database Programming with Java, Coriolis Group Books.

Meyer, J. 1997. Java Virtual Machine, O'Reilly.

Mohseni, P. 1997. JavaBeans Developer's Guide, M & T Books.

Morrison, M. 1997. Java 1.1 Unleashed, Sams.net.

Naughton, P. 1998. Java 1.1, Osborne McGraw-Hill.

Nickerson, D. 1998. Official Netscape JavaBeans Developer's Guide, Ventana.

Niemeyer, P. 1997. Exploring Java, O'Reilly.

Oaks, S. 1997. Java Threads, O'Reilly.

Orfali, R., and Harkey, D. 1997. Client/Server Programming with Java and CORBA, John Wiley & Sons.

Parnas, D. L. 1972. On the Criteria to be used in Decomposing Systems into Modules, Communications of the ACM, Vol. 15, No. 12, pp 1059-1062.

Patel, P. 1997. Java Database Programming with JDBC, Coriolis Group Books.

Rinehart, M. L. 1998. Java Database Development, Osborne McGraw-Hill.

Rumbaugh, J. et al. 1991. Object-Oriented Modelling and Design, Prentice-Hall.

Savit, J. 1998. Enterprise Java, McGraw-Hill.

Schneider, J. 1997. Using Enterprise Java, Que.

Siple, M. D. 1998. The Complete Guide to Java Database Programming, McGraw-Hill.

Snyder, A. 1986. Encapsulation and Inheritance in Object-Oriented Programming Languages, Proceedings of the 1986 OOPSLA, reprinted in Sigplan Notices, Vol. 21, No. 11, pp 38-45.

Sowizral, H. A. 1998. The Java 3D API Specification, Addison-Wesley.

Sridharan, P. 1997. Advanced Java Networking, Prentice Hall PTR.

Standish, T. A. 1998. Data Structures in Java, Addison-Wesley.

Van der Linden, P. 1997. Just Java, SunSoft Press.

Van Haecke, B. 1997. JDBC, IDG Books Worldwide.

Vanhelsuwe, L. 1997. Mastering JavaBeans, SYBEX.

Venners, B. 1998. Inside the Java Virtual Machine, McGraw-Hill.

Voge, A., Duddy, K., and Vogel, A. 1997. Java Programming With Corba, John Wiley & Sons.

Vogel, A. 1998. Java Programming with CORBA, John Wiley.

Wayner, P. 1998. JavaBeans for Real Programmers, AP Professional.

Weiss, M. A. 1998. Data Structures and Problem Solving using Java, Addison Wesley.

Wirfs-Brock, R. 1990. Variables Limit Reusability, Journal of Object-Oriented Programming, Vol. 2, No. 1, pp 34-40, May.

Zukowski, J. 1997. Java AWT Reference, O'Reilly.

Index